CONFRONTATIONS OF DEATH:

A Book of Readings and
A Suggested Method of Instruction

edited and compiled
by
Frances G. Scott, Director
and
Ruth M. Brewer, Librarian

Oregon Center for Gerontology
Eugene, Oregon

A CONTINUING EDUCATION BOOK
PORTLAND, OREGON

Text printed on 100% recycled book

ACKNOWLEDGEMENTS

Grateful acknowledgement is due the authors of the
selected readings included in this book, and to their
representatives and publishers for permission to use
the copyrighted material found in *Confrontations of
Death.*

1.   Agee, James. *A Death In The Family.* James Agee Trust, Inc. New York. 1956. Chapter 18, pp 304-316.
2.   Beattie, Ken. *Fang* (unpublished).
3.   cummings, e.e. *dying is fine) but Death* XAIPE (1950) in Poems 1923-54. Harcourt Brace Jovanovich, Inc. New York p 431.
4.   Gibran, Kahlil. *The Prophet* (an excerpt) Random House, Inc. New York. pp 80-81.
5.   Glaser, Barney G. and Strauss, Anselm L. *Dying On Time.* Transaction-Social Science and Modern Society, May/June 1965, Vol. 2, No. 4. New Brunswick, N. J. pp 27-31.
6.   Guthrie, George P. *The Meaning of Death.* Voices: The Art and Science of Psychotherapy, 1969, Vol.5, No. 1. The Process of Dying. The American Academy of Psychotherapists. Quality Press, Emerson N. J.
7.   Housman, A. E. *Is My Team Plowing?* A Shropshire Lad. Peter Pauper Press, Mt. Vernon, N.Y.
8.   Howard, Alan and Scott, Robert A. *Cultural Values and Attitudes Toward Death.* Journal of Existentialism, Vol. VI, Winter 1965. pp 161-174.
9.   Kazzaz, David S. and Vickers, Raymond. *Geriatrics Staff Attitudes Toward Death.* American Geriatrics Society, Vol. XVI, No. 12 (Dec 1968) pp 1364-1371.
10. Koestenbaum, Peter. *The Vitality of Death.* Journal of Existentialism, Vol. V, No. 18, Fall 1964. Libra Publishers, Inc. Roslyn Heights, N. Y.
11. Lasagna, Louis. *A Person's Right To Die.* Johns Hopkins Magazine, Spring 1968. Baltimore, Md. pp 34-41.
12. Leveton, Alan. *Time, Death and the Ego Chill.* Journal of Existentialism, Vol. VI, Summer 1966. Libra Publishers, Inc. Roslyn Heights, N. Y. pp 69-80.
13. McKuen, Rod. *Doug Davis, Three.* Listen to the Warm. Random House, Inc. New York.
14. Mitford, Jessica. *Fashions in Funerals.* The American Way of Death. Simon and Schuster, New York. 1963. pp 187-201.
15. Needleman, Jacob. *The Moment of Grief.* Death and Bereavement. Ed. Austin H. Kutscher, Charles C. Thomas, Springfield, Illinois. 1969.
16. Nettler, Gwynn. *Review Essay: On Death and Dying.* Social Problems, Winter 1967. Vol. 14, No. 3.
17. Pine, Vanderlyn R. and Phillips, Derek L. *The Cost of Dying: A Sociological Analysis of Funeral Expenditures.* Social Problems, Winter 1970, Vol. 17, No. 3.
18. Sandburg,Helga, *Father, Once You Said That In The Grace of God.* October 1968 McCall's Magazine, p96.
19. Saunders, Cicely. *The Moment of Truth: Care of the Dying Person.* Death and Dying: Current Issues in the Treatment of the Dying Person. Ed. Leonard Pearson. Copyright 1969 by the Press of Case Western Reserve University, Cleveland.
20. Thomas, Dylan. *Do Not Go Gentle Into That Good Night.* The Collected Poems of Dylan Thomas. Copyright 1952 by Dylan Thomas, reprinted by permission of New Directions Publishing Corporation. New York.
21. Thurmond, Charles J. *Last Thoughts Before Drowning.* Journal of Abnormal and Social Psychology. Ed. Gordon W. Allport, Evanston, Ill. The American Psychological Assoc. Inc. 1943.
22. Tolstoy, Leo. *The Death of Ivan Ilych.* Teller of Tales, Ed. W. Somerset Maugham, Doubleday, Doran and Company, Inc. New York, 1939.
23. Wolfe, Thomas. *Of Time and the River: A Legend of Man's Hunger in His Youth.* Charles Scribners Sons, New York 1935.

CONTENTS

FOREWORD

To Members of the Seminar "Confrontations of Death"

May I congratulate you on having the courage, while you are still young, to face up to a problem which I feared to tackle for over sixty years.

Through the ages, death, which happens to every one of us, has generally been considered chiefly in private and in connection with one's religious beliefs, not as a psychologic and physiologic event which it unquestionably is.

What has been thought and discussed concerning the subject has inevitably been highly tinged with fearful emotion. I expect that even when reason and logic are brought to bear we will find it impossible to avoid many of the earlier pitfalls. However, attempts such as you are making can help to show the way toward a better approach.

You will find, I am sure, little guidance from physicians. We are so bound up with the problems of living beings and, traditionally, in postponing death as long as possible that we have neglected too long to consider adequately the windup of life and how to deal with it well.

Clergymen have of necessity given more thought to the matter and have learned how to deal with dying, but each only according to the tenets of his particular faith. These may yield pointers toward helpful measures, but such measures may not be acceptable to everyone.

Your efforts to understand the problem, to discuss its various aspects and to aim for workable conclusions may lead to much good, I believe. For example, you may help doctors find better ways to accept responsibility in this field where we have been so backward.

I have found that by seeking ways to make my aging and death a useful process, much of the emotional strain and, as far as I can determine, all fears have been removed. Death has become a useful objective when it arrives and yet it is not an all consuming fetish. I still have many interesting ideas to work out while I live and I hope that this may be still a considerable time.

Maurice T. Root

Maurice T. Root, M.D. (retired)
51 North Main Street
West Hartford, Connecticut 06107

CHAPTER I

ORIENTATION TO A CONCEPT AND A METHOD

Frances G. Scott
Oregon Center for Gerontology

Pundits have commented that the current status of interest in and research about the phenomena of death is analogous to that in the phenomena of sex before Freud: everyone is obsessed with it, yet it is still a taboo subject in most quarters. In 1968 when the seminar "Confrontations of Death" was introduced at the University of Oregon, the subject was even more taboo than it is now (in 1971). Norman D. Sundberg, Dean of the Wallace School of Community Service and Public Affairs, Marvin M. Janzen, Field Instructor in Gerontology, and I were looked upon somewhat askance by fellow faculty members and friends when we began the seminar. People asked if we were morbid about dying. Students, however, were enthusiastic from the first.[1]

In this chapter, a short description of the origins of the seminar is given, along with a discussion of what we who introduced "Confrontations of Death" perceive as the objectives of the seminar, both for ourselves and our students. There is also an orientation to the use of this book of readings in similar seminars, and a discussion of some of the variations we inaugurate from time to time.

The selected readings are grouped together in chapters, with a short introduction to each one. The introductory comments provide insights into how we use the reading materials and how they are coordinated with the various other "inputs" of the seminar.

The final chapter is a discussion of the week-end "retreat" which is the culmination of the seminar; it is written by Saul Toobert, a psychologist who has served each time as a "trainer" and who has given empathetic support to our efforts from the very beginning.[2]

These chapters, taken together, give the student a preview of what to expect in the "Confrontations..." seminar, and enable our lay audience as well as our fellow academicians to understand what we offer under the rubric "Confrontations of Death" at the University of Oregon.

How It Began and How It Developed

In the Spring of 1967, a conference for physicians on "The Doctor and the Dying Patient" was held in Portland, Oregon. It was coordinated by Robert I. Daugherty, M.D., a general practitioner in Lebanon, Oregon, who was involved along with me in a training project for teaching general practitioners the concepts of psychiatry.[3] The remarkable thing about the conference is that it went far beyond the usual professional in-service training seminar – which at its best may be interesting and informative, but rarely inspiring, and at its worst is simply soporific. This conference electrified virtually all the participants, and informal follow-up interviewing revealed many physicians actually changed the way they dealt with dying patients as a result of the experience.

How was this remarkable effect produced? It seemed to be largely attributable to the method of instruction selected by Dr. Daugherty and the group of us who planned the physician's conference. This is what I shall call here a "modified T-group approach to helping adults learn," or a "modified T-group," to be brief.[4] Needless to say, we did not actually "T-group" or provide "sensitivity training" for the participants. However, the conference was preceded by an intensive two-day training session for group leaders, who were themselves introduced to rudimentary "T-group" methods by Leon J. Fine, a psychologist at the University of Oregon Medical

School. Dr. Fine began the conference proper with a set of "warm-up" exercises which consumed the entire first morning and resulted in a number of small groups, the members of which more or less remained together for the entire conference.[5]

The subject matter of the conference was in itself highly interesting, of course, but the use of the "modified T-group" method intensified the existential and personally meaningful aspects of the educational experience to the point where some participants were so highly involved and "turned on" that small groups of them remained together far into the night discussing the ideas and feelings they had experienced during the day.

The format of the conference was in most respects similar to that of ordinary professional meetings: there was an "input" of an hour or so, and then an hour or two of small group work, the object of which was to discuss the "input." However, "inputs" consisted not only of lectures — although there were those — but also a couple of plays, a bombardment at every free moment with art and music on the theme of death, and an almost unbearably insightful interview with a dying patient and his wife. In my opinion, and in that of most of the persons who attended the conference, it might still have been the same old tired professional meeting, had it not been for the "T-groups." The "T-groups" would not have been possible without prior training of the group leaders. Although the group leaders functioned imperfectly, judged by the standards of "professional" sensitivity group trainers, they were much more attuned to eliciting expression of feeling and to increasing personal involvement of group members than the average group leader under similar circumstances.

As an educator, I am interested in methods to increase the relevance and impact of the learning experiences of students. When I returned from this conference — from which, incidentally, I derived great personal benefit and satisfaction — I pondered about the method. How could we give university students an intensive, concentrated "T-group experience" like that? The method is expensive, requires a lot of staff, and is almost the antithesis of the usual university course with its series of well-thought-out lectures. Instead of trying to obtain

a *large* enrollment, the "T-group" method demands strict limits on enrollment (12-15 students per group leader is maximum). An entire three-day week-end is needed to allow the requisite number of classroom hours to meet university standards. When can university students devote three consecutive days to attendance at one course? And what would other professors think if we ask students to "cut" their Friday (or Monday) classes to attend our three-day week-end class? Such arrangements are obviously impossible in most university settings.

Two highly imaginative and interested colleagues helped me think through these and other problems: Dean Norman D. Sundberg and Marvin M. Janzen. Our decision was to offer the seminar on an experimental basis for one quarter and evaluate the results before pursuing it further. We all "donated" our time, in the sense that this was an extra teaching load for us, and we obtained six volunteer trainers (two for each group) for the planned week-end.[6]

What is the "Task-Oriented T-Group?"

Although it is difficult to describe in positive terms exactly what a task-oriented or modified T-group is, we can point to several things it is *not*: it is not a therapy group, "encounter" group or a marathon.[7] Our object is to provide an educational setting which maximizes the extent to which students become involved with each other as human beings, exchange information, share experiences, and in general learn from each other rather than from a "teacher." Students must be "trained" to operate in this independent (of the instructor), group-oriented fashion; hence, the "teacher" is a "trainer," whose function in the group theoretically will cease once the group has learned to forge ahead without him. To the extent that students are "trained" to share their feelings, fears, information, phobias, and so on with a group of peers who are exposed to the same educational process at about the same rate, they will be enabled to enjoy a healthy, psychologically satisfying and socially rewarding learning experience.

The "modified T-group" approach involves students in a discussion group in which they not only are able to consider objective or factual materials but also are encouraged to examine their own needs, attitudes, values, feelings and fears as these impinge upon the subject matter — in this case, the phenomenon of personal death. Some of the specific objectives or goals of the "modified T-group" model in this educational context are as follows:

1. Developing the capacity to relate the subject matter to one's personal feelings about that subject matter; we are not necessarily aware of our feelings about the subjects we study, but with the T-group method we make a conscious attempt to become aware.

2. Developing self-diagnostic skills — as the student becomes aware of his fears of death and his strong motivational needs for coping with this phenomenon,he will better be able to relate them to his current situation in life.

3. Developing communication and interpersonal relations skills. This facility might also be called "developing social relationship skills," or the ability to tell others of one's own feelings, fears,desires, and needs.

4. Developing attitudes of independence, rather than dependence.

5. Developing an awareness of one's present approach to life as a basis for evaluating if this approach is worthy of carrying "to the grave."

6. Developing skills and attitudes for effective problem solving, which we believe are necessary tools for coping with the reality of personal death.

7. Developing the attitude of "action taking," so that plans for living will be carried out after they are made.

The Suggested Format

The first seminar was, as the reader might anticipate, considered an outstanding success. The format developed and the one we have maintained because it seems to work well, is to meet for six weeks in the manner of a usual seminar, i.e., one evening a week for three hours. This gives us time for an "input" to the whole class followed by small group discussions each evening. On the Saturday and Sunday of the sixth week, we meet for a two-day week-end in a retreat situation in an intensive "T-group experience." Then we have one follow-up session on the seventh week at our usual class time. This completes the work of the term by the seventh week, as opposed to our usual 11-week quarter. It provides a compromise of the intensive learning experience we wished, but it allows us to meet the academic standards and to abide by the regulations of our university.

"Confrontations of Death" as a University offering goes against one of the important current trends in classroom instruction in large universities: we insist upon an extremely *high* staff/student ratio, rather than striving for a low (or even zero) ratio. We sharply limit the enrollment to between thirty and thirty-three students, and we have three instructors, one for each 10 or 12 students. When the three trainers join the staff for the week-end experience, the staff/student ratio is raised to about 1:5. We are not mass producing "graduates" of "Confrontations...": quite the contrary. However, we feel that only with very small groups — no more than 10 or 12 members — can we obtain the intensive kind of involvement we want to achieve. Interpersonal relationships must be close, warm, and trusting to provide the kind of learning situation we seek. One does not attain this kind of relationship in the lecture hall.

To develop close interpersonal relationships among small group members, we begin the seminar with a series of human relations "warm-up" exercises on the first evening. The exercises we use are essentially non-threatening ones; the purposes of the exercises are to 1) insure that all members of the seminar become at least superficially acquainted with all others, 2) develop skills in communicating one's feelings, 3) develop skills in giving feedback to other people about the group process, 4) to divide the large group of 30 or so students into 3 small groups of 10 or so, with equally distributed resources, and finally 5) to give the small groups a task to work on in which they can practice the ways of relating to each other that have been suggested in the warm-up.

In subsequent seminar sessions, the "inputs" to the seminar are made in the large group situation (all 30 students together). The students then adjourn to their small groups for discussion of the "input," of their feelings about it, or about the reading assignment or other relevant materials. Each instructor, functioning as small group leader, tries to refrain from "lecturing" and tries to facilitate the expression of feeling by modeling in his own behavior the kinds of verbalizations and actions he feels are appropriate. Each meeting of the small groups usually results in a closer, warmer inter-relationship of the members; frequently very significant "peak" experiences develop in the small group meetings. The instructors are encouraged to allow as much expression as they are themselves capable of tolerating; on occasion, the instructor may ask the group to postpone until the week-end experience discussion of a topic or a group process with which he feels unable himself to cope.

The result of the first six seminar sessions is normally three small groups, the members of which are very comfortable and trusting of each other, with each group having the ability to relate to "outsiders' in the large group situation (all 3 small groups meeting together) in a much more open, expressive manner than the usual university class of similar size is able to do within the same length of time.

After our very first seminar, in which we reorganized the small groups for the week-end experience, we kept the original small groups intact for the duration of the seminar. Although a majority of our students did not seriously object to being "reorganized," enough of them were thoroughly unhappy that we decided there was no overriding reason for not leaving the small groups intact. We then redoubled our efforts to teach the students to feel at ease in the large group situation, to minimize "out-grouping" of members of the other two small groups, and to realize both the close trustfulness of "their own" small group and the somewhat more formal atmosphere of the large group situation are valuable — although different — experiences.

Objectives: Intellectual and Existential

The reader has probably realized by now that the intent of "Confrontations" is to elicit discussion of *feelings* about death, rather than simply to examine research materials or other erudite writings on the topic. This is true: our intent is to come as close as we can to providing a situation within which each student can *confront his own death* in as realistic a fashion as he is capable of, with the help of his small group. We do not denigrate intellectual and academic instruction. We do not seek to downgrade research efforts. Rather, our teaching objective is to free up the student's emotions and enable him to confront and cope with feelings about his *own* death. The result is a person much better prepared to confront his own life. And, if he is preparing for one of the

"helping professions," especially in the field of gerontology, he will be much better able to deal with the problems of his clientele, many of whom are old and close to death, some of whom die and leave to the professional the job of helping families recover from the death of a member, and some of whom have extreme emotional difficulties in coping with their own mortality. Our students report that these are exactly the benefits they receive: **they are better able to live a full life, and to help others so live, as a result of the seminar.**

Since we have "academic" input, how do we use it in our instruction? We are listing in Appendix A of this volume the schedule for the quarter current at this writing, Winter, 1971. The reader will note that the "input" varies from a lecture, to music, to a movie, to a videotape—in short, the "inputs" are multi-media.

Reading assignments are also shown on the schedule. These demonstrate how we use the readings in this book. Both the "inputs" to the large group and the readings are discussed in the small group sessions each evening. We ask students not to read ahead in the book, because there is a certain psychological progression to the materials which is better experienced in a cumulative fashion than all at once. In general, the material presented to the student begins "far away" from the individual and proceeds to the level of his innermost feelings; learning should progress from fairly intellectualized "desensitization" types of experiences at first to almost entirely visceral or gut-level learning during the week-end experience. However, emotional-level learning is not reserved for the week-end; it is planned to occur in the small group each week, as we implied above.

The intended psychological progression works better with some students than with others, of course, and the teacher should not be disappointed if not every student responds enthusiastically. Furthermore, the student should not be disappointed if he does not reach the peak experience that most students report. We cannot all peak at the same time nor by the same method nor in the same subject. For students who are naive about "T-groups," the experience is almost uniformly one of extreme intensity. Students who have more experience with such groups, especially those who have had productive sensitivity training, may find the "modified T-group" method, which focuses more on content than most "T-groups," does not produce further helpful insights into themselves.

Such students (and such teachers) should remember that not everyone is as sophisticated as he, and unless he has previously considered the phenomena of personal death in the context of a "T-group" (in which case he should probably not be enrolled in the seminar) he very likely does have a lot to learn about himself if he will relax and not expect the same kind of "miracle" that his first "T-group" produced for him.

Variations on a Theme

It should be pointed out, especially for the benefit of teachers planning similar seminars, that the readings we present here are arbitrarily selected, although they were picked to focus upon an existential point of view, interspersed with "hard research" and information-giving selections. The selections from literature and poetry represent the personal preferences of the teachers and editors at the University of Oregon, and certainly could be expanded, changed, or omitted entirely if one prefers. In fact, the academic literature on death and related phenomena, including humanistic and existential treatments, is expanding very rapidly; new and exciting selections become available every month. The teacher should be aware that this is happening and look for additions and supplements to the current volume. We do this ourselves. We change the "inputs," as well as the readings, almost every term.

Change is perhaps the principal characteristic of "Confrontations of Death;" we have changed the format, we have changed the "inputs," we have changed the readings, we have changed the instructors, we have changed the trainers, we have changed the week-end experiences. The one thing that has not changed is our philosophy: *it is the existential components of the phenomena of personal death that are most important, and it is in this realm that we can all learn from each other.*

1   As it turned out, "Confrontations..." has become perhaps the most well-known seminar of all the curricular offerings of the Oregon Center for Gerontology. Publicity about the class started with a scholarly and insightful article by Belva Findlay, in *Old Oregon* (July-August,1969), the alumni magazine of the University. This article was cited in several other sources, resulting in the prominent inclusion of the "Confrontations of Death" seminar in an illustrated feature story by Terence Shea in the *National Observer* (January 5, 1970). The Findlay article also was reprinted (November, 1970) in the *St. Anthony Messenger*, a widely-circulated Catholic family magazine. At about this same time there were several requests to allow photographers or newsmen to attend the classes in order to document the work. Our first book of readings, a mimeographed collection intended for the use of our students and tied closely to the specific classroom presentations scheduled for the seminar, resulted in a deluge of requests from other universities as well as interested laymen, for copies of the book, for course outlines, and for any other materials we had available.

It is not often a teacher finds one of his courses achieving nationwide attention; we admit ambivalence about the "super-success" of our effort. However, the manifestation of such widespread interest increases the feeling of obligation to the academic and to the lay communities to provide full information about "Confrontations..." The present volume is the first step in this direction. A final step is also under way. Since we have adamantly refused to allow reporters or photographers from the media to attend this seminar, we feel it incumbent upon us to provide a documentary film of the "Confrontations..." experience. With the aid of a Special Projects grant from the Oregon Division of Continuing Education, the filming will soon be accomplished. The documentary film will be available in April, 1971.

2 In private life, Saul Toobert is my husband; our mutual experiences in this seminar have added an important new dimension to our marriage as well as to our professional lives.

3 This project is funded by the National Institute of Mental Health, Grant No. MH10544, 'General Practitioner Psychiatry Post-Graduation Education;" the project began in 1965 and is currently still in progress. A conference is held each year on a different theme of interest to general practitioners.

4 There are several excellent books describing the T-group method. Among these, see E.A. Schein and W.G. Bennis, *Personal and Organizational Change Through Group Methods: The Laboratory Approach*, Wylie, 1965; L.P. Bradford *et al, T-Group Theory and Laboratory Methods*, Wylie, 1968; J.R. Gibb *et al, Dynamics of Participative Groups*, National Training Laboratories, 1951.

5 In some groups, a few members had not planned to attend the entire conference, and thus dropped in and out of group sessions, sometimes seriously disturbing the "stable" group members. This kind of problem is likely to arise when the "modified T-group method" is used at a conference, or when one offers a program to any group over which he has tenuous control with respect to attendance requirements.

6 These men and women also volunteered their time for the first experimental seminar. They were: Carolin S. Keutzer, Daniel Langmeyer, Charles H. Pyron, Richard A. Schmuck, Patricia (Mrs. Richard A.) Schmuck, and Saul Toobert. In subsequent seminars, we used only three trainers (one for each group) and are usually able to pay them a consulting fee since the course has been incorporated into the curriculum of the Oregon Center for Gerontology. The Center is largely supported by a training grant from the Administration on Aging, Washington, D.C.

7 The student interested in general references on group therapy and its various theories and practices might examine: W.M. Lifton, *Working with Groups: Group Processes and Individual Growth*, 2nd ed., Wylie, 1966; or M. Rosenbaum and M. Berger (eds.), *Group Psychotherapy and Group Function*, Basic Books, 1963.

CHAPTER II

SOME TAXONOMIES OF THE PHENOMENA OF DEATH

Introduction

Maybe we are too cautious; maybe we are trying to overprotect the student or the reader. Maybe we should reveal to you—immediately and without reservation—what we regard as the most profound insights about personal death that we have discovered. Maybe we should not lead up to these excruciating insights gradually, by going from general or abstract considerations to specific and personal ones. Maybe.

For those of you who want to make the existential leap quickly, here is an exercise: *If you have never tried seriously to think about your own death, try it now. Set a timer for two minutes, and think intensely about how it is for you to be dead.* How long did it take you to **stop** thinking about your own death? Did you actually think intensely about it for two minutes? Almost no one does.

The chances are you would be better able to think about your own death if you were in reality about to die. Gwynn Nettler points out in the review essay introducing this chapter that most terminal patients seem to know they are dying, but that most physicians seem to want to keep confirmation of this state of affairs from the patient. Why should this be? As Nettler says, "...the definitions given death rest upon the meanings assigned to life." And these definitions and these meanings are very patently determined by our culture, by the society in which we live.

Howard and Scott underline this point in their ethnographic sketches of American and of Rotuman attitudes toward death. It is no accident that ". .most Americans do not really accept death as inevitable; they tend to feel invulnerable." All the relevant aspects of the American's upbringing emphasize the desirability of overcoming all obstacles, even the final one, death. Of course the average American cannot seriously consider his own death for two minutes! He must deny the possibility of his mortality, if only by the mechanism of letting his mind wander from this unwelcome subject. The Rotuman, however, is a different sort of creature. "(In)...the characteristic Rotuman attitude...death is described as an almost pleasant state, one that frees the individual from the burdens of obligation and work." The Rotuman might easily consider his own death for two minutes; in fact, the authors of our second selection imply young Rotumans "rap" together frequently about death and life. But Rotuman culture has its undesirable aspects, just as does American culture. You cannot impose a set of values toward death that is inconsistent with the other cultural values of a society. Howard and Scott do not advocate Americans' adopting Rotuman attitudes toward death; they simply italicize the fact that different and contrasting attitudes toward death are found among human beings.

The final selection in this chapter, while it still may be regarded as a taxonomic effort, moves closer to helping us feel that "...the essence of human existence is its mortality," as Koestenbaum so succinctly puts it. He draws a dichotomy between the *death of another* and the *death of myself*. He suggests that with the *death of myself* (the observer of the existing world) there is no longer any life; hence, my own death is literally unthinkable. No wonder we cannot concentrate upon it for two minutes!

Koestenbaum sounds a theme which echoes again and again through the present book, and builds to a resounding crescendo in the "Confrontations of Death" seminar: "A successful and happy life begins with the understanding that we must die..." I am poignantly reminded of a student who was "zapped" (see Chapter VIII for an explanation of this exercise) and decided to spend his isolation time acting as a "ghost" and observing, from a hidden distance, the activities of his living small group peers. He reported the uncanny sensation that if the group persisted in regarding him as dead, and speaking of him as dead, he must surely die. He further reported an extraordinary change in his attitude toward life and living as a result of this experience; he appreciated his wife more, he enjoyed his body more, all his senses were honed and sharpened. An already well-adjusted young man became an unusually "tuned in" individual.

REVIEW ESSAY: ON DEATH AND DYING   *

by

Gwynn Nettler

Dying, like living, is a matter of definition.[1]

This assumption regards attitudes towards life, and its end, as various and open to test.

We may test for the sources of these different definitions, for their correlates and consequences, and for their conformity with standards of right and wrong.

The last type of test seems the least interesting. It lacks interest because it is the easiest of the associations to establish — by fiat. It still lacks interest when one attempts to be reasonable about his morals because the usual tactic then is to justify one's ethic by reference to what-will-happen-if....[2] When such an attempt is made, the moral quarrel reduces to predictions, and we are back on the more rewarding ground of counting the consequences of attitudes toward life and death.

A recognition of the futility of moral debate does not lead to the inference that the subjects of our study, people who live and die, do not infuse their living acts, and dying ones, with moral meaning. They do. And they do as part of an effort to answer the mysteries of our arrival and departure. "Why am I here?" "Why do I die?"

Justice intrudes upon these questions, and with justice a cosmology. "Why did God have to take *my* child?" "Why this good man and not that evil one?"

To the positivist, these popular queries are often non-questions. No empirical predicate will answer them, although many non-empirical predicates will satisfy them. But the naturalist observer wants to know what difference the style of question and the mode of its answer make to the living — as they live, as they regard the dead and dying, and as they themselves come to their final scenes.

About all this we know little. Theologians, philosophers, and psychoanalysts talk much about the meaning of life and death, but there have been few empirical studies that would resolve their musings. Such studies as do have empirical content are blemished by the common imperfections of social science research: limited sampling and inadequate instrumentation (What does this measure measure?). When the empirical investigation is clinical or reportorial, it suffers also from a press to interpret beyond the data. We are accustomed to such stretching of the data in the ministerial meditations on dying; data-free interpretation is a priestly prerogative. But over-interpretation may be as common among psychoanalysts and journalists for whom the death scene has become "big."

Claude Bernard advised us that "It's what we think we know that prevents us from learning." His point is illustrated in some of the contemporary exegeses on death. Among these we swim in a sea of *non sequitur*, unsupported assertion, and conflicting readings of meanings.

---

[1]An excellent demonstration of the definitional quality of life and death is given by D. Sudnow, *Passing On*, New York: Prentice-Hall, 1966, particularly ch. IV. "Dying," "Being Dead," and, of course, "Being Alive (Human)," are shown to be social as well as biological conditions. An expelled fetus at Sudnow's "County Hospital" "... is either considered 'human' or not.... the dividing line is 550 grams, 20 centimeters, and 20 weeks of gestation. Any creature having smaller dimensions or of lesser embryonic 'age' is considered non-human ... and if 'born' without signs of life, is properly flushed down the toilet, or otherwise simply disposed of .... Any creature having larger dimensions or of greater embryonic 'age' is considered human, and if 'born' without signs of life, or if born with signs of life which cease to be noticeable at some later point, cannot be permissibly flushed down the toilet, but must be accorded a proper ritual departure from the human race" (pp. 176-177).

The fact that life is socially defined means that there are class connotations here too. Thus J. F. Kennedy is less dead socially, when medically dead, than the wino off the street (p. 169).

[2]It may be a useful definition of a moral norm, and a test of its presence, that its advocates do *not* change their stance when their justifying predictions are invalidated. Such a definition distinguishes a moral attitude from a reasonable or pragmatic one. It conforms with the thoughtful description of a moral code given by John Ladd, *The Structure of a Moral Code*, Cambridge: Harvard University Press, 1957, particularly pp. 102-103. Morals, when believed, are autonomous of their consequences.

*   Reprinted by permission of the author Gwynn Nettler, University of Alberta, Edmonton, Canada.
Social Problems, Vol.14, No.3 (Winter 1967.)

The temper of much recent writing on dying has been critical. Western societies are unsatisfactory because they "deny death," or pay it too much attention, or the wrong kind. Funerals are called expensive, vulgar, and a symbol of guilt.[3] They are both necessary and unnecessary and are perceived either as a test of our morbidity[4] or as signs of our unhealthy rejection of death.[5] Mourning is in decline[6] and we are told that this change in practice signifies a refusal to face the facts of our mortality. This denial, in turn, is supposed to lead to guilt and mental distress.[7]

Gorer discerns "... maladaptive and neurotic behaviour ... as a consequence of a denial of mourning ... "[8] and he includes his government's campaign against smoking as a further symbol of the rejection of death.

In a similar vein Fulton and Geis write that "... modern society rejects death in the most formidable and paradoxical fashion possible, by embracing casually and joyfully the delicately designed accoutrements of the grave."[9]

Children, too, take their lumps, particularly at the hands of their Freudian students. If children seem not to think much about death, this is, of course, "repression:"

> The predominant tendency we have found is that emotional response is inhibited, and on a level slightly below the surface the reality of the loss is denied. Inhibition of affect and denial of the reality of the loss mutually re-enforce each other. If one does not react to an event, it is as if it had not occurred.[10]

For the psychoanalyst, this alleged "inhibition of affect" on the part of male adolescents in response to the assassination of President Kennedy is "...ascribed to the arousal of vicarious guilt for a crime that bore the latent significance of parricide."[11]

These critiques on the end of life repeatedly advise us that the definitions accorded death tell us about our definitions of life. The question remains, "What?"

For example, Fulton assumes that when death "... is viewed merely as the inevitable conclusion of a natural process ... [it] lacks meaning, it is merely a fact in a world of facts, *and so too*, our lives lose their essence and we must search in vain for our lost selves."[12]

Is this so? Do those with a naturalistic attitude toward death live more meaningless lives, or lives harassed by a search for identity? Would any acquaintance dare assert this of such men a P. W. Bridgman, Ernest Hemingway, or George Lundberg?

In attempting connections between life and death attitudes, some recent essayists have labelled societies as "life-" or "death-oriented." Although independent, reliable criteria of a culture's "death orientation" are nowhere described, social scientists are not reluctant to draw inferences.

Fulton tells us that "We find ... both in death and life-oriented societies the same indifference to death, but stemming from quite different roots and social needs."[13]

[3]L. Bowman, *The American Funeral: A Study in Guilt, Extravagance and Sublimity,*Washington, D.C.: Public Affairs Press, 1959; R. N. Harmer, *The High Cost of Dying,* New York: Crowell-Collier, 1963; J. Mitford, *The American Way of Death,* New York: Simon & Schuster, 1963.

[4]Huxley, *After Many a Summer Dies the Swan,* New York: Avon, 1932; E. Waugh, *The Loved One,* Boston: Little, Brown, 1948.

[5]"On Death as a Constant Companion," *Time,* November 12, 1965, pp. 42-43; "The Necropolis," *Time,* September 30, 1966, p. 59.

[6]G. Gorer, *Death, Grief, and Mourning: A Study of Contemporary Society,* Garden City: Doubleday, 1963; *Time, op. cit.,* November 12, 1965.

[7]Gorer, *op. cit.*

[8]*Ibid.* p. xiii.

[9] R. Fulton and G. Geis, "Death and Social Values," in R. Fulton (ed.), *Death and Identity,* New York: John Wiley & Sons, 1965, p. 73.

[10]M. Wolfenstein, "Death of a Parent and Death of a President: Children's Reactions to Two Kinds of Loss," in M. Wolfenstein and G. Kliman (eds.), *Children and the Death of a President,* Garden City: Doubleday, 1963, p.64

[11]*Ibid.,* p. 202.

[12]Fulton and Geis, in Fulton, *op. cit.,* pp. 337-338 (emphasis supplied).

[13]*Ibid.,* p. 73.

On facing pages of the same volume, Octavio Paz can convince us that "The Mexican's indifference towards death is fostered by his indifference towards life. We kill because life — our own or another's — is of no value. Life and death are inseparable, and when the former lacks meaning, the latter becomes equally meaningless."[14] This sounds quite reasonable, but the next page dislodges us from this comfortable plausibility. "A civilization," Paz continues, "that denies death ends by denying life."[15]

A diverting game to play with such referent-free poetry is to alter a significant verb and see whether the declaration remains equally plausible.

"A society that *accepts* death ends by denying life." Or, "A society that denies life ends by *accepting* death." Or, to give Paz a Christian twist, suppose this were written, "A society that denies death begins to accept life."

There is no end to such word-games, as there is no end to philosophizing about life. The games and the philosophies give us hypotheses, but little information.

The psychoanalytic and literary death-metaphors, so conveniently adopted by some sociologists, will receive any data as their confirmation and none as their negation. The reader is entertained. There has been a verbal massage and one feels better, or worse, although he remains ignorant.

The critiques carried by this assemblage of recent monographs can be analyzed by the three types of problems they pose and intertwine.

The first problem is aesthetic and ethical:

How ought a person to die? What is a proper response to our own mortality and the loss of friends and enemies? Does "dignity" require that we maintain life against all consequence, or that we assist men to die on their own terms?

The second problem is interpretive. When one observes behaviors in others, what do they mean? What are the limits of inference, and the rules of correct conclusion?

If mourning practices change, does this signify an alteration in feeling? If children don't talk about the death of a president, does this mean "repression?" And Oedipal guilt? What does Forest Lawn signify? And family picnics on graves? If high-status persons express less grief than lower-status ones at the death of a Democratic president, can this be attributed, "in part," to guilt at having opposed the murdered leader's federal programs?[16]

The third problem is correlative and sequential. It is related to the second, but it has greater predictive implication. Where the second category of question is addressed largely to *post factum* explanation — making things seem plausible — the third type of question asks what attitudes and acts are connected with what others, and in what order. It leads to thoughts of the "if ... then" variety:

If you believe in a hereafter, will you die more easily? If you esteem yourself highly, does death come harder? If people don't mourn, do they become ill? If you have lived a ' good life" by your standards, are you better prepared to die? If the physician informs his dying patient of his probable fate, what happens?

It is not surprising that we can say the least about the last type of question (the most important one?) and the most about the first. Fulton and Geis conclude their literature-survey thus: "The social and psychological correlates of varying attitudes toward death remain to be established."[17]

Although this is true, some provisional facts about death and dying in America can be reported.

It seems most certain that it is "normal," statistically at least, *not* to think about the end. "The material from empirical sources reveals that on a conscious, verbal level people in our culture do not seem to be seriously concerned with thoughts of death," say Alexander and Adlerstein.[18] "Normal people," they tell us,

[14]*Ibid.*, p. 390.

[15]*Ibid.*, p. 391.

[16]B. S. Greenberg and E. B. Parker, eds.),*Kennedy Assassination and the American Public: Social Communication in Crisis*, Stanford: Stanford University Press, 1965, p. 372.

[17]Fulton and Geis, in Fulton, *op. cit.*, p. 74.

[18]I. E. Alexander and A. M. Adlerstein, "Studies in the Psychology of Death," in H. P. David and J. C. Brengelmann (eds.), *Perspectives in Personality Research*, New York: Springer Publishing Co., 1960, pp. 65-92.

"show very little conscious concern about death. Children, old people, and those in psychopathological or socially marginal states express somewhat more conscious interest in the problem."[19] Middleton reports that 93 per cent of a college sample only "very rarely" or "occasionally" think about death.[20]

Despite these facts, authors who cite such studies can hold that "... human beings find themselves increasingly caught up in the debate on the meaning of death."[21]

If people think little about death, except, of course, as it enters their homes, this statistical norm of low concern may coincide with an evaluative one: there may be a "wisdom of the psyche" in thinking of matters other than dying.

First, this normative "denial" of death flows from "good" sources. Children who are loved, it is said, are fortified against fear of death. Such acceptance "... enables one to effectively isolate the possibility of eventual death from ourselves (sic). This persistent feeling of personal invulnerability is puissant enough to enable the majority of mankind to remain relatively untroubled in the face of the vast array of facts which should convince us that death is the inevitable end of all men, even ourselves."[22]

Second, disdain of death may simply be a healthy — that is, an effective — attitude. Mortality is a fact of life. But how much ought one to attend to it if he is to go about getting his work done and living well?

> A centipede was happy quite
> Until a frog in fun
> Asked, "Pray, tell me,
> Which leg comes after which?"

We know the fate of the thinking centipede. It may similarly be questioned whether "facing reality," whatever that may mean, is the best way of handling all careers on this hazardous earth. The Scarlett O'Hara complex seems to succeed as often as it has failed, and there are, as yet, no psychic mathematicians who have solved the equations of this felicific calculus.

For example, the psychologist Feifel reminds us that "... it is far from being being established ... that all facing of death necessarily represents gains in mental health. Certain studies of airplane pilots in World War II, for example, revealed that those who did not break down psychologically retained, in the moments of most extreme danger, the illusion of invulnerability." [23]

Truth is not always the friend of Utility, as Pareto cautioned us and as some recent studies have demonstrated.[24] The muddied consequences of truth-telling and reality-facing are well described by Glaser and Strauss.[25] They demonstrate how, in confrontation with death, each condition of truth, and of deceit, has its price. In such a market-place, moral debate finds its commerce. Glaser and Strauss show awareness of dying to be multi-dimensional. Each dimension of expectation has rather patterned preconditions and consequences. Thus, many who die in American hospitals do so interacting with their helpers in a process of "closed awareness." The patient does not recognize his impending death, but his attendants do. In our society there are pervasive conditions of dying, and an associated mythology, that sustain this pattern.

1. Many who die are inexperienced with the premonitory signs of death.

2. Hospitals are structured to hide medical information from patients.

3. Physicians and family dissemble with the dying and justify their deceit by the assumption that dying men don't want to know their fate. As with most popular dicta, this is both true and false.

[19]I. E. Alexander, R. S. Colley, and A. M. Adlerstein, "Is Death a Matter of Indifference?" in Fulton, *op. cit.*, p. 83.

[20]W. C. Middleton, "Some Reactions Toward Death Among College Students," *Journal of Abnormal and Social Psychology,* 31 (1936). pp. 165-173.

[21]Fulton and Geis, in Fulton, *op. cit.*, p. 74.

[22]C. W. Wahl, in Fulton, *op. cit.*, p. 61.

[23]H. Feifel, "The Function of Attitudes Toward Death," Group for the Advancement of Psychiatry (eds.), *Death and Dying: Attitudes of Patient and Doctor,* New York: Mental Health Materials Center, 1965, pp. 639-640.

[24]V. Pareto, *The Mind and Society: A Treatise on General Sociology,* New York: Harcourt, Brace & Co., 1935, Π 2002 and *passim*; F. E. Fiedler, "Assumed Similarity Measures as Predictors of Team Effectiveness," *Journal of Abnormal and Social Psychology,* 49 (1954), pp. 381-38; G. Nettler, "Good Men, Bad Men, and the Perception of Reality," *Sociometry,* 24 (1961), pp. 279-294; I. D. Steiner, "Interpersonal Behavior as Influenced by Accuracy of Social Perception," *Psychological Review,* 62 (1955), pp. 268-274; J. A. Sprunger, "Relationship of a Test of Ability to Estimate Group Opinion to Other Variables," unpublished M. A. thesis, Ohio State University, 1949.

[25]B. G. Glaser and A. L. Strauss, *Awareness of Dying*, Chicago: Aldine Publishing Co., 1965.

One investigator who has counted the wishes of terminal patients tells us that between 77 and 89 per cent, depending on the study, want to know.[26]

Feifel reports that "In [a] sample of 52 persons ... the great majority, 82 per cent, want to be informed about their condition for such reasons as these: 'settle my affairs'; 'make various financial and family arrangements';[27] 'it's my life − I have a right to know'; 'do what I really want'; 'understand why I am suffering'; 'I would respond to treatment better if I actually knew what I was up against'; 'I don't want to be denied the experience of realizing that I am dying'; 'have time to live with the idea and learn to die' "[28]

In contrast with these expressed wishes of terminal patients, various studies report 69 to 90 per cent of physicians as opposed to telling the patient the truth.[29]

It will not constitute a genetic fallacy here to cite a possible source of physicians' attitudes: Feifel believes doctors themselves are more afraid of death, though they think less about it, than two control groups of patients and one of non-professionals.[30]

4. The process of "closed awareness" is also justified by the medical axiom that "it's better not to tell." Doctors give this rule anecdotal support and they transmit their "clinical experience" to those families that might serve as allies of the patient in the information-seeking contest. In practice this rule of silence protects the physician from an unpleasant task and throws the burden of the death-managing chore upon nurses.[31]

On this subject, the consequences of knowledge of one's terminal state, the babel of experts is deafening. Aronson lists four rules for psychiatric support of the dying person, two of which are sufficiently vague and potentially contradictory to guarantee hesitant treatment: "Hope must never die too far ahead of the patient;" "The gravity of the situation should not be minimized.'[32]

Feder reports that "People with skin cancer or cancer that presents a visible mass handle the threat far better than those who have an internal malignancy that cannot be kept under their observation and that they cannot follow very carefully." [33] This would suggest that knowledge allays anxiety. But before we can settle upon this assumption, Feder himself rejects it, "The implication is that the acceptance of death eases the conflict. I can't agree."[34]

Perhaps telling doesn't matter much anyway. Boland tried an experiment at Christie Hospital in which every other cancer patient was told of his malignancy. Follow-up interviews revealed that those who had been told "sometimes acted as though they never heard anything about it."[35] Further, the conditions of much dying makes disclosure irrelevant. Sudnow comments, "The deaths that I witnessed seldom involved a patient whose condition was such that interaction with him was likely. It is my feeling that a considerable number of deaths involve the circumstance where awareness of 'dying' is irrelevant, from an organizational perspective, with a chief exception being cancer, where both patients and staff members are involved in daily social interaction. Deaths of patients suffering from other diseases, e.g., heart disease, kidney disease, CVA's (strokes), and liver diseases, have a course such that at that point when 'dying' becomes noticeable, during the patient's 'last admission' ... the patient is, so to speak, out of the picture. The greatest 'cause of death,' heart disease, typically 'produces' death in the course of a short term hospital admission, eventuating from an 'attack' and is not preceded by that lengthy period of consciousness which is the fate of the cancer victim."[36]

[26]Feifel, *op.cit.*, p. 635.

[27]Concordantly, one study found that physicians are more likely to tell businessmen of their fatal condition so they can clean up their business affairs. D. Oken, "What to Tell Cancer Patients: A Study of Medical Attitudes," *The Journal of the American Medical Association*, 175 (1961), pp. 1120-1128.

[28]Feifel, *op. cit.*

[29]*Ibid.*

[30]*Ibid.* p. 634.

[31]J. C. Quint, *The Nurse and the Dying Patient*, New York: The Macmillan Co., 1966; Glaser and Strauss, *op. cit.*, p. 45.

[32]G. T. Aronson, "The Treatment of the Dying Person," in H. Feifel (ed.), *The Meaning of Death*, New York:McGraw-Hill Book Co., 1959, pp. 251-258.

[33]S. L. Feder, "Attitudes of Patients with Advanced Malignancy," in Group for the Advancement of Psychiatry *op. cit.*, p. 617.

[34]*Ibid.*, p. 622.

[35]*Ibid.*, p. 620.

[36]*Op. cit.*, p. 100, fn.

"Closed awareness" seems most satisfactory, then, when the patient dies quickly. Otherwise it tends toward instability, and other modalities of being aware of dying develop: those that Glaser and Strauss call "suspicion," "mutual pretense," and, finally, "open awareness."

The likely consequences of each process of interaction between the dying man, his helpers, and his family differ. And all conclusions about consequences, particularly those concerning the effects of "open awareness," are qualified by the intersecting feelings about the certainty of the prognosis and the time assumed to be remaining. The influence of these variables is, in turn, compounded with the personality of the dying man, the manner in which he is told, and the setting in which he is dying. The "death-setting" includes, too, the victim's perceived reasons for dying.

In hospitals such as those of the Veterans' Administration, where "captive patients" are often told abruptly of the approach of death, an initial response is depression. In most cases depression is dissolved in acceptance or denial of the imminence of death. And these "choices," in turn, have their respective results.

But our powers of predicting individual responses to the certainty of death are negligible. We know some minor things:

1. "... sharp, abrupt disclosure tends to produce more denial, then dulled disclosure."[37]

2. In a highly selected sample of terminal patients who submitted to group research, the communal awareness of dying is said to have had happy consequences, *a la* the "Hawthorne effect."[38]

3. When groups of men are confronted with certain death in a hopeless situation, they do not seem differentially vulnerable to neurotic breakdown.[39]

4. Attitude toward death does not vary with judged degree of mental disturbance. A possible qualification of this finding is that mentally ill persons may more often conceive of themselves as dying violently.[40]

5. Old people are *not* noted for their fear of death and, when in poor health, "... tend actually to look forward to [it] ...."[41]

6. Individuals of lesser education show less concern for imminence of death.[42]

7. Being alone increases fear of dying.[43]

8. Old people who are "actively religious" seem more favorably inclined toward dying than those less religious.[44]

However, Feifel reports that those religious persons who expect to be judged in an after-life are more frightened of dying, as well they might be.[45] On this issue, Feifel is careful to point out that "being religious" is multifaceted. It would be of interest to assess the dimensions of supernatural belief and their relationship to joy in living and strength in dying.

Beyond a chronicle of this nature, sociologists can offer no definitive advice that would answer the physicians' justifications for "not telling."[46] We cannot yet predict who will die denying his departure or who, aware of his passage, will exit screaming.

If our knowledge of the determinants of graceful dying is thus qualified, so too is our information about the bereavement process. " We rarely understand how to treat our sorrow or those of others," Trollope wrote.[47]

[37]Glaser and Strauss, *op. cit.* p. 126

[38]R. Fox, *Experiment Perilous,* New York: The Free Press of Glencoe, 1959.

[39]W. R. von Baeyer, H. Häfner, and K. P. Kisker, *Psychiatrie der Verfolgten,* Berlin: Springer, 1964.

[40]H. Feifel, "Attitudes of Mentally Ill Patients Towards Death," *Journal of Nervous and Mental Disease,* 122 (1955), pp. 375-380.

[41]W. M. Swenson, "Attitudes Toward Death Among the Aged," in Fulton, *op. cit.*, pp. 105-111.

[42]*Ibid.* p. 110.

[43]*Ibid.*

[44]*Ibid.*

[45]H. Feifel, "Some Aspects of the Meaning of Death," in E. S. Shneidman and N. L. Farberow (eds.), *Clues to Suicide,* New York: McGraw-Hill, 1957, p. 53, fn.1.

[46]"... readily ascertainable and unambiguous general criteria are needed for deciding when to disclose terminality and when to keep the patient unaware of it. Criteria that require 'intimate knowledge of each patient' offer no better a solution to the doctor's dilemma than does a universally applied rule of telling or not telling." Glaser and Strauss, *op. cit.*, p. 135.

[47]A. Trollope, *Framley Parsonage,* London: 1861.

Loss is differentially perceived, of course, and we know something about the correlates of emotional expression in response to the death of others. For example, when President Kennedy was assassinated, the mass media reached almost everyone in the nation,[48] and this event generated more empirical social science research than any previous single event with the possible exception of the Kennedy-Nixon debates.[49]

Some 400 pages of report on these studies lead to such conclusions as:

— people were shocked.
— people who liked JFK were more shocked than those who didn't like him.
— shock and disbelief were followed by the need to know, by emotions of sorrow, fear, despair, and anger, and by a return to normalcy.
— lower-class people tended to express more emotion and sorrow than others[50] and to hold more extreme beliefs about the murder.
— women were more emotionally upset than men.
— women resorted more frequently than men to religion.
— Negroes were more upset than whites.
— children and adults seemed to respond similarly.
— lower-class people were more punitive and concrete in their recommendations than others.[51]
— "Collective responsibility for the assassination ('we're all to blame') was assumed by people from all regions studied,"[52] but more frequently by women, Democrats, and liberals.
— hostile people responded with hostility ("The respondent who is ready to attack when frustrated is the one who was likely to be pleased by Oswald's death, to feel that Oswald's act was politically inspired, and to believe that Ruby was a patriot who should be let free with a suspended sentence or, contrastingly, a conspirator who ought to be shot.")[53]

One need not be an Arthur Schlesinger to question whether this yield justifies such extensive study. Study that elaborates the obvious. Study that does not resolve the empirical questions of consequences, and that leaves unanswered the aesthetic and ethical questions of how one ought to behave when others die.

The processes by which we acquire attitudes toward life and death have been described. A fair conclusion seems to be that what has been so learned could have been taught differently. Children ingest our superstitions about death along with those we hold about life.[54] These attitudes later intrude upon our research and our interpretations of the behavior of others. As an illustration, Gorer is led to equate ritual mourning with grief. But it is apparent to others of us, less socialized in the psychoanalytic style, that the etiquette of response-to-death can allow many feelings, and that the association between public observance and private sentiment is far from the linear one Gorer assumes.

Wolfram demonstrates this. She wields Ockham's razor to cut the crust of presumption from Gorer's thesis. She shows the ritual of mourning to express more closely one's formal relationship to the deceased than one's feelings of loss.[55] Similarly, one doubts the meaning of much behavioral research that asks questions stimulated by the investigator's assumptions, where such assumptions may have little relevance to the worlds of the observed actors. Pollsters, particularly, are guilty of putting the "vacant question," a "vacant question" being one that elicits a response out of "nothing" — neither opinion nor information, neither feeling nor disposition to act. "Nothing" is perhaps too strong a term: since there is a response, one may infer a motive. But the answer's motivation may not be what the student assumes; it may be courtesy or the socially approved feeling that "one ought to have an opinion."[56]

[48]S. P. Spitzer and N. S. Spitzer in Greenberg and Parker, *op. cit.*, pp.99-111. "If a hard core of know-nothings existed in the community studied, we were unable to find them" (p.110).

[49]*Ibid.*, p. 361.

[50]*Ibid.*, p. 187.

[51]*Ibid.*, pp. 372-373.

[52]*Ibid.*, p. 253.

[53]*Ibid.*, p. 304.

[54]M. E. Mitchell, *The Child's Attitude to Death,* London: Barrie & Rockliff, 1966.

[55]S. Wolfram, "The Decline of Mourning," *The Listener,* May 26, 1966, pp. 763-764.

[56]"An opinion is considered a free gift in a culture where privacy is at a minimum, and people will feel that the interviewer is entitled to an opinion irrespective of whether they also try to guess which of several possible opinions he may want of them." D. Riesman and N. Glazer, "The Meaning of Opinion," *Public Opinion Quarterly,* 12 (Winter, 1948-1949), pp. 633-648.

On this possibility, cf also P. R. Hofstaetter, "The Actuality of Questions," *International Journal of Opinion and Attitude Research,* 4 (1950), pp.16-26; H. J. Parry and H. M. Crossley, "Validity of Responses to Survey Questions," *Public Opinion Quarterly,* 14 (1950), pp. 61-80; S. L. Payne, "Thoughts About Meaningless Questions," *Public Opinion Quarterly,* 14 (1950), pp. 687-696.

Silence *is* sullen, and the polite pollster is given "something" when he asks, "Who or what should really be blamed for the assassination of President Kennedy — aside from the man who actually fired the gun?" "Did the assassination teach the American people a lesson of any kind?" "Why did Oswald do it?"[57] So contagious is interrogation that investigators may even riddle themselves with presumptuous questions: "... why did this event provoke such deep reactions among those who are so often untouched by the events of the political world."[58]

An exercise among the mortuary literature does not end merely in the revelation of the repetitive frailties of attempts to study man "objectively." It leaves one impressed with the possibility that death need not be assigned the importance we give it.[59] And there is a return full circle to the acknowledgment that the definitions given death rest upon the meanings assigned to life.

The bridge across this Styx remains to be built.

[57]Greenberg and Parker, *op. cit., passim.*

[58]N. M. Bradburn and J. J. Feldman, *ibid.*, p. 284. This question assumes that, because the man who died was a political figure, reaction to his death must also be a political function.

"Today, some 90 percent of social science research is based upon interviews and questionnaires. We lament this overdependence upon a single, fallible method. Interviews and questionnaires intrude as a foreign element into the social setting they would describe, they create as well as measure attitudes, they elicit atypical roles and responses, they are limited to those who are accessible and will cooperate, and the responses obtained are produced in part by dimensions of individual differences irrelevant to the topic at hand." E. J. Webb *et al., Unobstrusive Measures: Nonreactive Research in the Social Sciences,* Chicago: Rand McNally & Co., 1966, p. 1.

[59]Death is not believed to be an exigency in all cultures. Thus, for example, Kardiner maintains that the Tanala fear neither death nor the dead. Whether this actually means that death simply is not an exigency in Tanala culture, or whether it means that a need "not to die" cannot become articulated in this culture, is a nice question.

G. K. Zollschan & P. Gibeau, "Concerning Alienation," in Zollschan & Hirsch (eds.), *Exploration in Social Change*, New York: Houghton-Mifflin, 1964, p. 153, fn. 2.

CULTURAL VALUES AND ATTITUDES TOWARD DEATH *

by

Alan Howard and Robert A. Scott

Attitudes toward death, like so many other aspects of a people's "world-view", are strongly influenced by dominant cultural themes. In this paper, we propose to analyze some of the cultural values that appear to affect American attitudes toward death, and to explore their social consequences. We shall also contrast American patterns with those of a Polynesian people, the Rotumans, among whom one of the authors has recently completed twenty-one months of field work.[1]

In comparison with other attitudes such as prejudice, attitudes toward death have received little attention from social scientists in this country; yet few attitudes are more central to human motivation. Any satisfactory comprehension of human behavior requires a knowledge of the significance that people attribute to being alive; and to understand this requires a knowledge of their attitudes toward death. The paucity of systematic studies in this area reflects the morbidity with which the subject is regarded in our society. Nevertheless, a few highly significant studies have been made which should stimulate further research.

Previous studies have reported that the predominant attitude toward death in American society is one of dread. Such a disposition has been found to prevail in the population as a whole,[2] and in such subgroups as older persons,[3] college students,[4] adolescents,[5] and physicians.[6] But perhaps the most thoroughly studied group has been young children. Various studies have dealt with children's feelings about death,[7] how they cope with the idea of death intellectually,[8] the theories they employ to explain it,[9] the impact of their first experience of the death of another,[10] and the effects of their own impending death upon their fantasies.[11] It should be noted in passing that this focus upon children's attitudes is not entirely rooted in their theoretical relevance, nor does it seem to stem solely from the intellectual curiosity of the investigators. Perhaps a more important factor is the ease with which the investigators are able to avoid identification with young subjects, thereby reducing the danger of their own self-involvement with the fact of death. Furthermore, children are less apt to communicate a sense of morbidity, and so are less threatening subjects than adults.

Additional studies have dealt with various other aspects of death. Among these are studies of bereavement and its social impact,[12] and of the sociological and cultural significance of funeral rites.[13] Anthropologists have contributed some special studies on attitudes toward death in other cultures,[14] while most standard ethnographies describe beliefs and rituals concerning death.

These studies provide an excellent basis for attempting to comprehend and explain the predominance in our society of a fearful attitude toward death. Some noteworthy progress has already been made toward illuminating the psychodynamics involved,[15] but as yet the sociocultural determinants have gotten little attention. What little speculation there has been on those determinants has come either from general essayists,[16] or from writers on philosophy,[17] art,[18] and literature.[19] The purpose of the present paper is to systematically explore some of the links between dominant cultural themes and attitudes toward death, with a view toward stimulating further research.

There is a distinction between attitudes toward death and attitudes toward dying. Death is a state or condition into which every organism passes. It refers to the complete cessation of all vital functions of the organism. Dying, on the other hand, is a process, the process of life drawing to a close. Hence, dying usually involves the possibility of avoidance or delay, whereas death is final and inevitable.

The fear of dying seems to be universal. Philosophers and students of human behavior have long pointed out that self-preservation is a fundamental human motive, and some have even suggested that it is the most basic of all human motives. Every society regards human life as precious and takes precautions to preserve it. From time to time, under very special circumstances, other values may supersede the value of life itself — clan

* Reprinted by permission of the Journal of Existentialism, Vol.VI (Winter 1965.) Libra Publishers, Inc., Roslyn Heights, N.Y. pp 161-174.

and kindred, honor, patriotism, self-glorification, etc. — the nature of these values varying from society to society. But in every society, individuals willingly give their lives only under extreme conditions. Nowhere is dying taken lightly, and to die for nothing is everywhere regarded as a great misfortune.

The fear of death, however, is not universal. Persons may also regard the state of death with acquiescence, friendly anticipation, or even fanatical hope. This fact is well documented in the studies of Bromberg and Schilder, who note that "the fear of actually dying is apparently uppermost. It seems that the act of dying more than being dead or death completely overrides the notion that the individual is removed from the land of the living. Most of the subjects stress the dislike of the dying process."[20] As Wahl notes, "death is itself not only a state, but a complex symbol, the significance of which will vary from one person to another and from one culture to another, and is also profoundly dependent upon the nature of the vicissitudes of the developmental process."[21] It is the cultural context of this developmental process that we shall explore here.

Three aspects of death are of special relevance to our discussion. First, death may be conceived of as a defeat of man by nature. Men everywhere have at their disposal a variety of cultural techniques — notably medicine, magic, and prayer — with which to challenge dying. But despite all men's efforts, death is the ultimate victor.

Second, death results in separation. Foremost is the physical separation of the deceased from friends and relatives, and from society in general; but also implied is a total cessation of social interaction between the deceased and his survivors. The degree to which this separation is dramatized differs from society to society, but it is usually expressed in the specific funeral custom.[22] At one extreme are those societies which sanction the preservation of corpses or of relics from them, or which keep the corpse within the village and allow it to deteriorate slowly. Under such circumstances, the drama of separation is mitigated. At the other extreme are those societies in which corpses are destroyed with the greatest possible haste; in these societies, the physical separation, at least, is dramatic and abrupt. Cultural beliefs regarding the fate of souls may also affect the rapidity with which separation is experienced. Where tradition holds that the souls of the dead remain socially active for a period of time following death, one would expect separation to be experienced less abruptly than where souls are believed to depart directly from the social sphere, or not to exist at all.

Third, death is a state of inactivity. It is true, of course, that most people profess to believe in a life after death — a state in which the soul is active. Yet the very way in which this is usually stated — *life* after death — merely emphasizes the association of life with activity and death with inactivity. Regardless of beliefs concerning the soul, the quiescence of the physical organism after death is readily apparent and dramatizes the association of death with inactivity.

It is our basic thesis that the dread with which death is regarded in American culture can in part be explained as the result of a conflict between the aspects of death discussed above and basic American values.

American Values and Attitudes Toward Death

At the core of the American value system is the belief that man can master nature, a belief which has motivated the phenomenal technological progress that we now enjoy. The belief, itself, however, has been nurtured by the fact that man has been able to gain a greater control over his environment than previous generations thought possible. Technological progress has enabled man to solve problems that previously had been regarded as unchangeable facts of life. Man has moved into an age in which it is not only hoped, but accepted as certainty, that with enough money, knowledge, and hours of work, it is possible to resolve any problem, surmount any obstacle, or change any part of nature.

One result of these beliefs is that most Americans do not really accept death as inevitable; they tend to feel invulnerable. As Wahl has noted, these beliefs are "puissant enought to enable the majority of mankind to remain relatively untroubled in the face of the vast array of factors which should convince them that death is the inevitable end of all men 'even themselves.'[23] Thus our cultural conditioning makes us feel shocked at the realization of death's finality. In its presence we are forced to re-evaluate our belief system. In the words of Jung, "the question of the meaning and worth of life never becomes more urgent or more agonizing than when we see the final breath leave a body which a moment before was living."[24] In sum, death may be conceived of as a thwarting of man's struggle for ultimate supremacy; it hence constitutes a serious threat to his sense of mastery over nature. As such, it is a source of anxiety and fear.

In America, separation and isolation are also associated with death. To some extent, this is a consequence of two features of our sociocultural system. First, our modal funeral custom involves interment of the corpse in a closed box, which is hastily transported to the outskirts of a town or city and placed in a hole in the ground. The process of cremation is hardly a less dramatic form of separation. Second, since the network of interpersonal relations with significant others tends to be narrowly confined in our culture, death usually involves a certain measure of social isolation for the bereaved. To fully understand this association of death with social isolation, it is necessary to probe further into the significance of social isolation in America. As a general rule, the threat of social isolation generates considerable anxiety for Americans. This is implied in our system of social control, in which social isolation is second only to death in severity of punishment. Perhaps the most dramatic example of its effectiveness can be seen from its impact on prisoners of war.[25]

There are several reasons why separation is threatening to persons in our society. One is that most individuals live within a tight security circle, relying upon only a few people for emotional gratification. This tends to produce intense, rather than diffuse affective relationships, rendering separation from only a few people a potentially critical emotional experience. The possibility of finding adequate substitutes for significant others is remote. As a consequence, the whole self-image of an individual is under maximum risk when he is faced with separation. A factor of even greater consequence is the nature of the socialization process in America, particularly in the middle class, among whom social isolation, along with reasoning and "love-oriented" techniques, are dominant forms of discipline.[26] Moreover, many of our child-rearing practices result in periodically isolating the child from his main source of emotional security. He is often put in a separate room to sleep at an age when isolation and punishment may be synonymous in his mind.

It should also be noted that a number of crucial social experiences encountered by most children involve facing new and sometimes threatening experiences alone, without the presence of someone on whom they can rely for emotional support. The first days of school, being lost in a crowd, or spending time in a hospital are examples. Whatever other threats or dangers might be associated with these experiences, it is clear that the factor they have in common is separation from significant others, which in our society is tantamount to social isolation.[27] One would expect, then, that persons exposed to such socialization experiences, would anticipate social isolation with anxiety; and, since death is the epitome of social isolation, it is not surprising that it is regarded with dread by persons so raised.

The association of death with social isolation is not simply a one-way affair, however. While a fear of death may stem from anxieties about social isolation, it seems equally true that the process of becoming socially isolated stimulates a concern about death. There are exceptions to this, of course, particularly in cases of voluntary exile. In fact, social isolation for some may be a means to a valued end, such as mystical experiences. When social isolation is involuntary, however, the individual experiencing separation from others may become obsessed with the idea of death. Ordinary values, those previously associated with primary groups or with society in general, may pale into insignificance when they are no longer shared with significant others. As these values lose their saliency, behavior patterns once structured by culturally shared imperatives may come to be based upon only the grossest considerations of life and death. As a result, the fear of death may come to outweigh the fear of dying, and the person may be motivated toward ego-destructive behavior. On the other hand, the equation of social isolation with death may lead the isolate to regard death with indifference, since he is, in effect, already "dead." In either case, the potential social consequences are profound. Fearing death more than dying is probably instrumental in suicide, dope addiction, alcoholism, and other forms of psychological self-destruction; while feeling indifferent toward death probably motivates such nonpassionate aggressors as professional killers. In any case, when people cease to care about dying, society is deprived of its ultimate deterrent to deviant behavior — execution.

The activity orientation of Americans is so well-known that it hardly requires comment. Indeed, one could make a strong case for considering it the dominant theme in our culture. The value placed on improving one's status by hard work and the traits associated with success — ambition, ingenuity, and assertiveness — are indicators of this activity bias. Those who spend their time wisely, attempting to improve themselves, are praised. Wasting time is looked upon with disfavor by nearly everyone, and as sinful by many. The only acceptable justification for resting seems to be to regain strength, so that work may be attacked with renewed vigor. That this value has a religious basis makes it especially significant. As Weber pointed out, the pre-eminence in capitalistic societies of the value of success through hard work has its root in the Protestant ethic, and particularly in the theology of Calvin. According to Calvin's doctrine of predestination, the only tangible indications a person has of his fate after death are his attainments on earth; thus, a great value came to be placed upon success, particularly when it was achieved through hard work.[28]

But the American emphasis on activity goes beyond simply encouraging productive endeavor. So thoroughly engrained is this value that even leisure time is not often spent idly, but rather in some form of diversionary activity. It is the rare person who is able to remain inactive over a period of time and actually enjoy it. One indication of this fact is that persons inactivated against their will, by illness or involuntary retirement, often say, "I might as well be dead." And, with the increasing amount of leisure time among the active, boredom seems to be emerging as a major social problem. A desperate search appears to be on to find more things to do, more games to play, more places to go. It does not occur to many Americans that much time could be spent loafing. One of the important consequences of this over-all association of activity and virtue is that Americans tend to feel guilty and anxious when faced with inactivity, and since death is clearly associated with the latter, it is a state to be feared.

Finally, let us consider some of the behavioral consequences of these cultural themes and of their resultant attitudes. It is apparent that most Americans do not become so thoroughly isolated that they cease to care about death. On the contrary, they manifest acute anxiety about the prospect of death. Symptomatic of this problem is the obsessive spectatoritis concern for death. There is little doubt that many people go to see automobile races because they are attracted by the possibility of human destruction; and televison ratings have repeatedly demonstrated the appeal of death and violence. The attraction seems to consist of both fascination and anxiety. (In this respect, American attitudes toward death parallel those toward sex.) Yet, possibly because the idea of death is so threatening, there exists a strong defensive attempt to deny its significance. This pattern is perhaps most clearly manifest in Western and gangster films, in which a "bang-bang-you're dead" aura prevails. The impersonality of those killings is striking. One wonders whether the fact that some of those who are "killed" ride again in a new picture may not further support Americans' apparent inability to thoroughly grasp death's finality. Other defensive responses are significant. One is the withdrawal from activities which may be construed as a threat to life, such as flying or sailing. It may be found that the overall worship of security that characterizes a large portion of our population is rooted in the fear of death, as distinct from the fear of dying.

Rotuman Values and Attitudes Toward Death

The Island of Rotuma is somewhat isolated, lying approximately 300 miles north of the Fiji group on the western fringe of Polynesia. The current population of the island is about 3000, and about 1500 other Rotumans now live in Fiji, with which Rotuma has been politically affiliated since 1881, when it was ceded to Great Britain.[29] The culture of the people is basically Polynesian, although influences from Micronesia and Melanesia are also evident. In order to provide a background for comprehending Rotuman values and attitudes toward death, we shall describe some basic features of the social organization and life cycle.

The Rotuman kinship system stresses bilateral principles, with the personal kindred (*kainaga*)[30] providing the basis for social relations. Kinship is recognized broadly by American standards; third and fourth cousins, and even more distant relatives, are known and treated as close family members. Relatives assist one another in various social and economic activities, and come together enmasse for important social ceremonies, including funerals. The most important social unit, however, is the individual household, which for the most part is economically self-sufficient. The average household contains seven or eight persons, although many are considerably larger. Most households consist of a nuclear family, with various attached relatives of either the husband or wife. Social relations within the household are generally warm and cordial, even between in-laws, although as elsewhere, antagonisms sometimes develop between even the closest of relatives. In general, although there are somewhat definite rules of behavior among various categories of kin, within the household spontaneity rather than formality is the norm.

Households are organized into social units called *ho'aga*, which work together on community projects under the direction of a subchief, the *fa es ho'aga*. They also assist one another in projects demanding resources beyond the scope of an individual household, including ceremonies. The *ho'aga*, in turn, are grouped into seven districts, each under the direction of a paramount chief, or *gagaj es itu*.

Following its discovery by Europeans at the end of the eighteenth century, Rotuma was subjected to intensive acculturation from whalers, traders, and missionaries. The missionaries were Methodist ministers and Catholic priests, who divided the island between them. Today, approximately two thirds of the population is Methodist, and, except for a few individuals belonging to other Christian sects, the remainder are Catholic. But despite this subjection to prolonged acculturation, Rotuma remains today quite conservative culturally,[31] and, in 1960, when field work was being carried out, it was a well-integrated community.

The Rotuman life cycle can conveniently be divided into six stages: infancy (prelinguistic), childhood, school years, youth, adulthood, and old age.

During infancy the child is indulged to the utmost. Rotumans are open in showing their love of children, and youngsters are the focus of attention in nearly every household. Since the households usually contain many people, there is almost always someone available to hold the infant; and, as a rule, until a child can walk, he is held in someone's arms most of the time. A child is rarely permitted to cry without some attempt being made to soothe it. Such neglect would bring ridicule from neighbors, who would accuse the guardians of being unloving and unkind. The affection displayed for children does not signify a possessive love, however. As in many other Polynesian societies, adoption is a common practice and serves to distribute children from those who have too many to those who have too few. A mother is pleased to give her child to a friend or relative who can give it more attention than she can afford.

Indulgence continues throughout childhood. To Rotumans a loving parent is one who indulges a child's every wish, or at least all of those with which he can possibly comply. Indeed, "to love" (*hanisi*), for Rotumans, implies "to give" — to behave in a loving way — rather than to experience an emotion. A Rotuman parent would find incomprehensible the English statement, "I am punishing you because I love you. It is for your own good." We do not, however, mean to imply that Rotuman children are not disciplined. As soon as a child is capable of understanding shame, ridicule is used as a primary discipline technique. The most important behavioral lesson a child must learn is to discern whom he must respect and with whom he may take license. He must also learn not to show off or act proud. Moreover, Rotuman parents sometimes slap their children simply because of anger or annoyance. The tone of child rearing is, however, unmistakably warm and indulgent.

During the school years [32] the children encounter a somewhat different situation. It is impossible for any teacher — even a Rotuman teacher — to indulge a large number of children all at once, and to teach them besides. Children make obvious overtures for teachers' attention, but at the same time they are restrained by previous training from showing off. In doing school work they generally perform well as long as they are able to maintain mastery, but they usually stop trying in the face of difficulties which are not easily overcome. This low tolerance for frustration, coupled with the withdrawal response, is apparently rooted in the unconditional indulgence experienced in the home. Prior to attending school, a child has to bear little frustration, and subsequently poor performance in school is more likely to be met with sympathy than by admonishments or exhortations from parents. It is significant that withdrawal from frustration takes place when superiors are involved (objects of respect); in athletic competition, with people of equal rank, the response to frustration is more apt to be overt anger directed toward the opponent or opponents. In neither case, however, is the frustrating challenge likely to become a spur to greater effort until all obstacles are overcome and mastery achieved.

Youth begins when a boy or girls leaves school, which on Rotuma goes only to Form IV, our equivalent of the tenth grade. After that, a student wishing to continue his education must take a standard examination; if he passes it, he may go to an advanced school in Fiji. But the majority stop school at about age sixteen, and assume the roles of young men and women.

Youth is a period of little responsibility, when the most important interpersonal relations are among members of one's own age group. Comradeship between members of the same sex is intense, but the predominant concern is with surreptitious courtship. At this stage, the young men ordinarily sleep away from their parental homes in special sleeping houses, although they customarily eat with their own family. They form the nucleus of communal labor in every village, but aside from the obligation of participating in community efforts they enjoy a maximum of personal freedom.

The young women are considerably more restricted than the young men. They live at home and are expected to make a serious contribution to the family economy by cooking, washing, cleaning, making mats, and fishing on the reef. Customarily, girls are expected to remain virgins until marriage, which is supposed to be arranged between families. Careful measures are usually taken to restrict a young girl's freedom, so that she cannot get involved in sexual affairs that might cause her family embarrassment. Despite these restrictions, or perhaps more accurately because of them, courtship is a focal point of cultural elaboration, and evokes a great deal of ingenuity and cunning.[33] Romantic attachments take place frequently and with considerable intensity. Jealousy is easily aroused between partners, and suicide (or more often, attempted suicide) is not unknown among rejected suitors. Intense romantic attachments occur because of the indulgence the person receives as a child. Expectations of comparable indulgence persist, and if the focus narrows to one lover, the mood is apt to be further intensified.

Adulthood ordinarily begins with marriage. At this time, both man and wife are expected to assume full social and economic responsibilities within their own household and within the community. Residence at marriage is theoretically uxorilocal, but statistically it is bilocal — the choice depending on various economic and social circumstances. In some rare cases, residence is neolocal. Most newly married couples, therefore, assume a subordinate role in one of the partners' parental households. For the visiting spouse, the situation may prove a difficult one: because relations between in-laws are supposed to be governed by respect, the visiting spouse, initially at least, may find a sharp contrast with his or her previous history of indulgence from one's own parents. If this period of adjustment is experienced as emotionally too demanding, the visiting spouse may request that his or her partner come to his or her parental home. If such a request is refused divorce or separation may ensue (another manifestation of the Rotuman tendency to respond to frustration by withdrawing). Before too long, however, most men become heads of their own households, and in-law problems are alleviated. On the whole, divorce is infrequent; and, despite the fact that husband and wife are expected to manifest respectful behavior to one another in public by showing restraint, most couples develop a genuinely warm and affectionate attachment, whether or not their union had followed a romantic courtship.

In old age, most individuals yield authority to their mature children. Many old people remain economically productive until their ultimate illness, but their proportionate contribution tends to decrease with time. As grandparents, their greatest emotional pleasures come from the superindulgence with which they treat their grandchildren. Some old people express loneliness, and a few have been completely neglected by children immersed in their own affairs, but most of the elderly are able to maintain an adequate network of interpersonal relations as long as they live.

The characteristic Rotuman attitude towards death markedly contrasts with the morbidity found in American culture. Death is described as an almost pleasant state, one that frees the individual from the burdens of obligation and work. Also striking are the sense of reality and acceptance that Rotumans manifest when confronted with death. This acceptance is partially due to the fact that most Rotumans are confronted with death far more often than most Americans. Until recent years, the death rate has approximated the birth rate, and since each person is intimately concerned with a large number of relatives and community members, several deaths are likely to affect each person annually. This contrasts with the American pattern, especially among the more mobile elements of the population, in which families are dispersed and community involvement minimal. Since this fact is combined with a low death rate, it tends to make most people's association with death remote; and this makes it easier to maintain an unrealistic attitude about death.

To further understand the Rotuman attitude towards death, we shall examine the prevalent cultural values and relate them to socialization experiences and their apparent behavioral consequences.

First, in contrast to the American pattern, the Rotumans value passivity above activity. Although they are capable of working hard at times, they regard labor as a distasteful though necessary burden. Leisure time is usually spent in relaxation; just sitting around and talking, or preferably eating, is regarded as the most pleasant way of using time. Only in certain recreational activities are Rotumans self-motivated toward substantial physical effort, and even then the resistance of the more conservative old folk is pronounced. They hold that vigorous exertion is a cause of tuberculosis, and warn their children against it. This passivity orientation would seem to be another consequence of childhood indulgence. The loved child is held and fondled; everything is done for him, and he does not have to achieve for this love to continue.

That the resultant passivity has significance for Rotuman attitudes toward death was dramatized during the investigator's conversation with a Rotuman youth of twenty who served as chief informant. One evening, while sitting around, the young man introduced a conversation with the question, "What do you think is better, to be alive or to be dead?" After receiving an evasive answer and being asked his opinion, the young man suggested that it was better to be dead. When asked why, he replied that when one is dead he no longer has to worry about the future, or to work; he can simply rest. He compared death to dreamless sleep. His response aroused curiosity, since he was overtly a devout Catholic. When questioned about Catholic conceptions of afterlife, he indicated that he had never thought about it. Further evidence from other Rotumans demonstrated that his views were widely shared, and that commitment to religious dogma, and to ideology in general, plays a minimal role in the islanders' practice of religion. Their strongest ontological concerns are not otherworldly. They maintain that by being "good," which includes following the appropriate religious ritual, one can avoid misfortune in this world. This is an important consideration, since it indicates that the absence of fear about death is not simply the result of a belief in eternal life.

Second, a person in Rotuma is rarely if ever isolated, particularly during his formative years. Children are virtually never separated from loving adults, and even emotional separation is rare, since one person's withdrawal of love almost invariably brings compassion and sympathy from another. A few individuals — some old people and a few deviants — can be considered as suffering from social isolation, but only when compared to the extensive social relations of their fellows. Such persons still participate in community affairs; their circumstances cannot be compared to the anonymity that characterizes social isolation in an American city. As a result, social isolation is not a real threat to most Rotumans; and since it is a state never encountered by most youngsters during the socialization process, it is associated neither with punishment nor with loss of personal security.

The inevitable separation at death is also softened. Funeral ceremonies bring together family and community, and people bring gifts (mats or money) to the deceased and say farewell with a nose-to-nose kiss, or by touching the corpse on the forehead. Even when the corpse is taken to the cemetery and buried, his actual isolation is minimized by the fact that the body is buried in an ancestral grave, among "friendly bones." In this respect, the Rotuman conception of death is closer to the Japanese notion of "joining one's ancestors" than to our notion of the "dear departed." Finally, a belief that the ghosts of deceased persons remain active for an indefinite period following death further alleviates the drama of separation.

The most striking feature of a Rotuman funeral, however, is the complete lack of morbidity that pervades the social atmosphere within which it is carried out. Close relatives sit near the corpse, which is laid out in state, and may weep or even wail, but among all but close relatives and friends an attitude of conviviality prevails. As long as one does not flaunt a lack of concern, there are no restrictions on light-hearted play or joking. No one is chastised for not feeling sad.

The association of death with social isolation is also minimized by the fact that almost all bereaved persons have a widely diffused set of primary social relations, and are therefore able to absorb the loss of a love object without significantly increasing their personal isolation. As has been previously pointed out, the network of kinship relations is extensive; and most Rotumans have no difficulty in finding a household into which they are welcome if need be.

Finally, the Rotumans are less concerned than Americans with trying to master the forces of nature. Implicit in their world-view is a complementarity of man and his natural environment. Man exists within nature; he attempts to control it in part, but not to conquer it. Consequently, natural events, including death, are not regarded as enemies or as challenges to man's mastery, but simply as facts of existence. Although not entirely fatalistic, the Rotumans do not seem to suffer from the sense of personal defeat that characterizes Americans when death occurs; nor do they display the same shock. This acceptance of natural events appears to be corollary of the passivity orientation derived from child-rearing practices. Instead of attacking frustrating events with an eye to eventual victory, they tend to withdraw effort and to reserve their energies for problems which they feel capable of dealing with successfully.

To the Rotumans, then, death is surrounded with neither the morbidity nor the sense of unreality that characterizes it in the United States. It is difficult to trace with any degree of certainty the full effects of the Rotuman attitude, especially in comparison with the American attitude, since many of the problems inherent in complex urban society do not exist in this remote Polynesian community. There are, however, some behavior patterns that tempt speculation. Perhaps most impressive is the lack of a sense of impending disaster that characterizes Rotuman culture. People undertake the most hazardous circumstances with incredible casualness, as long as they are in reasonably familiar surroundings. Near disaster is always laughed at, rather than responded to with warnings of caution. It is not unusual to see a three- or four-year old child swinging a macheta knife in playful imitation of his elders. No one gasps with fright, and his play may be permitted to continue if he is handling the implement reasonably well.

Also impressive is the ease with which Rotumans are able to leave their families and community, and adapt to a totally new environment. Separation from significant others appears entirely untraumatic, although abundant tears may be shed at the time of departure. Many Rotumans have gone abroad to New Zealand, Australia, or Canada and have expressed no homesickness whatsoever. This ability to easily separate from significant others seems to result less from a weaker degree of personal attachment than from an ability to face a new environment without fear. What anxieties they do manifest are related to social acceptance, but these are easily overcome by learning appropriate behavior patterns. Anxieties stemming from a fear of death are less easily mastered, but it also seems to be the result of an acquiescence in the life cycle.

Conclusions

It is difficult to estimate the impact of a dominant attitude toward death in a given society. A fear of death may well be found to underlie many forms of free-floating anxiety, at least in Western culture. Such anxiety can be interpreted as a general threat to the human organism's sense of personal mastery — the result of being confronted with the unsolvable problem of avoiding death.

The purpose of this paper has not been to answer questions, but rather to raise them. We do not believe that the solution to our problem lies in an imitation of Rotuman culture. Our attitudes toward life and death, are so basic, so deeply implicit in our view of the world, that we may fail to recognize their importance. The need for research in this area is profound, but until recently ontological problems have been left to philosophers and poets. Behavioral scientists must not avoid such inquiries simply because our culture regards death so morbidly. We must recognize the cultural basis of such an attitude. This is an area pre-eminently suited for interdisciplinary effort, in which psychiatrists, psychologists, sociologists, anthropologists, and historians all have important contributions to make. Research could begin in areas most obviously associated with death, such as bereavement behavior. The passing of a significant other is apt to trigger all of the connotations which death holds for the individual. In addition comparative research on this topic, a study of the role of attitudes toward death in various types of destructive behavior could yield fresh insights.

Perhaps the most profound argument for urging study of the problem is that adequate knowledge could lay the foundation for intelligent programs of preventive social psychiatry. Attitudes are subject to guided change — through altered socialization techniques, through education and by means of mass media. If persons were freed from misconceptions about death, many whose creative energies are now stymied could seek solutions to genuinely resolvable and vitally important problems of existence.

References

1. Field work was carried out between 1959 and 1961, by Dr. Howard under a grant from the National Institute of Mental Health, U.S. Public Health Service. Twelve months were spent on the island of Rotuma, and nine months among Rotumans in Fiji. The authors would like to express their appreciation to the Human Ecology Fund for a supporting grant which has made their collaboration possible.

2. W. Bromberg and P. Schilder, "Death and Dying: A Comparative Study of the Attitudes and Mental Reactions Toward Death and Dying," *Psychoanalytic Review,* 20 (1933), 133-185. H. Becker and D. Bruner, "Attitudes Toward Death and the Dead and Some Possible Causes of Ghost Fear," *Mental Hygiene,* 15 (1931), 828-837.

3. H. Feifel, "Older Persons Look at Death," *Geriatrics,* 11 (1956), 127-130. S. D. Shrut, "Attitudes Toward Old Age and Death," *Mental Hygiene,* 42 (1958), 259-266.

4. W. C. Middleton, "Some Reactions Toward Death Among College Students," *Journal of Abnormal and Social Psychology,* 31 (1936), 165-173.

5. R. Kastenbaum, "Time and Death in Adolescence," in H. Feifel, ed., *The Meaning of Death* (New York: McGraw-Hill, 1959), pp.99-113.

6. A. M. Kasper, "The Doctor and Death," in Feifel, ed., *The Meaning of Death,* pp.259-270.

7. P. Schilder and D. Wechsler, "The Attitudes of Children Towards Death," *Journal of Genetic Psychology,* 45 (1934), 406-451.

8. I.E. Alexander and A. M. Alderstein, "Affective Responses to the Concept of Death in a Population of Children and Early Adolescents," *Journal of Genetic Psychology,* 93 (1958), 167-177.

9. M. H. Nagy, "The Child's Theories Concerning Death," *Journal of Genetic Psychology,* 73 (1948), 3-27, S. Anthony, *The Child's Discovery of Death* (New York: Harcourt, Brace, 1940).

10. A. Weber, "Concerning Children's Experience with Death," *Monotsschrift für Psychiatrie und Neurologie,* 107 (1943), 192-225.

11. R. McCully, "Fantasy Production of Children with a Progressively Crippling and Fatal Illness," unpublished doctoral dissertation, Columbia University (1961).

12. T. D. Eliot, "The Adjustive Behavior of Bereaved Families: A New Field for Research," *Social Forces,* 8 (1930), 543-549; "The Bereaved Family," *Annals of the American Academy of Political and Social Sciences* (1-7 March, 1932). E. Volkart, "Bereavement and Mental Health," in A. Leighton, J. Clausen, and R. Wilson, ed., *Explorations in Social Psychiatry* (New York: Basic Books, 1957), pp. 281-307. J. L. Moreno, "The Social Atom and Death," *Sociometry,* 10 (1947), 80-84.

13. D. G. Mandelbaum, "Social Uses of Funeral Rites," in Feifel, ed., *The Meaning of Death,* pp. 189-217.

14. W. H. Kelly, "Cocopa Attitudes and Practices with Respect to Death and Mourning," *Southwestern Journal of Anthropology,* 5 (1949), 151-164. E. A. Kennard, "Hopi Reactions to Death," *American Anthropologist,* 29 (1937), 491-494.

15. C. W. Wahl, "The Fear of Death," *Bulletin of the Menninger Clinic*, 22 (1958), 214-223. M. Chadwick, "Notes Upon the Fear of Death," *International Journal of Psychoanalysis*, 10 (1939), 321-334. G. Zilboorg,"Fear of Death," *Psychoanalytic Quarterly*, 12 (1943), 465-475.

16. H. Marcuse, "The Ideology of Death," in Feifel, ed., *The Meaning of Death*, pp. 64-76.

17. W. Kaufmann, "Existentialism and Death," in Feifel, ed., *The Meaning of Death*, pp. 39-62.

18. C. Gottlieb, "Modern Art and Death," in Feifel, ed., *The Meaning of Death*,pp. 157-188.

19. F. J. Hoffman, "Grace, Violence and Self," *Virginia Quarterly Review*, 34 (1958), 439-454.

20. Bromberg and Schilder, "Death and Dying," pp. 147-148.

21. Wahl, "The Fear of Death," p. 217.

22. Mandelbaum, "Social Uses of Funeral Rites."

23. Wahl, "The Fear of Death," p. 216.

24. C. G. Jung, "The Soul and Death," in Feifel, ed., *The Meaning of Death*, p. 3.

25. P. E. Kubzansky, "The Effects of Reduced Environmental Stimulation on Human Behavior: A Review," in A. Biderman and H. Zimmer, ed., *The Manipulation of Human Behavior* (New York: John Wiley and Sons, 1961), pp.51-95.

26. U. Broanfenbrenner, "Socialization and Social Class Through Time and Space," in E. Maccoby, T. Newcomb, and E. Hartley, eds., *Readings in Social Psychology* (New York: Henry Holt and Company, 1958), p. 419.

27. See A. Green, "The Middle Class Male Child and Neurosis," in R. Bendix and S. M. Lipset, eds., *Class, Status, and Power* (Glencoe, Ill.: The Free Press, 1953), pp.292-300.

28. M. Weber, *The Protestant Ethic and the Spirit of Capitalism* (New York: Charles Scribner's Sons,1956).

29. See A. Howard, "Rotuma as a Hinterland Community," *Journal of the Polynesian Society*, 70 (1961), 272-299.

30. In the orthography being used, the *g* should be pronounced like the English *ng*, as in "singing;.. apostrophes are used as glottal signs.

31. See A. Howard, "Conservatism and Non-Traditional Leadership in Rotuma," *Journal of the Polynesian Society*, 72 (in press).

32. School is compulsory in Rotuma. The school is modeled after the British system, part being controlled by the Catholic mission, and part by the Colonial Government.

33. For a more detailed account on courtship behavior and its relationship to socialization, see A. Howard and I. Howard, "Pre-Marital Sex and Social Control among the Rotumans," *American Anthropologist* (in press).

THE VITALITY OF DEATH   *

by

Peter Koestenbaum

The most dramatic reminder of man's limitations and of the decisive effect of them on his life, that is, on the problem of finding meaning in life, is to be found in the phenomenological analysis of the anticipation of death. Although no one has experienced death, everyone has confronted directly the anticipation of an inevitable personal death. Mortality is an essential characteristic of life. It is the task of this paper to examine how that anticipation affects the quality of human existence.

According to the phenomenological method used by existentialist philosophers, the only genuine and legitimate way in which we can develop a theory of man is to understand what it means to be alive or to exist as a human being in the world. We achieve such understanding by *describing* accurately, sensitively, and perceptively the general characteristics of this experience or cluster of experiences. And in engaging in such descriptions, we must be prepared to ignore all our preconceived opinions and theories about what Man is or what he ought to be. It follows that in the analysis of man — that is, in the effort to develop an adequate theory of man or philosophical anthropology — we must examine what it is that we think about, fear, stand in awe of, etc., when we envisage our own personal death. We must place in limbo, at least temporarily, our beliefs about the immortality of the soul, our theories that death might be an eternal sleep, our thought of death as bodily disintegration, as survival through children and influence, and the like, since these matters are hypotheses and inferences and not items in our immediate first-person experience. With this reminder of the methodological commitments of existential thought, we are ready to begin the descriptive analysis or self-disclosure of the experience of the anticipation of death.[1]

The Various Meanings of the Word "Death"

The primary distinction to be drawn in the congeries of meanings of the concept or experience termed the "anticipation of death" is that between the death of another and the death of myself. But in order to understand the difference between the death of myself and the death of others, we must first explore the more general meanings of the word "death." Death means *fascination, terror,* and *tragedy.*

The idea of death appears to us and comes to us in variegated forms. Surprisingly, death as a mental presence can be relaxing, fascinating, and entertaining, in addition to showing its more common characteristics of horror, dread, despair, and of tragedy. We read, for example, in a newspaper about murder while we relax over our morning cup of coffee. We also read with fascination of Custer's men and how they were all killed in the Battle of Little Big Horn. Moreover, some individuals find it relaxing and above all entertaining to watch people getting shot on television or in movies.

On the other hand, we read avidly, but also with dismay and horror, about death in the gas chambers of Nazi concentration camps. Also we respond to the death — or the threatened death — of a relative or someone else close to us with concern, panic, and anxiety. The feeling that the world is coming apart at the seams, that the universe is caving in, overcomes us when a person for whom we have complete responsibility — such as a son — or on whom we are totally dependent — such as a father or husband — is threatened with death or is actually dead.

[1] For an analysis of the scientific character of the phenomenological method, see my article, "The Interpretation of Roles," in Farber and Wilson, eds., *The Potential of Woman,* New York: McGraw-Hill, 1963. See also my article, "Existential Psychiatry, Logical Positivism, and Phenomenology," in the *Journal of Existential Psychiatry,* No. 4, Winter-Spring, 1961, pp. 399-425.

* Reprinted by permission of the Journal of Existentialism, Vol.V, No. 18 (Fall 1964.) pp 139-166.
Libra Publishers, Inc., Roslyn Heights, N.Y.

This last experience is a close reminder of our own death. We feel sick, weak, and queasy at the prospects of our own immediate death. We cannot easily control the anxiety, hysteria, and nausea that overcome us when we are confronted with the immediate threat of our own death. Thus, the word "death" refers to a large number of conscious states, some of which are relaxing to us and some of which are destructive of the total structure of our personality. The death of myself, as interpreted here, is not only filled with *anxiety* but it is also tragic. Note Edna St. Vincent Millay's lines:

> Down, down, down into the darkness of the grave
> Gently they go, the beautiful, the tender, the kind;
> Quietly they go, the intelligent, the witty, the brave.
> I know. But I do not approve. And I am not resigned.[2]

The life-world is the creative or constituted totality of a human being. That life-world comes to naught, vanishes, is destroyed with death. All the great experiences, loves, hopes, all wisdom and education, the learning of, let us say, eighty-eight years, all comes to nothing. What is the point, we might say, in creatively structuring our human existence if it all is to be destroyed? It is sad to destroy anything precious, anything that took much human creativity to bring about — as the loss of an ancient cathedral in a bombing raid. But it is tragic to lose the most precious thing of all: a full human life — full of fulfillment or full of promise.

The Two Basic Meanings of the Word "Death"

When we classify the various meanings of the word death that were suggested above, we discover two general types of meaning that this word possesses. On the one hand, the word refers to the death of *others*, and on the other, it refers to the death of *myself*. Perhaps the terminology introduced here, that is, the distinction between the death of another and the death of myself, is somewhat coarse and crude; but it does make the necessary theoretical point. Let us examine, in some greater detail, what we mean when we think of the death of another or others as opposed to when we reflect on the death of myself, that is, our own death.

The death of others is, first of all, an occurrence within the world. We conceive of the world as going on. We may think of funeral arrangements, tearful scenes, maybe a funeral oration, the settling of the estate, and the like. The death of another means the cessation of heartbeats, the cessation of respiration; in general, it means termination of all bodily processes. The death of others — as seen from the perspective of my own subjectivity and inwardness — is usually not accompanied with any overwhelming invasion of anxiety, dread, and nausea; it is merely one event occurring amongst many in a highly variegated and nigh interminable world.

What is characteristic about meaning of the death of another is that it involves the *elimination of an object within the world, and not of the observing ego or subject.* In other words, if a man examines closely — that is, phenomenologically — what he means by the death of another person, he recognizes that *he himself is still in the picture:* he is the observer contemplating the scene, even if the scene may be only in his imagination. Death is an event within the world, while the life-world, the world of human experience perdures.

The situation is altogether different if we subject the conception of *my own* death — the death of myself — to a similarly careful phenomenological analysis. This, of course, is the kind of analysis existentialists have engaged in to discover the real meaning of death in the life of man. In analyzing my own death, I must examine more than merely the physical disintegration of my body. My own death means the total disintegration and dissolution of my *world.* The *death of myself* is well described phenomenologically by the terms "void" or "encounter with Nothingness." At least such is the manner in which we anticipate our death. Since the death of myself is the disintegration of my world, the death of loved ones — who make up this world of mine — has many of the disintegrative features of the death of myself.

My own death, when I am immediately confronted with that threat, presents itself to me in terms of extraordinary and unspeakable anxiety. Such a terrifying confrontation immobilizes my normal responses and

[2] Edna St. Vincent Millay, "Dirge Without Music" in *The Buck in the Snow and Other Poems* (New York: Harper and Brothers, 1928).

what is most important, transforms the value of everything in my life. Whereas prior to the confrontation with the threat of my own death such things as having a greener lawn than the neighbors, a better grade in school than my friend, a higher income than my associates, and the like, loomed large and important, now, in the face of the ultimate threat, their value is totally transformed: in fact, these things no longer mean anything at all to me. It of course cannot be maintained that man lives in constant terror of death, or that the thought of his death fills him with unspeakable anxiety. What is asserted here is that the full awareness of what death involves, the clear confrontation with the anticipation of death, the unconscious presence, as it were, is the source of deep anxiety. We are not honest with ourselves in thinking about our own death. When we are forced to do so, as in the presence of a corpse, or upon hearing of the death of one who occupies a central and large part of our life-world, then the anxiety attending death emerges and the essential brittleness of the world becomes apparent.

However, just as with the death of others the central fact was the continuous presence of my own self or ego as the inescapable *observer, so,* when contemplating my own death, the central fact is that *the observer himself dies or vanishes.* When I think of my own death with candor and honesty, then I must recognize that one of the reasons why the immediate confrontation with my own death submerges me into the deepest state of anxiety is that it entails the disappearance of the observer himself; in fact, it entails, in a sense, the disappearance of the world itself.

If I think of my death as the end of everything, then, in a manner of speaking, I must think as well of the termination of the universe itself. After all, what mental image is present when I think of the real meaning of the death of myself? Honest analysis will disclose that there is then no image of the world left. Thus, my image of the death of myself is tantamount to asserting the end of the world.

There is a fundamental phenomenological error in the thought that the death of myself means the cessation of heartbeats, burial, and yet assures the continuation of the world. That is *not* how the threat of my own death presents itself to me. That threat is the death of the observer, and if I should think of my own burial, the settling of my estate, the cessation of my breathing, etc., then I tacitly — and erroneously — also think of myself as some eternal observer contemplating the tragic scene of his own death! What the observer has done here, in effect, is not to have considered candidly enough the reality of his own death. The understanding of what it means for him to be dead cannot include the presence of himself as an observer at his own death. He has, in fact, slipped back surreptitiously into the picture of his own death as some sort of eternal observer. But we must remember that *his* death is supposed to be the death of the *observer itself.* And with the extinction of that observer, the entire scene vanishes as well.

The structure of the death of myself involves certain ambiguities and an attempt to clarify these must be made at this time. The "death of myself" is an expression designating that part of human experience which may be described as the anticipation of total nothingness and its emotional concomitants. The meaning of the death of myself does not always coincide with the extinction of the individual subjectivity. It sometimes refers to the extermination of the life-world. For example, a mother may have greater concern over the death of her children than over her own death. Her life-world — that region of experience into which she has totally projected herself — is her children. Her death is but a passing and natural event. Her life-world is her children, and even though she die, her children will have been given a good start in life. In one sense, her real anxieties are connected with the death of her children and not her own. The possibility of the death of her children becomes for her the symbolic form of the death of herself (i.e., the death of myself). Should the catastrophe occur, should her child or children die, she will exist in a state of "living death." That "living death" — impossible to bear — will soon resolve itself into one of two possible directions. The living death may become a real death: she may die of a "broken heart," physical neglect, of unconscious or even of deliberate suicide. In that case — like Oedipus, who tears out his eyes to make real the blindness with which he has lived all his life — she makes manifest what has been true all the time anyway. On the other hand, she may "get over" her sorrow by doing what the ancient Stoic philosophers had recommended all along, namely, to detach herself sufficiently from her children — to avoid excessive projection onto them or ego-involvement — so their death can be accepted with equanimity. Epictetus suggests that a father whisper into his beloved child's ear upon leaving in the morning the sweet nothing "you may be dead tomorrow." Excessive attachment to that over which we do not have total control — as the life of a child — can lead to despair and is therefore to be avoided. By getting over the shock, by adjusting herself to the death of a child, a mother has ceased projecting her ego onto the life-world, so that gradually that death is transformed from the intolerable "death of myself" to a tolerable "death of another." It follows that the image evoked by the expression "the death of myself" need not be associated exclusively with the subjective ego. In actual fact, the constellation of the experience is highly complex and difficult to localize uniformly and consistently.

The phenomenological definition of *the death of myself* is to be construed, roughly, as follows: The death of myself is the anticipation of the extinction of the Transcendental Ego or of the ultimate subjective observer of the world. The anticipation of the death of myself is experienced as the ultimate threat of Being itself. What Tillich has called the threat of non-Being is in effect here referred to as the phenomenological constellation of the death of myself. The death of myself need not mean the death of the body that is associated with my person. Any threat that is experienced as a threat to all of Being as that presents itself to me (cf. the illustration above of a mother and her children) becomes the death of myself. The death of a child is experienced by the mother not as the death of another but as an instance of the death of myself. In a parallel manner, the death of another requires a phenomenological description and definition: The death of another is the death of one item within the life-world or within Being. The death of another implies the continuation of the matrix within which the death (or general threat) occurred. It is therefore quite possible for my own bodily and personal death to be experienced as an instance of the death of another. In fact, the latter is usually the case. Under these circumstances, we can say that the unbearable death of her child is to a mother an instance of the death of myself, while her own contemplated death is bearable, is perhaps a solution to her problems, because it is but the death of another.

The Ambiguity of the Word "Death" as Deliberate

The previous sections have called attention to a very serious and altogether fundamental ambiguity of the word "death." Although we use but one word, and although there are of course significant similarities, it does remain an undisputed fact that the total constellation of meanings in the expression "the death of another" differs from that of "the death of myself." The death of others is conceived to be an occurrence within a larger world, and is often, although of course not always, devoid of heavy emotional content. The death of myself, on the other hand, is the anticipated termination of any confrontation with or conception of the world itself. In addition, the anticipation of the death of myself, as the termination of a life-world, is interwoven with deep anxiety and tragedy; borrowing a phrase from Nietzsche, it entails a complete "transvaluation of values." As suggested earlier, the word "death" is ambiguous in two dimensions. It refers first of all to (i) the death of another and (ii) the death of myself. Translated into our phenomenological analysis, the death of another reduces to the "continuation of the world" and the death of myself to the "annihilation of the world." Seen in this light, the ambiguity of the word "death" suggests the need for further investigation, since it in effect stands for two opposite meanings. In the second dimension we saw that the word death means (iii) fascination, (iv) terror, and (v) tragedy. These are also to be sharply distinguished from one another. Fascination, terror, and tragedy are significantly opposed to each other in meaning. Fascination attracts, terror repels, while tragedy is a feeling unique to itself. That the word "death" means all of these suggests that the word serves the function of hiding from us certain crucial facts of experience.

This ambiguity may be no accident, but, on the contrary, may serve a most useful function. By means of the semantic and linguistic *confusion* between the death of myself and the death of another, I *protect* myself from the tremendous and dangerous amount of anxiety that is released when I am confronted with the phenomenologically accurate recognition of the meaning of my own death. I circumvent facing the tragedy of death. We tend to think of death as the death of another. We hopefully maintain that the death of another is the only kind of death there is. In fact, we think of the death of myself as nothing worse than the death of another. We believe that the death of another is characteristic of all forms of death, even my own. Through this device, we hide from ourselves the true and demolishing nature of our own anxiety about and tragedy of our own death. But such ambiguity is an escape, and no meaningful existence is possible without the honest recognition of the unadulterated facts of human existence. One of the most important of these facts is that of my own inevitable death.

A successful and happy life begins with the understanding that we must die, and with the knowledge that, to us, our death is generically different from the death of others.

The Problem of Immortality

At this juncture, the reader might be tempted to make the observation that the preceding statements about the differences between the death of another and the death of myself apply only to the consciousness of those people who do not believe in the immortality of the soul. The deeply religious person, that reader may argue, needs to have no anxiety about death because he knows he has an immortal soul. For him, all death has the characteristics of what we have here called the death of another. His soul, he continues, remains always as an observer.

The present discussion, however, is intended as an analysis of the experience of feeling human, irrespective of any religious beliefs whatever. The fact is that all men are concerned about their own death. The religious believer who is convinced of his own immortality is perhaps more anxious and more concerned about his death than the agnostic or the atheist, who may never give this matter much thought. As a matter of fact, the *belief* in immortality is one of mankind's most pervasive and cherished efforts to handle the persistent and anxious problem of the death of myself.

To believe in immortality does not mean to have overcome the primal anxiety about our own death; it means that we have decided to make a strenuous effort — both psychologically and intellectually — to lead an existence which works constantly at convincing ourselves that the anxiety about our own death is unfounded and can be overcome. It means that the individual focuses his attention on those aspects of his experience which tend to support the existence and the presence for him of a loving God into whose bosom the soul will retire after death. Rather than ignoring the importance of death, the life of such a man is determined by the everpresent anticipation of his death far more than is that of the average individual. To lead a life which is centered about such effort is one form of the religious life. The possibility, as well as the frequency, of such a life, far from being evidence that for some there is no anxiety about death, is testimony to the wholehearted dedication of that life to the issue of death. The religious person who lives for immortality has focused his entire life on the fact of his own death. And such concern is precisely what existentialism as a philosophy urges, since, in the last analysis, such concern is inevitable. Thus, belief in immortality is decidedly not contradictory to the existentialist theory of man as seen in the problem of death.

The Fascination of Death

The experience of our anticipated death is not exhausted by calling attention to its elements of terror and tragedy; it shares with other terrifying and tragic experiences the element of fascination.

The subject-matter of death, seen from any of its levels, has always provided fascination to mankind. Death in novels, movies, plays, newspaper reports, military history, etc., provides us with "relaxation," although we may often feel guilty over the disturbingly paradoxical fact that what to another is the ultimate threat turns out to be a kind of relaxing pleasure to us.

Death more closely linked to our own is perhaps even more fascinating to us, although that type of fascination is morbid indeed and unravels a welter of deeper and otherwise hidden emotions. A good example of this second, morbid kind of fascination we see in the curiosity that almost everyone displays about accidents.

It will be profitable for our purposes of exposition to subject the sense of fascination that an individual may experience in the presence of an accident — together with the anxiety, horror, distress, transvaluation of values, and nausea that it may engender within us — to careful and honest introspective scrutiny. This also serves as a felicitous illustration of the operation and the application of the phenomenological method.

What is our response when we see the tangled remains after a car accident? Our experiences can be grouped into two classes. The first group consists of emotions of anxiety. The second group consists of a reevaluation of our values, our relations to other people, and to ourselves, and a reassessment of the total plan and meaning of our life. This response obtains in any serious confrontation with the reality and realization of our death.

On the one side there is anxiety. Seeing an accident is different from reading about it. In seeing an accident we are immediately confronted with the realization that "but for the grace of God, there go I." Our identification with the actual or potential victims is so close that we are suddenly faced with the clear, unmistakable, and overwhelming presence of the phenomenological constellation that we have termed the "death of myself.' This presence fills us with deep anxiety and concern; it shakes the stability and equilibrium of the world of our experience to its very foundations. It makes us realize — if but for a fraction of an unpleasant moment — that the world in which we live, with its goals, prejudices, and institutions, is not the solid existence that we had believed and hoped. For a moment, our otherwise secure and predictable world has disintegrated itself into total chaos. Whereas before witnessing the accident we felt comfortable and at home in a familiar world, we now, suddenly, feel like an alien in this world, we are like a falling body in a dark and infinite abyss. This feeling of total alienation, this experience of being completely homeless, this undermining of the most basic foundations of the world on which we depend is characteristic of how it feels to realize that we are indeed finite and mortal beings.

On the positive side, the inevitable corollary of the experience of the dread of the destruction of our world leads to a complete revaluation and transformation of the meaning of our individual human existence. We become aware of the urgency to find meaning in life. We are forcefully impressed with the necessity of taking the bull of our lives by the horns and subduing it into a meaningful existence. We are eased into a situation which gives us the courage and the decisiveness to re-assess our lives, to rethink our values, and, eventually, to act on these insights, and to be enabled to act *now* — and not in an indefinite future. We experience the pressure — which has always been present in latent form — of deciding what it shall be to which we dedicate our lives, of how we shall spend our existence. And the pressure is to decide on this issue immediately and to act without delay.

We thus see that the morbid fascination that the average person sees in an accident is merely a clue — as are many other events in our human existence — to a crucial element in human nature. That element is the inescapability of death, with its negative and its positive impact on our life. We shall see presently that the enormous anxiety generated by the full understanding of the meaning of the death of myself leads, like a catharsis, to the determination and eventual acquisition of a meaningful life.

But before we may be permitted to dwell on the positive aspects of death we must remember that by the phrase "the death of myself" we mean infinitely more than the cessation of heartbeats and the other concomitants of the physical conception of death.

A "scientific" or "positivistic" analysis, account, or description of an accident will be in terms of sense data — *i.e.,* what can be photographed — the laws of mechanics, and the laws of physiology. Such a description will also include reference to the psychological reactions of the subject witnessing the scene. A phenomenological description spreads the proper mood over the entire scene, and claims that the scene is given pervaded with this mood. To overlook the mood that covers the scene like morning mist — or to relegate this striking fact to an obscure and minor position by saying "the scene made me sick" without any further experiential or phenomenological analysis of "sick" — is to be false to the facts of experience; it is to distort and misrepresent the nature of the experience itself, as that experience is present to empirical investigation.

An accident combines fascination with terror, that is, nausea. Man is curious about accidents — newspapers capitalize on this pervasive curiosity. Yet in the presence of an accident man is also gripped by fear and is likely to re-evaluate — at least temporarily — his entire mode of life. By the unique combination of fascination and terror, the experience of an accident becomes a symbol or reminder of the fundamental paradox of man. The terror of the accident means death — the inevitable defeat of man's quest for indefinite and infinite transcendence. The fascination of the accident indicates to man that he must resolutely face death if he wishes to handle the human paradox successfully, and that there is hope — and even possibly bliss — if he can successfully deal with this great issue.

Practical Callousness With Respect to Death

Let us subject our experience in witnessing an accident once more to phenomenological disclosure (that is, description and analysis) in order to discover what it reveals to us about ourselves. We have examined it in the light of two dimensions. The first dimension is the distinction between the death of myself and the death of another. The second dimension — which applies to both types of death mentioned — consists of the elements of fascination, terror, and tragedy. Of these, most important for this section is the question "Why are men curious about accidents?' which is the element of fascination. The answer proffered has been that the presence of death is rich in profound revelations to us about our essential nature, and is likewise a cornucopia of clues about the meaning of life. We add a *third* dimension, mentioned here for the first time: it is the distanced or *callous* and *practical* response to or meaning of death. It is the response of the professional soldier, the policeman, the nurse, and the doctor. The second (*fascination, terror,* and *tragedy*) and third (*practical callousness*) dimensions of death apply separately to both aspects of the first dimension of death (the *death of myself* and the *death of another*). However, the second and third dimensions are as mutually exclusive as are the two elements of the first dimension. An overpowering sense of fascination, terror, and tragedy interferes with the practical attitude of the physician needed to help in a situation of death. Sympathy and efficiency are frequently mutually exclusive attitudes towards human existence.

We have explored the meaning of most of these dimensions, that is what they tell us about ourselves. Let us think about the last. An individual who faints at the sight of blood is not able to apply a life-saving tourniquet. A man who sees clearly the staggering terror and tragedy of nuclear war may not be able to shift his thinking into the practical detached frame of mind required to plan for civil defense and survival after attack. It is well worth our while to examine the nature of this shift in attitude to see what it discloses about existence. The shift is related to that between passionate promises while in love and practical far-sighted decisions when rational. It is the difference between solving a personal problem by giving in to depression and relishing the consequent introverted reveries of introspection — as suggested by Meister Eckhart's statement that "God would sooner be in a solitary heart than any other" — on the one hand, and adopting a practical, aggressive, rational, fighting extroverted attitude on the other. The first solution *discloses ourselves to us* whereas the second solves the problem, at least temporarily. In fact, both attitudes attempt to solve the problem but they do so in two altogether different directions.

Can these two ways of life be reconciled? The first seeks the innermost self, while the second seeks satisfactions in external realities. In the last analysis, the external reality is no different from the internal life. In adopting the practical attitude, an individual seeks to identify himself with the external world. In adopting the introspective attitude, he identifies himself with his inner ego. The distinction between the innermost ego of man and the external world as he sees it and has constituted it is highly ambiguous. Possibly the two are manifestations of, as some philosophers have stated it, one and the same underlying consciousness.

Real Death and Symbolic Death

The word "death," when used in the expression "the death of myself," is a symbol that signifies complete destruction, total annihilation, the utter elimination of support, substance, and sustenance, the everlasting absence of any meaning whatever. In addition, the word "death" refers to the state of anxiety that accompanies the realization of the fact that total destruction threatens me.

It is quite evident that this experienced threat to my existence, consisting, as it does, of total annihilation, does not have to be associated with the physical death of my body. On the contrary, it is quite possible that most of us do not think primarily of the death of the body when we think of man's mortality, but that we think of something that might be called the death of the spirit or the extinction of the mind or of consciousness. We shall refer to non-bodily or non-physical (that is, non-literal) fears of death as stemming from the anticipation of what we call *symbolic death.*

For the purposes of finding meaning in life, a symbolic death has all the reality of a so-called "real" death. Every man lives in a self-created world. The businessman lives in the world of his business, his associates, his clients, and his business goals; the musical conductor lives in the world of his music, his orchestra, and his audience; the research chemist lives in the world of his laboratory, his problems of chemical synthesis, and occupational advancement; the salesman lives in the world of his product, his industry, and his profession. A symbolic death is the collapse of the particular world towards which our energies and goals are directed. The collapse of his business is a symbolic death for the businessman; the loss of his job is a symbolic death for the chemist, and so on.

A personal slight is a further example of symbolic death. To be ignored by others, especially by those whose attention we prize and esteem, is to be thought dead. A somewhat urbane form of expressing anger, hate, hostility, or chagrin is to refuse to speak to the person with whom we are so related. What we in fact do is that we refuse to acknowledge the very existence of that person; we act as if that person were dead. And the effect of our actions are similar to those facing a person in what we are inclined to call real or genuine death.

A subtler form of the same type of emotional symbolic death is involved in the manipulation of personal acceptance. To *accept* a person — by being understanding, forgiving, friendly, cordial, open-hearted, and sympathetic — is to act as if he were alive. To accept a person is to embrace him in our world. In the act of acceptance, his world reaches out to ours. On the other hand, to *reject* a person — by criticizing, disapproving, or ignoring what is important to that individual — is to threaten him with symbolic death.

Take the illustration of a secretary to an important executive. She has a good position, good salary, status, good working conditions, and a most pleasant, cordial, and friendly boss. He is a strong personality and she is relatively submissive and weak. Irrespective of the obvious and enviable advantages of her position, she is beginning to feel that she is getting on in years and should think about marriage and children. Her excessive dependency on her job makes it impossible for her to see any man as a serious marriage prospect. It appears to her — not very clearly, of course — that she should quit her present job and either select one that gives her more emotional freedom, that she can leave without elaborate preparation, or abandon work altogether for a while to acquire the necessary emotional independence from her present employer to make eventual marriage a serious possibility.

Our secretary is heavily dependent emotionally on the strong personality of the executive. He is married and has no serious romantic interest in her. However, he finds her services most useful and is quite determined not to let her go. As long as she makes it apparent to her boss that she is committed to staying — and he helps her make such a commitment by frequent raises as well as gifts and flowers for special occasions — he is ready to *accept* her. But as soon as she but insinuates that she might quit her job, he becomes cold and indifferent. She literally dreads this cold indifference. As a matter of fact, she dreads it so much that she finds it impossible to quit! Why does she fear this coldness so desperately?

Traditional psychological explanations might make reference to such items as early upbringing, early relations with her father or her mother, specific learning-responses, conditioned reflexes based on early experiences, and the like. However, from the perspective of the existential analysis of her problem, considerations as those adduced above are theoretical inferences and hypothetical constructions, although they are very illuminating. Important as these inferences and constructions might be, in matters such as these we can err easily. The existentialist finds that there is another, prior, and far more direct approach to understanding human problems. Although the psychological and the existential approaches are by no means mutually exclusive, the existentialist approach has certain methodological advantages in that it does not base itself on the multifarious presuppositions that are involved in any application of the scientific method. The existentialist, using, as he does, the phenomenological technique, prefers the more immediate and direct analysis of experience to account for life's situations. In the existentialist analysis, the predicament of our secretary must be accounted for in terms of her confusion about the nature of her own death. Only the correct appraisal and full acceptance of death will free her from this painful, anxiety-filled, and guilt-ridden predicament.

Speaking then in terms of direct experience, we can say that a great portion of the secretary's world lies in the acceptance provided by her employer. Rejection by him means, in effect, that he is ignoring her existence, that he is *destroying her world.* Since she has become dependent on his acceptance of her, he possesses a god-like power to uphold or to destroy her whole world. His rejection of her, even if it is only by means of minor gestures and relatively insignificant omissions, is a clear and distinct form of symbolic death for her. While rejection is a symbolic threat of death, her employer is also offering her symbolic immortality. As she interprets her relation with him, he is saying, in effect, "Stay with me and I shall give you eternal life!" Since she has not learned to respond maturely to the general problem of death in life, she is not able to manage any more successfully a symbolic form of death when she meets it in her daily experiences.

What creates anxiety, guilt, a sense of self-dissatisfaction, and above all, a complete paralysis of the will in the mind of the secretary is that the world of her concerns does not lie exclusively in the acceptance of her boss. If that were the case, all she would need to do is to remain in her present employment and the threat of symbolic death would vanish. The fact is, however, that the world towards which she directs herself in order to achieve fulfillment in life goes also towards marriage and family. And, of course, the two worlds conflict.

Only through the proper management of the threat of the death of myself — first in general and then in particular instances — will she be able to achieve genuine happiness and authentic success in her life. The specifics of how this is to be achieved will be discussed beginning with the section after next.

Aging and the Sense of Time

One of the most striking phenomena connected with the inexorable fact of the death of myself is the sense of aging and the passage of time. What is behind the pressure of time? We always seem to be in some sort of hurry or under some kind of pressure to "get things done" and "catch up," and "get organized," etc. Above all, we feel anxious, guilty, and left out about getting old. We engage in endless stratagems to hide our years — from others as well as from ourselves. We worry over grey hair and wrinkles; we are concerned over the fact that we are getting old and are not getting anywhere in life; we are disappointed about early promises unfulfilled, and about innocence lost. Of course, the process of getting old and the many and severe problems associated with it arise only because of the conviction that the death of myself is inevitable. As we get older we increasingly get the feeling that we have not achieved the kind of fulfillment and found the kind of meaning in life which in our youth we promised to ourselves. This feeling is the acknowledgment of the overwhelming, inescapable, and depressing truth that "time is running out." The problems and anxieties connected with aging testify to the persistent, if underlying, presence of the dread of the death of myself.

Many existentialist philosophers and psychologists make an effort to set all human experiences in the dimension of time. In so doing, the life of man becomes the experience of duration and of time. In the background of such a world-view, just beyond the horizon, there is death, the termination of duration and of time.

Our secretary who served as example in the previous section was plagued — as we all are — by the feeling that time is running out. The fact of death was the real background of her problem. After all, if man did not die, then the solution to her problem could easily be postponed indefinitely. The fact of death makes us guilty about procrastination. Unconsciously, perhaps, we feel that we must get somewhere in life — in small matters as well as in large. And the indefinite approach of death increases the pressures impinging upon us to achieve whatever our confused goals may be.

Death and Courage

Let us now examine in our deliberately pedestrian example how our secretary might acquire the will-power, decisiveness, and self-assurance that she needs in order to quit her job in good conscience and with a full measure of self-respect. The courage and determination to make sense of this life while it lasts and fulfill all its possibilities — in the face of death — was forcefully stated in these lines of the fifth century Greek poet Pindar:

> O my soul, do not aspire to immortal life,
> but exhaust the limits of the possible.[3]

---

[3]·Quoted in A. Camus, *The Myth of Sisyphus,* J. O'Brien, trans. (New York: Random House, 1959), p.2.

First of all, she must recognize that the threat of death — real and symbolic — is inevitable and inescapable. She will quickly recognize that the symbolic promise of immortality (in the form of her employer's emotional acceptance of the person of the secretary) is a fraud. Once she has accepted — and this part is the hardest part — the inevitability of her real death, and accepted it from the bottom of her heart, she will no longer be intimidated by symbolic threats of death. She now recognizes full well that her employer's eventual rejection is inevitable — just as is her own death — and that she is being a fool in hoping secretly that life is different from what it really is, which means that she hopes that there is no death.

She also recognizes, once she honestly focuses her attention on death, that time is running out, that she has but one life to lead, that if she throws away this life she will have lost, as far as she is concerned, *all there is!* It will soon become apparent that her boss is not worth all that and that his symbolic promise of immortality can be fulfilled no more reliably than immortality in relation to our real death.

If she keeps the fact of her inevitable death clearly enough in mind, she will develop the courage and decisiveness needed to quit her job and to engage forthwith in the task of building a family for herself.

One of the most nefarious problems plaguing our secretary is self-deception. Because she dreads leaving her job, she procrastinates making and executing a decision; she accepts stupid excuses as rational. As a matter of fact, most of the time she avoids thinking about the matter altogether.

However, the realization of death places immediate and tremendous pressure upon her. It makes the problem of the meaning of life a problem of the first importance to her. She realizes that she has no time to waste, that she must face the facts, and that she must come to a decision.

Her first decision will be *not to deceive herself* in this matter. Self-deception, the harmful and dishonest practice of hiding the facts from our own selves, is possible only if in the background we tacitly accept our own terrestrial immortality. The man who has been condemned to death, by the very fact that he has a human nature, cannot afford to deceive himself and sees no merits whatever in such self-deception.

Thus, our first point illustrating the vitality of death, and the point of departure from which all subsequent considerations derive their merit, is that authentic success and happiness in human existence demand uncompromising realism: we must understand and acknowledge the facts of life. And paradoxically, the most vitalizing fact of life is the utter inevitability of death! Man must constantly keep before his eyes the reality, the nature, and the inevitability of that fact. He must make every effort to understand exactly what his own death means to him. He must see the consequences of the knowledge that he is mortal. He must never let go of this insight.

The fact of his own inevitable death will place his problems in an altogether new light. What may have seemed depressing, frustrating, hopeless, now achieves meaning. The student who sits in the library and falls asleep instead of studying his assignment might find help in conquering his problem if he has learned to see his present moment in relation to his eventual death. His life unfolds itself in the direction of death; his life points to his death. Realizing this, his studying is suddenly placed in its proper perspective. The thought of death suffuses his life with a liberating sense of urgency. He is able to view his torpor as a minor inconvenience rather than as a major obstacle or an insurmountable barrier. He may also be able to stop the process of repression and self-deception. Before, he refused to recognize that his slipshod study habits were threatening his college career and his future. Now, seeing the reality of death, for him the process of repression and self-deception becomes altogether pointless. Repression ceases to be a temptation. He sees the fraudulence of self-deception. He thus achieves increased objectivity about the manner in which he conducts his life. He suddenly is able to see his life rationally and in perspective. He is thus helped to handle and overcome his problem.

One of our greatest problems in making a success of life is the chronic inability to make decisions, especially decisions that demand courage. How can the thought of death give courage? Courage is the opposite of fear and fear is ultimately the fear of death — real or symbolic death. The person who gives in to one's fear is based on the acceptance of a fraudulent promise: death. On the other hand, the man who has admitted to himself, once and for all, that he is going to die will no longer act out of fear. He understands the fear of death, and he certainly can handle fears of symbolic death. To give in to one's fear is based on the acceptance of a fraudulent promise: that of symbolic immortality.

Consider the further tribulations of our secretary. Let us assume that she has quit her job, found herself a man, received a marriage proposal, accepted it, informed her family, and set the wedding date. Now she has serious second thoughts and wants to break off the engagement.

She needs courage and decisiveness for two reasons. First, it takes courage to admit to herself that she made a mistake in getting engaged to this man and in permitting the relationship to reach an ill-advised deep level of emotional entanglement. It takes courage to admit that she has been weak in this relationship and that she has allowed a personality stronger than her own to make fundamental decisions for her. Second, it takes substantial courage to break off the engagement itself, especially after she got as involved as she did. Out of timidity and indecisiveness, out of sheer lethargy and inertia, she may yet get married to this man — and regret it for the rest of her days!

The clear understanding of death, as well as its ever-present awareness, will make certain facts amply clear to our secretary. She will be fully conscious of the fact that she has but one life to lead and that she can either make the most of it or throw it away. She must also remember that, in the light of her death, her life is all she has, her life is her sole value; her life, in fact, is all of existence for her. Seeing her engagement from this liberating perspective, her pain in breaking it off will indeed seem minimal compared to the alternative of throwing away her entire life, her total being. After all, her life is her only possession. We possess nothing but our human existence, since we *are* that existence.

We must not labor under the illusion that the recognition of the "death of myself" will make it any less painful for her to break off the engagement. What this realization *will* do for her, however, is to give her the courage and the decisiveness to carry out that decision. Furthermore, the thought of her death enables her to see her life as a total project; it enables her to look ahead towards a complete plan for life. In seeing her human existence thus "from the aspect of eternity," she recognizes that breaking off the engagement would be but a passing ripple in the totality of her life, while getting married to this man against her innermost wishes would be a major catastrophe for that life. In the face of death, to her it is obvious that she has no recourse but to steer her life in the best possible direction. She will thus be dissuaded from hiding from herself the true facts of her relation to this man. The immediacy of death leads to honesty with oneself. She knows that she has no time to waste; she has no choice but to be thoroughly honest with herself.

Finally, getting married against her wishes — just as keeping her job against her wishes — would be a symbolic promise of infinity and immortality, while, conversely, breaking off the engagement entails the anger of her fiance. And we remember that such anger — which is a form of rejection — represents a symbolic death to our secretary. But she now recognizes that *there is no escape from death.* She has accepted death and resigned herself to it. She can now focus all her energies on the creative reconstruction of the only existence that she has. The existence and threat of death, especially symbolic death, are no longer the same type of considerations that they were earlier in her life. She will now say to herself, "If I break the engagement he will threaten me with symbolic death." She will continue with "So what! The threat of death hangs over me anyway! I have accepted that fact. I no longer allow that threat to intimidate me in the regulation of my life, because if I allow it, then I will lose whatever happiness and success I can achieve in life. I used to think that if I were to allow myself to be intimidated by that threat I could escape it. But I now realize that I cannot escape the threat of death, therefore, since it is pointless to submit to it, I shall not submit myself to that threat."

The person who is aware of his death and the consequent limit to his time on earth will thereby concentrate on essentials. He will not waste time in useless details, since detail is often but an excuse to avoid the real issues in life. Recognizing his death, man is prompted to get immediately to the point of his life — and to stay there. He will always look ahead; he will see every action of his in the light of a total plan. The realization of death leads automatically to what in the business world is called "thinking big."

A man, with a family, who is thoroughly confused about his values and goals, will develop a clear outline for his life once he accepts the fact of his mortality. He will, let us say, decide to change jobs, since his present one does not provide him with either a challenge or a future. He will dedicate his energies to what, after all, is the *raison d'etre* of his job: the happiness and success of his family. He wants to see his wife fulfilled, cheerful, and loyal; he wants to see his children thrive emotionally, physically, and intellectually; he wants to see that they have the very best opportunities to succeed in life, in education, health, and character. He may have thought of these values as not *real* values, or he may have postponed his serious dedication to them into some indefinite future. Now, however, recognizing the limitation of his life and the pressure of death upon him, he will make a quick and final decision about what is really important and, in everything he does, focus his immediate attention on these long-range plans. By thus constantly looking ahead he is guaranteed constant stimulation, courage, decisiveness, and hope. He is not like the suitor who never marries because he does not find the perfect mate. The decision of what things matter most must be made now. We may make a mistake; but the greatest mistake is to make no decision at all and miss all opportunities whatever.

Let us focus on the example of a salesman who has had a bad week. He has been rejected by customer after customer. He retains no reservoir of good will towards his job. He is depressed; he is convinced that he is a failure. He cannot see his way out of the vise that his life is to him. He is too old, he feels, to learn another profession, and, at the same time, he has too many family obligations to merely resign from his job. The more depressed he gets, of course, the greater becomes his inefficiency as a salesman. Whereas only last month he had a happy outlook on life — he was cheerful and outgoing — this month life has lost all meaning to him. He may try to forget his depression by buying himself a drink, going to a movie, washing his car, escape into the reverie of daydreams, etc. He may engage in any number of equally ineffectual means of handling the sudden surge of meaninglessness and despair that has overcome him. He may even consider suicide.

How can the knowledge of the truth about his own death help him? To think of one's eventual death as an absolutely necessary aspect of human existence is to look ahead to a complete plan for life. Life becomes a project with a point of termination. This insight prevents man from *drifting* into situations — rather than making these his own — and from "getting into a rut." To have a total vision of life has the effect of placing him, at all times, at the helm of his life. If the ship runs aground or merely drifts, it is he who has allowed it to flounder by simply not looking ahead far enough.

Depression is, in effect, the inability to look ahead. But when we think about our human mortality, we have looked as far ahead into the future as it is possible for us to see. We thereby overcome the block that is immediately before us. We then realize clearly that life is not merely a lost sale, a week or a month of lost sales, or even the selling profession itself. The bad week or month is then but a passing moment in the larger scheme of things. Furthermore, by reflecting on his recurring depressions, our salesman may discover that he is basically unsuited for his job. If he now couples this reflection with the time-pressure that the thought of his death imposes upon him, then he may be prompted to rethink the entire configuration of his present life. He may gradually make some basic decisions, decisions which will eventually introduce a genuine sense of meaning and fulfillment into his life. All this represents far more intelligent and rational behavior than the escapes of drink, busy-work, or suicide.

The thought of death forces him to think above and beyond the cloud of depression that hangs over him as a consequence of the bad week that he has had. To concentrate on this depressed state is to escape from the facts of his life. The thought of his eventual and inevitable death, like a sun ray in the rain, forces him to pierce through this oppressive cloud. All he needs to regain *terra firma* is to see the present sense of hopelessness within the context of his total existence, within a total plan for his life.

The knowledge and awareness of death leads the consciousness of man straight to essentials. Students, in high school or college, are often deeply disturbed over what occupation or career to choose. The problem of whether to go to college or not, and the problem of what jobs to seek and accept, what subject to choose as major, and the like, these are some of the troublesome questions facing young people. In fact, the weight, anxiety, and guilt associated with these problems may not leave him even in later life. The thought of death — leading, as it does, to the vision of life as a whole — forces him to think seriously and immediately about how he is going to spend that life. It coerces him to face the issue of the meaning of life, to face it centrally, and come to a decision — perhaps not the best — but to make it now.

For example, it is not enough for a student to say "I like cars, I think I'll become a mechanic;" or "I like poetry, so I think I'll become a poet;" or "I like money, I think I'll study business practices." He has to go deeper into the problem of making life meaningful than these answers suggest. He has to wrestle — and do so immediately, continuously, and honestly — with problems such as "What do I really want out of life?" "What is the purpose of my human existence?" "What will yield the highest fulfillment in life?" Every person is condemned to face these difficult problems, and everyone must answer for himself. Our decisions have to be confirmed day after day, or revised, as the case may be. Just to decide once to become a mechanic, a poet, a businessman, etc., is not enough. Constant rededication is more important than the initial decision.

Thinking along these lines, the student will become far more serious than he would be otherwise. He will be soberly motivated to explore vocational counseling. He will investigate literary, philosophic, and religious ideas. It follows that the thought of death is not morbid or depressing. On the contrary, it is revitalizing; it will lead the student directly to the path which will make him an educated person. He will learn quickly how to distinguish essential knowledge from inessential frills; he will be able to separate important questions and activities from mere pastimes and bagatelles. He will be able to see his frustrations and failures as part of a much larger scheme. He can ask for no more.

The thought of death can also be an anodyne for serious illness, grave pain, and major loss. A student told the author that her fiance, a senior in medical school, was recently killed by a drunk driver in an automobile accident. The shock of this fact completely destroyed the life of the girl: it has destroyed her fondest hopes. She feels that she no longer belongs in the world. The world has lost its familiar shape, its solidity. The universe is, to her, disintegrating into some abysmal chaos. Can the thought of her own death help to extricate her from such desperate emotions?   First she will recognize that the feeling of the disintegration of the world (*i.e.*, death) is not just something that happened to her and does not happen to others. On the contrary, she has acquired an important insight into the inevitable condition of man. She sees life now in a true light, as mortal, while those happy and insouciant souls surrounding her have repressed these facts of life. We are always directly before the disintegration of our world, whether we happen to be thinking of it or not. In the presence of her tragedy, she is immediately forced to take her life into her own hands, recognize that death is inevitable, and quickly make the most of what she has.

She will discover that time is not to be wasted, that life must be subjugated to an ideal that is greater than life itself. That is, she is forced to become a total realist. She is forced to recognize life for what it is, dispell all illusions about life that our culture has taught her, and handle her life from that factual basis. Such approach to life's problems may indeed be hard. However, in the long run it is not only the most successful approach, but it is the only one available. The sooner she realizes that inevitability the better for her eventual happiness and fulfillment.

The fact that a major catastrophe has befallen an individual does in no way change the truth that he will die eventually; that whatever life he has left is all that he ever will have, all that he is; and that fulfillment can be achieved solely by molding that life into a meaningful form. He will thus not be tempted to waste time by "giving up," or by hiding the truth about himself from himself. He will then not give in to sulking over any calamity, no matter how severe. He will never indulge in self-pity. He will always get right down to the business of managing his life intelligently, rationally, and purposefully. He will accept his fate stoically. He will face all human contingencies with calmness, cheerfulness, equanimity, and peace of mind. No situation that life offers will make him "lose his mind." Discouragement will have vanished from his vocabulary.

A final illustration of how the realization of the nature and inevitability of the death of myself leads to courage and decisiveness in life we can find in the following situation. Let us imagine an individual who goes to his physician for a yearly check-up and is told, to his complete surprise and utter dismay, that he has at best one year to live.

He has been told nothing fundamentally new. And yet, his existence is shaken to its foundation! Whereas before the idea of his death was always something just beyond the horizon of his consciousness and his planning — even while he may have been discussing various alternative programs with his life insurance agent — now, all of a sudden, his death becomes an immediate, certain, and terrifying reality. What is his response? He may go to pieces. That changes none of the facts, and he will realize it soon enough. Presently he will regain his composure and take stock of his life. He is now forced to decide what is important in life and what is not. He is compelled to face the question of the ultimate meaning of life, and to face it immediately. We all realize the importance of the question of the meaning of life, and we all, likewise, postpone coming firmly to grips with it to some indefinite and fuzzy future. Now, fully realizing the truth about death, he is forced to be brutally honest with himself. He becomes aware, in every action that he performs or omits, of the limit imposed on his life. He will not even dream of procrastinating. He may suddenly experience an extraordinary and almost inexhaustible surge of energy. There is an old Arab proverb which says that in victory, no one is tired. He will now decide to do — without further delay — the "things he always wanted to do." He will have acquired the power and motivation to make a success of his life because he realizes that he *must* have it. He realizes that he cannot escape from the obligation to fulfill his life, and that he cannot postpone that obligation any longer.

Quite aside from this illustration, he can ask himself "How much life have I left?" The author had a brilliant student in one of his classes: one day he came to class and made some acute observations on the lecture; the next day he was dead. He had run his car into a moving house on a major highway. The house was improperly lit! We do not know how much of our life is left. Maybe less than a year, maybe a year, maybe a great deal more. Some of that, of course, depends on us, on our physical and mental health habits. But most is out of our hands. Our generic problems are, in the last analysis, the same that confront the man in the above illustration, the man told by his doctor that he has but a year to live. Authentic success, decision, genuine happiness, full meaning, these goals can be achieved only in light of the clear insight into the fact that all of us have been condemned to die.

The foregoing analysis of death is prior to any favorable or unfavorable religious commitment. We are going to die irrespective of our religious beliefs. The believer in immortality is no less subject to the vicissitudes and the vitality of death than is the disbeliever or the agnostic. The fact of death does not relate itself, in one way or another, to the religious belief in immortality.

Let us assume that our man who was told by his physician that he had but one year to live decided to handle the problem of death by becoming deeply religious. In that case, we can say that it took the shocking realization of the inevitability of his death — an insight that occurred only after his visit to the physician — to cut through the pseudo-goals of his life, such as status, money, education, and sex, and direct his mind to the ultimate of all problems. His goal of life, then, is to acquire the steadfast conviction — or to discover irreproachable proof — for immortality. His last days will then be spent in the preparation for immortality.

For good or for evil, such decisions every man must make for himself. The seriousness and gravity of the existential outlook on life correspond well to these words of Cyril Connolly, "Melancholy and remorse form the deep leaden keel which enables us to sail into the wind of reality; we run aground sooner than the flat-bottomed pleasure-lovers, but we venture out in weather that would sink them."[4]

In general, our response to death follows four clearly delineated stages. First, we repress the thought of our own death by projecting it onto external realities (such as onto the stage in plays, the newspapers, etc. Also, we flirt with death — in war or daring acts — to prove that death cannot assail us). Second, when we recognize the reality of the death of myself, we experience anxiety. In fact, death, as symbol of my finitude, may well be the source of all authentic, *i.e.* ontological, anxiety. Third, after the anxiety of death has been faced, the anticipation of death leads to courage, integrity, and individuality. Finally, by opposing, contradicting, and fighting death, man feels his existence and achieves some of his greatest glories — in art, religion, and self-assertion.[5]

Summary of the Salutary Consequences of Death

Let us summarize the salient features of the positive and salutary aspects of the fact of death.

1. Man cannot escape death — real *or* symbolic. He must construct his life — daily actions as well as major, over-all plans — with the full and clear realization of that fact. He must accept, once and for all and without any reservation, misgiving, false hope, repression, or bitterness, the fact that he has been condemned to death. Then he can start living.

In accepting death, he will neutralize an otherwise completely demoralizing and paralyzing fear. This is one

[4] Cyril Connolly, *The Unquiet Grave.*
[5] For a more extensive and systematic development of these and related ideas see my article, "Outlines of an Existential Theory of Neuroses," in the *Journal of the American Medical Women's Association,* Vol. 19, No. 6, June 1964, pp.472-488.

key to the successful management of human existence.

2. Once he has recognized and admitted the inevitability of his death, the individual is on the way to becoming courageous, fearless, and decisive. Whenever he feels indecision and lack of courage, he must remind himself that life will end for him. The symbolic threat of death, which often is the cause of his indecision, will then disappear, since its basic fraudulence will have been made manifest. He will be able once more to steer his life with courage and decisiveness.

3. By remembering the certainty and finality of death, man immediately sees the urgency of concentrating on essentials. He cuts red tape in his life. He abandons excuses and procrastinations. He does not indulge in the luxury of wasting time — under the guise of getting work done — by getting lost in an endless amount of detail and busywork.

4. Only through the constant awareness of death will an individual achieve integrity and consistency with his principles. Since there is, basically, no threat other than real or symbolic death, and since he has accepted that threat, he is well beyond fraudulent bribes and threats alike. In the last analysis, all man owns is the integrity of his character. No one can threaten him in the matter of his principles, since he is always in the presence of the ultimate threat anyway. What criminal would think of holding up a convict on the way to the death chamber?

5. The man who knows he will die wastes no time in attacking the problem of finding meaning and fulfillment in life. The pressure of the thought of death is a persistent and nagging (and most effective) reminder that he is coerced to make some sense of his life, and that he is to do it *now*. He who has faced death adopts a no-nonsense approach to the business of living successfully.

Precisely what these goals are is an individual choice. It may not be desirable to be burdened with such choice; but it is a fact of life that every man must commit himself personally to whatever values he chooses to consider highest. We all have strong predilections; we all have some idea of what it is we really want. Under pressure of death we will quickly dedicate ourselves to these goals. Existentialism is not an ethical commitment or a normative proposal on how life should be conducted. The existentialist philosopher can not, as philosopher, decide questions of ultimate values. Existentialism is a theory of man and as such it either corresponds to the facts of lived experience, in which case the theory is true, or it does not correspond, in which case the theory is false. Existentialism is religiously and axiologically neutral. Death is a fact of life — that is a universal truth. The recognition of the nature of the anticipation of death has rejuvenating and revitalizing effects on human existence. That is another fact of life. What the decision is, or should be, about the meaning of life is, perhaps unfortunately, a burdensome individual decision. But the decision will come — since we often know what we really want — as soon as the urgency of reaching a conclusion is brought home to us through the fact of inexorable death.

6. The vitality of death lies in that it makes almost impossible the repression of unpleasant but important realities. We do not accept any excuses to postpone dealing with our basic problems or to hide these from us. The realization of death carries with it the successful management of many unconscious and repressed problems. He who is about to die does not practice the art of self-deception. Death makes man honest.

7. The realization of the death of myself leads to strength. To be strong means not to be intimidated by real or symbolic death. Having conquered these threats, man faces no others. The world of self-fullfillment belongs to the strong, decisive, and courageous man.

8. To accept death means to take charge of one's life. The man who sees the genuine function of death in life is no fatalist. He does not feel strictured. On the contrary, he is the freest of all men. Nothing holds him back but his own free decisions. He has nothing to fear, nothing to be timid about, nothing to make him feel dependent, inadequate, or inferior, for he has once and for all conquered the ultimate threat.

9. The thought of death urges one to assume a total plan for his life. The vitality of death leads one to adopt an ideal or goal, a noble life, or a major achievement as the purpose of existence. Through the vitality of death, one is able to see all events in life from the perspective of his total existence. This enables one to perform tasks that might otherwise be boring, discouraging, and senseless.

10. The thought of death enables man to laugh off vicissitudes and pains. Every man has a certain type and amount of raw material out of which he can fashion for himself a good life. The amount and quality of the material out of which man may construct his life varies greatly from one human existence to another and from one situation to another. But the pliable nature of the raw material is universal. To take defeat too seriously, to be thrown off balance by disappointments, is still secretly to harbor the hope that death may not be real after all and that perhaps man was "meant" to be immortal but, somehow, has missed his chance.

The above has been an outline of one result of the phenomenological exploration of the life-world. Part of the existential theory of man is that the essence of human existence is its mortality.

CHAPTER III

SOME PHILOSOPHIES OF LIFE AND DEATH

Introduction

One of the paradoxes of modern man, or the contemporary alive in the "Age of Aquarius," is that he places his reliance in *man,* not in God or some other supernatural being, and yet he finds man a frail vessel, not altogether worthy of trust and reliance. While we have no empirical evidence except as the written word has come down to us through the generations, that the man who organized his life around a system of religious beliefs was somehow "happier" than the man of today, beset as he is by moral confusion and agnosticism, we tend to think this was true. Many of us long for some kind of return to a simple religious faith which gives us explicit principles by which we can live and die.

Chapter III presents two selections which essentially examine the question: Is life a preparation for death, or is a confrontation of the certainty of death a preparation for life? Guthrie is concerned with whether or not an awareness of the certainty of death is conducive to good mental health. Is the meaningfulness of life asserted in one's stance toward death, or is this a morbid point of view? Needleman brings up a series of metaphysical questions about death, and leaves to the reader the task of answering these questions for himself.

THE MEANING OF DEATH   *

by

George P. Guthrie

The following remarks have grown out of ten years of experience, both in teaching a course in existentialism and in counseling with students. During this period I have found that the subject of death invariably provoked a strong and mixed response. Students, though initially wary of the topic, were unusually intrigued by it and many seemed to undergo a certain catharsis in being able to look at it and talk about it. Moreover, I found that the course became increasingly attractive to more mature, middle-aged students who enjoyed the leisure and the adventuresomeness to audit a course. Out of these experiences I have tentatively come to three observations: First, people may have a need to deal more concertedly with the problem of death than our culture usually permits. Second, death may be a more pervasive human problem to all of us than we ordinarily admit. And lastly, for many reasons death cannot be treated as just another fact of life. Death itself and especially our modes of relating to it of necessity partake of a strangely paradoxical quality.

In the twentieth century death seems to have usurped the role that sex held during the Victorian era as a fundamental, powerful, universal experience about which little is said. In our culture death, just as the Victorian sex, seems to be deliberately and consistently shunted to the periphery of our conscious awareness. Except for those whose professions throw them into intimate contact with it, death has become a phenomenon encountered only accidentally. Insofar as possible, death is confined to the hospital and to institutions for the aged and infirm.

Yet some cracks are apparent in this solid wall of disregard. Beyond the perennial interest in medicine and health there have appeared recently a popular concern with the economics of "the high cost of dying" and a criticism of the appropriateness of "the American way of death." Even more important, psychotherapists such as Frankl and Binswanger and philosophers such as Heidegger and Sartre have pointed to the apprehension of death as a prime source of existential anxiety. Indeed though death has symbolically, as well as literally, gone underground in the popular cultus of our day, at the same time there has developed a body of insights about death which is perhaps unequalled since the Middle Ages. It is my own belief that any approach to the fact of death that would prepare us to cope with it and prepare us to help others to cope with it must avail itself of these insights in order to challenge and counter the prevailing common sense opinions about death.

In the following remarks about death I would like to provide a theoretical background for considering the process of dying by highlighting the strangeness of death and the ambivalence of our responses to it. Hence my concern is with the *meaning* of death, i.e., both with what death is and with its broader significance. What strikes me most strongly is that our ideas about death have been confused and obscured under the impact of the very fact of death itself. Death is simply not a phenomenon that we can readily think about in a disinterested fashion. Death is a final, boundary line situation which sums up the whole of our life. Because of this, anxieties about death continually threaten to distort our attitudes and thoughts concerning it. I believe in some measure death must always strike us as ultimately absurd, and accordingly our responses to it must always remain highly ambiguous. To state it differently, there are many ways in which death partakes of a paradoxical character. I want to explore four of these paradoxes that may be relevant to the process of therapy.

The first paradox of death is that though it is an inevitable and universal event about which little can be done; yet at the same time it is an event which we cannot take lightly, cannot denote to the status of a common, everyday happening.

* Reprinted from Voices: The Art and Science of Psychotherapy, 1969, Vol.5, No. 1. The Process of Dying. Published by permission of the author George P. Guthrie, University of Toledo, Toledo, Ohio.

On the one hand death is *widespread;* it is *certain* for each of us; it is an experience which *all* men undergo. From the long point of view death remains something largely beyond our control. In these senses death is an ordinary, everyday, commonplace event. Because of this generality of death there have periodically been those who sought to treat it as something natural and "nothing to get excited about." This would appear to be the sanest response to it.

On the other hand there is something about *my* death that resists this kind of treatment. It asserts itself as an *extra*-ordinary event! Objectively speaking, along with my birth, death is one of the two boundary situations of my life. Certainly it is the most important situation toward which I must take some kind of conscious or unconscious stance — a stance which undoubtedly affects the whole of my orientation toward the future. Psychologically I am not free simply to remain indifferent to it.

Moreover, although when seen from the outside death is a general experience, seen from the inside it is very unique: It is one of those experiences everyone *has* to go through. It is an experience I go through *only once.* My death is *uniquely mine* in that no one else can do my dying for me. Thus death individualizes and throws us back on ourselves. My death is intensely personal to me; and it may well be that awareness and appropriation of this is at the root of personality. For all of these reasons, at least in modern Western culture, one cannot regard death as just as everyday occurrence, just an ordinary event.

The second paradox surrounding death is that while intellectually we know we are going to die, experientially we have difficulty in believing it.

It is sometimes said that man differs from the animals in that though animals die, man alone *knows* he is going to die. At an early age we learn that death is universal. We read accounts of it in the newspapers. We are exposed to actuary tables. In college we are introduced to logic through syllogisms beginning, "All men are mortal."

Yet, notwithstanding this overwhelming knowledge of, and evidence for, the fact that we are going to die, experientially we still have difficulty in believing in the reality of our own death. I am persuaded that this is due not simply to wishful thinking or to fear of death, but also to the fact that our actual experience in part disconfirms the fact that we are going to die. For example: By the time we are twenty years old we have gone through approximately 7,000 instances in which we went to bed at night and awakened with the morning sun to find ourselves alive. This idea of a new day and finding oneself alive becomes directly associated and strongly reinforced in our own immediate experience. This more intimate inductive experience affects our belief and tends to counteract what we more vaguely know in general. This belief probably reaches its peak during the high school and college period. With the coming of age and illness this conditioned, quasi-instinctive response gradually becomes chastened and tempered. But it is nevertheless true that there is a factor in conscious experience that encourages us to avoid considering that which, in another sense, we know is our destiny.

The third paradox of death is probably the most important. Death is both a biological and a spiritual phenomenon.

The sense in which death is biological is both obvious and indisputable; but humanly speaking we must also always confront the question of what death means to us. The meaning of death has to do with the spirit of man: It primarily involves consciousness and awareness. What I fear about death in one sense has very little to do with the physical. What I fear about death is the ultimate loss of consciousness, the end of all meaningful experience, the cessation of my creative engagement in life, or the dissolution of my personality. If it were possible for meaningful involvement to continue, what happens physically would be a matter of relative indifference. I believe it is the awareness of this paradox that occasions the eeriness which overwhelms us when we view the corpse of someone we have known. In a sheer massive, physical way there is not much difference between the dead body and one that is asleep. Yet vaguely we are aware that there is somehow *all* the difference. Consciousness with all it entails is gone forever.

If it be true that death (or at least its meaning, i.e., the way it comes at us) is primarily a spiritual concern, then certain consequences follow that may have been obscured for us by our reliance on materialistic interpretations. An elementary consequence would be the clear insistence that the only justification for prolonging purely physical life for someone in a coma would be the expectation that some change might be effected by which consciousness could be restored.

A much more important consequence would be the realization that there do occur situations of mental disease, despondency, etc. in which one may experience spiritual death in almost every sense of the term: One enjoys no sustaining relationships; one ceases to be creatively involved with the world; and one senses an impending dissolution of one's personality. In these situations one may even long for physical death to free one from consciousness of the pain of the living death in which one finds oneself entangled.

The last paradox of death is that though it occurs as a terminus of life, it is not "simply located" at the end — its reality permeates the whole of our existence. Here I am not referring merely to the biological fact that apparently we begin to die as soon as we are born; but rather to the way in which awareness of the fact of death may impose a pattern on our lives of which we are often unaware.

Notwithstanding any experiential inductions to the contrary, it would seem that man derives intimations of mortality from a somewhat early age. The English poet Gerald Manley Hopkins in a brief poem, *Spring and Fall,* describes the reactions of a very young girl to the fall of leaves in a woods in autumn. As the young girl, Margaret, contemplates the unleaving of the trees, she is disturbed by a vague disquietude. Hopkins interprets this in the poignant concluding lines:

> What heart heard of, ghost guessed:
> It is the blight man was born for,
> It is Margaret you mourn for.

If it be true that we have these intimations of mortality, they are not the sort of thing we can afford to keep in conscious awareness — it would engender too much anxiety. In this respect the situation with regard to death is the precise opposite of Mark Twain's jest about the weather: Everyone talks about it, but no one does much about it. We do not do much serious talking about death; yet we may be more thoroughly engaged in attempting to do something about it than we realize. Not only are there the obvious efforts in the areas of health and medicine; but there are more subtle and pervasive projects around which we organize our lives. We spend considerable time amassing empires of material security in an attempt to insure the future. We erect structures of psychological security to ward off awareness of the end. When we sense the inadequacy of these, we still long to leave some kind of enduring mark on the world. This longing to leave something tangible behind us has great potential for both creativity and violence. Undoubtedly our inordinate desires for things and for power and our propensities for creation and destruction reflect in some measure our awareness of the end which for the most part we do not name.

What conclusions can we draw from these paradoxes concerning the event of death and the process of dying? Perhaps the following are most relevant.

First, in relating to one who is facing the imminence of death, we need to realize that we are dealing with a set of stances and behavior patterns that usually have a long history for the individual concerned. A person's whole style of life is involved in a person's way of dealing or not dealing with death. There may be much guilt connected with these situations. Perhaps a person's life has been dominated by fear of death and perhaps this fear has motivated compromises of which the person is ashamed — compromises which, furthermore, at this point are seen to be in vain. Whatever we say in these situations should be said in relation to what death has come to mean for that specific person with whom we are concerned.

The second conclusion is that we probably need to take more seriously the question of whether awareness of death, as an existential anxiety, may not enter into and subtly qualify some more ordinary instances of mental illness. Here the concern is that some neuroses, though apparently rooted in more mundane considerations, may yet have anxiety concerning death as one of their ingredients. For that matter some mundane projects themselves may need to be considered as in part derived from such anxiety. Accordingly, it might be fruitful to ask when it may be important overtly or covertly to deal with death and its attendant anxiety as part of therapy in even ordinary counseling situations?

The final conclusion is a broad query. To what degree is our present cultural tendency to avoid reminders of death healthy or unhealthy? This tendency has already resulted in our culture's extreme emphasis upon youth and its values, as well as in the tendency toward the physical separation of the old from the young. In sharp contrast to these tendencies and attitudes there have been periods in the past when the function of philosophy was seen to be "preparation for death." Such a view was not quite so morbid as it may appear to us; for such preparation was also regarded as the most profound and effective preparation for life. Times have changed and the religious and cultural ideologies that buttressed such views have largely lost their hold upon us. Nevertheless, the question remains as to whether or not there may be some wisdom in this approach. Perhaps no one is in a better position than the therapist to assess to what degree a more or less conscious opening ourselves to, taking into ourselves, and affirming the fact of our death may not only be the best preparation for dying but also the most creative way of affirming the meaningfulness of life as well.

> *The gods conceal from the living how pleasant death is, so that they will*
> *continue to live.*
> Lucan: Pharsalia

THE MOMENT OF GRIEF *

by

Jacob Needleman

Surely, few of us believe that life is a preparation for death. As historical events and scientific progress nullify our trust in traditional religious forms, this idea is one of the first to fall — that there will come a final moment when we will be tested and weighed in the balance of some higher universal purpose, and that the central concern of our day-to-day lives should be to ready ourselves. All our knowledge seems to lead us to the certainty that death is our destruction, meaningless, which only madmen glorify and whose factuality only cowards avoid. We know that we are cowards but at least we value those rare moments when life seems so rich that death loses its terror. For the rest, we refuse to brood morosely.

And so, when a philosopher like Plato tells us that we should spend our life learning to die, we cannot really listen to him, or even wish to. But in the time of grief we do turn to such thoughts and to many others which we avoid in the course of our lives. Are we simply looking for comfort in the form of some intricate denial of the death we have encountered? For, when we recover our customary balance, when we pass through this time, our attention is drawn far away from those thoughts.

Let us consider the possibility that in that moment of grief our consciousness comes into a new sort of relationship to the rest of us, and that it is precisely this relationship, and not the outer event, for which we are unprepared. And that a better meaning of the idea of preparing for death has nothing at all to do with the gradual relinquishing of vital experience. What we wish to explore is the thought that the preparation for death is a preparation to be alive.

Obviously, this line of thought will yield no consolation in the ordinary sense. It cannot lead to proofs of life beyond the grave or to prescriptions about heroic acceptance of our destruction. On the contrary, it begins and ends with the thought that we *do not know* what death is. The agony of the search for proofs and prescriptions is not rooted in our ignorance about death, but rather, in the fact that we are afraid to distrust our fears and imagination.

The point is this. It is a commonplace to say that man is afraid of the unknown. But is it really so? When I am afraid to enter a dark room, isn't it because my imagination make me *forget* that I don't know what is in there? And if someone then reminds me about my imagination, doesn't the fear lift for an instant? In other words, if somehow I were able to stand in front of my imagination, to see it, then at least that portion of myself which saw it would not be afraid. But somehow I cannot wish to do this. In some way I value my imagination and the fears that are in it; I trust it; I believe that it gets me through life, or that it brings me my satisfactions.

If we think of death as being like that dark room, then many of the proofs and prescriptions in the literature of philosophy and psychology read like reactions to the imagination, rather than attempts to awaken us to it. In the main stream of modern thought, this usually takes the form of proving that the mind cannot exist without the body, or that there is no soul. Of course we can also find proofs that go the other way: that there is a life after death, an immortal soul, etc. Both sorts of effort are essentially the same, whatever the content of the particular proof. Each moves away from the fact of ignorance rather than toward it or into it.

The fact of ignorance is a fact about oneself, and to move away from it is to move away from oneself. This is to suggest that thought must be distinguished from self-awareness, since the thinking process is but one of the functions of that self or organism. Just as my fear lifts when I become conscious of my imagination, so it may be that if I can become conscious of my thought about death, I may begin to stand in a new relationship to that thought.

The ignorance about death is not an ignorance of some facts about the external world. Rather, it is possible to see this ignorance as the sensing of the inadequacy of thought, perhaps even the sensing of its surprisingly

* Reprinted from *Death and Bereavement*. Ed. Austin H. Kutscher. Charles C. Thomas, Springfield, Illinois. (1969.)

dependent place in the totality of our life.

It was also Plato who showed that our thought does not guide us, though we imagine it does; rather that thought always follows and serves some impulse, desire or fear in us, creatures of the cave. The same Socrates who in *Phaedo* offers his pupils several external proofs of immortality, also, in the *Apology,* reminds the whole Athenian community that no one but God knows what takes place after death.

Kierkegaard, a modern Christian pupil of Socrates, writes:

> All honor to him who can handle learnedly the learned
> question of immortality! But the question of immortality
> is essentially not a learned question, rather it is a
> question of inwardness, which the subject by becoming
> subjective must put to himself. Objectively, the question
> cannot be answered, because objectively it cannot be
> put, since immortality precisely is the potentiation
> and highest development of the developed subjectivity.
> Only by really willing to become subjective can the
> question properly emerge, therefore how could it be
> answered objectively?...the consciousness of my
> immortality belongs to me alone, precisely at the moment
> when I am conscious of my immortality I am absolutely
> subjective...Immortality is the most passionate interest
> of subjectivity; precisely in the interest.lies the
> proof...Quite simply, therefore, the existing subject,
> asks, not about immortality in general, for such a
> phantom has no existence, but about his immortality,
> about what it means to become immortal, whether he is
> able to contribute anything to the accomplishment of
> this end, or whether he becomes immortal as a matter of
> course, or whether he is that and can become it.

We thus come to the tentative conclusion that there is something valuable about this ignorance and that perhaps we should not be in too great a hurry to get rid of it. Whatever else they may be, are not the great sorrows of life also confusions? That is, don't they — and the death of loved ones more than any — bring us at least momentarily to the awareness that we do not understand? That we are ignorant? And are not our efforts to assuage our suffering often attempts to fly from that awareness back to our former "understanding"? When we suffer and we say "I don't understand" are we not searching for some way to fit what has happened into our old categories?

So the question arises: What would it mean to want a new understanding, rather than the retaining of our old understanding? Surely, the first thing it would mean would be the wish to remain cognizant of our ignorance and to see it as something which cannot be "corrected" by the selection (under the aegis of the old understanding) of external facts, proofs or exhortations.

However, it is surely life and not we ourselves that brings us to moments of this awareness of ignorance. If we are to speak of any preparation, it would have to be preparation for these moments.

We know we cannot change our emotions; we cannot, by thinking, change hate to love or erase our fears. In a minor sort of way, every emotional surprise in our life is thus such a moment as we are speaking of. Thus the material basis of any preparation lies right in front of us in the person of our everyday emotional life.

Our discussion having come to this, we can now connect it again with Socrates. In that same dialogue, *Phaedo,* which takes place on the day of Socrates' execution, he explains to his pupils that those who really apply themselves in the right way to the search for wisdom are directly and of their own accord preparing themselves for dying and for death. At this

> Simmias laughed and said, Upon my word, Socrates, you have
> made me laugh, though I was not at all in the mood for it.
> I am sure that if they heard what you said, most people
> would think — and our fellow countrymen would heartily
> agree — that it was a very good hit at the philosophers to
> say that they are half dead already, and that they, the
> normal people, are quite aware that death would
> serve the philosophers right.

Socrates answers:

> And they would be quite correct, Simmias — except in thinking
> that they are "quite aware." They are not at all aware
> in what sense true philosophers are half dead, or in what
> sense they deserve death, or what sort of death they deserve.
> *Phaedo* 64

It is in precisely this context that Socrates explains this preparation as the turning of the attention toward the mind (or soul) and away from the pleasures and pains of everyday life. Most people are quick to see in this the thought that we should gradually relinquish the most vivid and valuable side of life. But, once again, does not this ready interpretation come also from the fact that we forget our ignorance about death? What could preparation mean if we are to continue, in our thought, to relate to our everyday emotions like undiscriminating beggars? If it is true that in our thought we are surprised by our emotions and confused by our powerful emotions, how else could we prepare ourselves than by searching for a new relationship to our thought? But we forget our ignorance, we forget that our emotions surprise us and lead us, we forget that they confuse us; we forget that we do not understand ourselves.

We think of the idea of preparing for death as preparing for something beyond the grave without our taking the initial steps of preparing for our fears and griefs. We reject the former idea as based on a presumption about life after death without realizing we live under the presumption that we stand in a right relationship to our fears and desires.

And so, when Socrates tells his pupils to despise everyday pleasures and pains, it is advice that follows from his (and the Oracle's) evaluation of ignorance. The Oracle said of him that he was the wisest in Athens because he alone was aware of his ignorance. We also recall the famous inscription "Know Thyself" which was Socrates' watchword as well. Together, these two formulae about Socrates' wisdom and self-knowledge can lead to the practical goal of becoming aware of our ignorance about ourselves. And thus, to despise our everyday emotions is to despise the illusion that we are not confused by our emotions, an illusion that often takes the form of believing it is the world out there which confuses us, or perpetrates injustice, or destroys us, or (on the other hand) rewards us and makes us happy.

A man would have to be a fool to think lightly of the anguish of the moment of grief. But precisely because such an emotion is overwhelming and sweeps everything else in us aside, precisely because of this the question of preparation becomes important. If emotions are our source of life and yet not our responsibility it would seem that when we prepare for them we are preparing for being alive. It would follow that our search must be to struggle directly only with what is in our power to meet. Where, then, is our responsibility? What *is* in our power?

This question may perhaps reveal something about that weakening of trust in traditional religious forms which was mentioned at the beginning. For if the religions of our present culture take it as their task directly to legislate our emotions, the result may be for us only that we overlay the actual emotions which willy-nilly occur in us with imaginary feelings, i.e., thoughts about our emotions which are out of all congruity with the emotions themselves.

Nothing, of course, could be further from the awareness of ignorance, and nothing would more effectively block the growth of that awareness. For if I am told and if I believe that I ought to love my neighbor, how will I ever relate to my hatred of him? No wonder modern psychiatry seems realistic in reminding us of our actual emotions. But unfortunately, psychiatry, in passing judgment on our thought, just as effectively blocks our vision of confusion. Self-knowledge surely does not begin with the attempted refusal to judge my emotions, but with the search to see both my judgments and my emotions.

Yet what else but religion has the office of relating man with the question of death? In a sense, this is its main, perhaps its only task. It may be, however, just because we go to religion to escape our ignorance rather than to discover it, that it can become undermined by such things as psychiatry, science, and political events. Thus, when a great fear or anguish overwhelms us, we soon afterwards turn to religion either to have a counter-emotion evoked in us or to be commanded to feel something else, both of which serve the purpose of reinstating the illusion that we understand our emotions. And once it is reinstated, once we have "regained our balance," "passed through the difficult time," etc., we then avoid religion because it seeks to give us what we think we already have: a sense of moving in the right direction, or — to put it in the language of this discussion — a turning away from our emotions in the form of a "contented relationship" toward them.

Thus religion, psychiatry, and science all leave us unprepared for death. And the moment of grief, a moment in which we may be genuinely face to face with the enormous forces that act in us in the form of our emotions, fails ultimately to make the rest of our inner life a question. On the contrary, our reactions to that moment pull us out of ourselves in the search for philosophical systems, proofs, exhortations, consolations, substitutes — in short, the search for a return to our former quality of life, a life which those very moments reveal to us, momentarily, as far less than our human right, as far closer to the death we confusedly fear than to the real life that lies hidden within us.

A Note About Metaphysical Speculation

When the fact of death compels us outward to more recognizably metaphysical questions about man's place in the universe, perhaps it need not be wholly at the expense of an awareness of ignorance. Let us, therefore, assume that there is a difference between fantasy and speculation, taking fantasy as the absolutizing of partial or relative knowledge, and taking speculation as the effort to maintain a sense of the relativity of our thinking and our concepts of the universe. Thus, it is not only grandiose metaphysical systems that are fantasies. Equally fantastic is the absolutizing of those common standards of intellectual satisfaction associated with logical consistency, ordinary language and pragmatic scientific theory.

How, then, are we to avoid fantastic thinking about death? And in what directions might metaphysical speculation about death take us?

One point is clear: for us, death is conceptually linked to a great many other things such as time, identity, consciousness, life, matter, change, birth. It would, therefore, be a great mistake to think about death without trying to see how these other ideas present themselves in our minds.

We may take as example what seems a truism: Death is the end of life. Yet this simple proposition contains many questions which, if totally avoided, leave us with nothing more than an empty verbal equation. *What* is that of which death is the end? How do we understand life? Biologically? Personally (my life)? If biologically, do we think of life as a complex trick of matter, an intricate organization of what is essentially dead? Does it seem more *natural* that things should die rather than that they should live? What concept of reality underlies this thought?

Or are we willing to settle for an unbridgeable dualism of the living and the nonliving in our universe? If so, what becomes of our *universe*? And in such a universe, how could anything die, that is, change from living to nonliving? What is lost or what is ended in such an event? How, in fact, do we understand an *end*? Disappearance? What is that — vanishing into nothingness — or disappearance from our view?

Furthermore, if we think of life as purposive activity, how do we recognize purpose? Is *our* activity the only sort of purpose that could exist? What is our standard of time against which we measure the accomplishment or effort towards purpose? Is there life that exists on totally different scales of time — incommensurably smaller or greater — than our own? If so, how would we ever perceive it?

For that matter, how can we perceive our own time scale? From what perspective, from what *place* could we ever perceive our scale of time? Or are we condemned forever to stay within it, never directly perceiving how or if our beginnings are related to our endings? Is there in *us* the possibility of another order of time within which we can see the processes and changes which constitute the time of our everyday lives, both as individuals and as mankind? If not, is there no other order or time other than our own? Or are we so cut off from the time of galaxies, planets and molecules that it is foolish to think about them in this way? What sort of a universe would that be? And are we necessarily so cut off?

Or should we avoid these questions as unanswerable or meaningless? Unanswerable, meaningless to whom? What sort of answers do we insist on? Why? What sort of meaning would we like to find? Why do we stop looking when we fail to find it? What sort of purposes is our thought supposed to serve? Are these purposes consonant with what exists in the universe? What kind of certainty are we looking for? Why do we get weary of questions, and more questions? Why do we want to stop? What kind of resting-place is the sense of certainty we prize? Is it that of fantasy?

Perhaps we take death as the end of *my* life. What kind of end can I have? What is it which ends? Can I believe in my own death? Can I imagine it? If not, why? Is it because I have no understanding of what I am? Can I even imagine my own life, not to mention my own death? Do I assume, only because of the rules of grammar and dictionary definition, that death is the end of experience? The end of consciousness? What are these? Is consciousness some weird, metaphysically unique phantom in a blind unconscious universe? If so, how could I begin to *think* about it? Do I even have it? or does it, can it, have me? Is it I?

And what do I ever experience? Is our past already dead? Is what dies, when I die, only the final member of a bundle of perceptions? Or is there a self that persists "through time"? If we would like to believe the latter, how do we experience it? Do we remember our life? What is there to do the remembering — one of the bundle? Or something above and beyond the bundle? And, again, if we believe the latter, who or what is believing? Another member of the bundle? That is, is this, too, fantastic thinking, a taking of the part for the whole?

There may be an interesting relationship between the notion that my self will be either destroyed or preserved in death and the degradation into fantasy of the impulse toward metaphysical speculation. The fantasist asks: What is the place in the universe of this being, man, who is destroyed by death? Or, alternatively: What is the place in the universe of this being, man, who is immortal? Fantasy would seem to be inevitable as long as we rely on part of our thought while questioning the other part. But in speculating about our place in the universe, is it not a fact that we have no real idea of what purpose our thought is to serve?

That our lives are dominated by fantastic thought may be because there is so little relationship between the *impulse* to speculate about our place in the universe and the *content* of our "speculative thought." If the emotion of the moment of grief represents one such impulse, surely another is what the ancients called *thaumazein* — what we speak of as "wonder."

Most of us remember the rare moments when we have experienced this emotion: perhaps on a night away from the city, looking up towards countless worlds; perhaps as children directly observing some living thing; it would be futile to try to put this emotion into words. But what is it we forget when this moment passes and we are trying to think about the questions which we then associate with that moment: What is the meaning of my smallness? How can I know my part in this magnitude which I sense? Isn't this what we forget: That at the moment when we are presented with the emotion of wonder, that emotion and that state of mind *are themselves an element in the answer to our questions*. We know this at the moment — though perhaps not in so many words — and we forget it later.

Might it not be that such an emotion and state of mind is itself a kind of knowledge that truly takes us out of ourselves toward the universe? Might it not be that, just as in the moment of grief, this emotion is a brief individual connection with what, to thought, seems so far above us or outside us? What do we trust when this emotion is no longer present? What do we then take to be knowledge? Is our fantastic thinking a mere expenditure of the knowledge or force with which we were temporarily connected? When we think of metaphysical systems which speak of man as a microcosm, embodying in himself in some way and to some degree all of the reality of the universe, do we value or even remember that our questions about the universe came to us originally in the form of an answering direction, and that this partial answer itself came in the form of a certain quality or force of questioning? Isn't it so, however, that our thinking flies away from that moment, forgets it by classifying it and distrusting it?

Thus, in this light, metaphysical speculation can be the study and the search for questions, or, rather, for questioning, the study of what we desire and the possible attempt to be alert for help and direction when it appears. Do we want thoughts about death and immortality, or do we want immortality? Do we want answers or do we want to be?

CHAPTER IV

THE THEME OF DEATH IN POETRY AND LITERATURE

Introduction

Artists, poets, sculptors, musicians, actors, dancers—masters of the creative arts—are able to catch in a phrase, a motion, a line, the essence of the human condition in all its aspects. As a student in "Confrontations..." on the Oregon campus, you read the selections which follow, and when you meet with your seminar group, you hear music on the theme of death, and sometimes you see artistic representations, too. We have never managed to present a ballet or a modern dance ensemble, but we would like to do so some day. The reader who is not a student must seek out these other media for himself; in this book of readings, we can present only the printed page and not the multi-media bombardment of the senses available to on-campus students.

The selection of works of art is a very personal, subjective process. There are hundreds and hundreds of poems on the theme of death, from Chaucer to cummings. The poems we picked mean something special to us. We begin with a poem commemorating the death of a dog, a real dog which lived with a real poet. Ken Beattie shares with us his experience when his dog Fang died, and who among us did not first learn of death through the trauma of a beloved pet's demise? To a child, such an experience is usually his first brush with the death of an important "other."

Friends are much more important than pets, and the selections by Rod McKuen and by A.E. Housman present different aspects of the loss of a friend; Houseman's poem shows us the ill-concealed joy we feel when it is the death of **another**, and not of **myself**, though the other was friend.

The excerpt from Gibran's *The Prophet* and the poem by e.e. cummings contrast two views of how dying is perceived. The chapter from *Of Time and the River* by Thomas Wolfe is, to us, one of the most poignant scenes of the moment of death ever written. And Tolstoy's *Ivan Ilych* is a classic short novel whose theme is the resolution of life's meaning, a process without which a man cannot die peacefully.

Dylan Thomas, in the oft-quoted ' Do Not Go Gentle Into That Good Night," and Helga Sandburg in "Father, Once You Said That in the Grace of God," provide startlingly different portraits of how the death of a parent might be mourned.

The student is urged to think of other selections from poetry, literature, art, or drama which are his favorites. It is perhaps surprising that most of us have a "favorite" poem or literary piece about death, and you may well find this true of yourself. You may not have considered your favorite as being "about death" until you review those selections which are outstanding in your mind. Housman's "Is My Team Plowing" was one of my favorites for many years before we began "Confrontations of Death;" I had thought of it as a poem largely about friendship, but it took on added dimensions in the context of the meaning of death.

There are two autobiographical accounts of the death of a beloved husband, written by women who have unusual empathy and emotional strength, which we highly recommend to the earnest student. These are:

1. Lael Tucker Wertenbaker, *Death of a Man.* N. Y., Random House, 1957.
2. Laura Anchera Huxley, *This Timeless Moment: A Personal View of Aldous Huxley,* N.Y. Farrar Straus & Giroux, 1968.

Both of these books recount a terminal illness of considerable duration and suffering, during which the dying husband was helped by the wife to live his remaining life to the fullest, during which the wife was helped by her husband to mourn his death before it actually happened, and at the end of which the wife was with the husband at the moment of dying. The insightfulness of these books almost hurts, but the reader will be better able to confront death—that of another or that of self—for having read them.

FANG *

April 1967 —

When my dog dies I shall stuff her
With hand-woven textiles, clay pots
Toys and grass,
I'll strap to her side
A tray of incense and candles
To have when she needs them
Then invite her on her way
Sorry it's not in my power
To lengthen her stay —
But wonderfully happy
She came.

                                        Ken Beattie

DOUG DAVIS, THREE   * *

While you were dying
I was going to the beach.
Unaware your smile
had caught fire at Orly
ten thousand miles away.

It was days later I learned
that you had walked your last deserted street,
crossed the line of infinity you had always tried to paint.

No longer smiling.
No more to run and chase the dappled dragonfly.

I would rather you had died breathing sea
          instead of smoke.
I lost your smile going down the stairs.

                                        Rod McKuen

* The unpublished poem *Fang* printed by permission of Ken Beattie, author.
* * Reprinted from *Listen to the Warm.* Used by permission of the publisher Random House, Inc. New York.

IS MY TEAM PLOWING *

"Is my team plowing,
　　　That I was used to drive
And hear the harness jingle
　　　When I was man alive?"

Aye, the horses trample,
　　　The harness jingles now;
No change though you lie under
　　　The land you used to plow.

"Is football playing
　　　Along the river shore,
With lads to chase the leather,
　　　Now I stand up no more?"

Aye, the ball is flying,
　　　The lads play heart and soul;
The goal stands up, the keeper
　　　Stands up to keep the goal.

"Is my girl happy,
　　　That I thought hard to leave,
And has she tired of weeping
　　　As she lies down at eve?"

Aye, she lies down lightly,
　　　She lies not down to weep:
Your girl is well contented.
　　　Be still, my lad, and sleep.

"Is my friend hearty,
　　　Now I am thin and pine;
And has he found to sleep in
　　　A better bed than mine?"

Yes, lad, I lie easy,
　　　I lie as lads would choose;
I cheer a dead man's sweetheart.
　　　Never ask me whose.

A. E. Housman

* Reprinted from *A Shropshire Lad* by A. E. Housman, published by Peter Pauper Press, Mt. Vernon, N.Y. p 33.

THE PROPHET   *

(an excerpt)

Then Almitra spoke, saying, We would
ask now of Death.
    And he said:
    You would know the secret of death.
    But how shall you find it unless you seek
it in the heart of life?
    The owl whose night-bound eyes are
blind unto the day cannot unveil the mystery
of light.
    If you would indeed behold the spirit of
death, open your heart wide unto the body
of life.
    For life and death are one, even as the
river and the sea are one.

    In the depth of your hopes and desires
lies your silent knowledge of the beyond;
    And like seeds dreaming beneath the snow
your heart dreams of spring.
    Trust the dreams, for in them is hidden
the gate to eternity.
    Your fear of death is but the trembling
of the shepherd when he stands before the
king whose hand is to be laid upon him in
honour.
    Is the shepherd not joyful beneath his
trembling, that he shall wear the mark of
the king?
    Yet is he not more mindful of his trembling?
    For what is it to die but to stand naked
in the wind and to melt into the sun?
    And what is it to cease breathing, but to
free the breath from its restless tides, that
it may rise and expand and seek God unen-
cumbered?

    Only when you drink from the river of
silence shall you indeed sing.
    And when you have reached the moun-
tain top, then you shall begin to climb.
    And when the earth shall claim your
limbs, then shall you truly dance.

Kahlil Gabran

* An excerpt from *The Prophet* by Kahlil Gibran. Used by permission of the publisher Random House,
Inc., New York. pp 80-81.

dying is fine) but Death   *

?o
baby
i

wouldn't like

Death if Death
were
good: for

when (instead of stopping to think) you

begin to feel of it, dying
's miraculous
why? be

cause dying is

perfectly natural; perfectly
putting
it mildly lively (but

Death

is strictly
scientific
& artificial &

evil & legal)

we thank thee
god
almighty for dying

(forgive us, o life! the sin of Death

    e.e. cummings

*   Reprinted from XAIPE (1950) in Poems (1923-54) by e.e. cummings. Used by permission of the publisher Harcourt Brace Jovanovich, Inc. New York. p 431.

OF TIME AND THE RIVER *

by

Thomas Wolfe

XXXI

The dying man himself was no longer to be fooled and duped by hope; he knew that he was done for, and he no longer cared. Rather, as if that knowledge had brought him a new strength — the immense and measureless strength that comes from a resignation, and that has vanquished terror and despair — Gant had already consigned himself to death, and now was waiting for it, without weariness or anxiety, and with a perfect and peaceful acquiescence.

This complete resignation and tranquillity of a man whose life had been so full of violence, protest, and howling fury stunned and silenced them, and left them helpless. It seemed that Gant, knowing that often he had lived badly, was now determined to die well. And in this he succeeded. He accepted every ministration, every visit, every stammering reassurance, or frenzied activity, with a passive gratefulness which he seemed to want every one to know. On the evening of the day after his first hemmorrhage, he asked for food and Eliza, bustling out, pathetically eager to do something, killed a chicken and cooked it for him.

And as if, from that infinite depth of death and silence from which he looked at her, he had seen, behind the bridling brisk activity of her figure, forever bustling back and forth, saying confusedly — "Why, yes! The very thing! This very minute, sir!" — had seen the white strained face, the stricken eyes of a proud and sensitive woman who had wanted affection all her life, had received for the most part injury and abuse, and who was ready to clutch at any crust of comfort that might console or justify her before he died — he ate part of the chicken with relish, and then looking up at her, said quietly:

"I tell you what — that was a good chicken."

And Helen, who had been sitting beside him on the bed, and feeding him, now cried out in a tone of bantering and good-humored challenge:

"What! Is it better than the ones I cook for you! You'd better not say it is — I'll beat you if you do."

And Gant, grinning feebly, shook his head, and answered:

"Ah-h! Your mother is a good cook, Helen. You're a good cook, too — but there's no one else can cook a chicken like your mother!"

And stretching out his great right hand, he patted Eliza's worn fingers with his own.

And Eliza, suddenly touched by that word of unaccustomed praise and tenderness, turned and rushed blindly from the room at a clumsy bridling gait, clasping her hands together at the wrist, her weak eyes blind with tears — shaking her head in a strong convulsive movement, her mouth smiling a pale tremulous smile, ludicrous, touching, made unnatural by her false teeth, whispering over and over to herself, "Poor fellow! Says, 'There's no one else can cook a chicken like your mother.' Reached out and patted me on the hand, you know. Says 'I tell you what, there's no one who can cook a chicken like your mother.' I reckon he wanted to let me know, to tell me, but says, 'The rest of you have all been good to me, Helen's a good cook, but there's no one else can cook like your mother.'"

"Oh, here, here, here," said Helen, who, laughing uncertainly had followed her mother from the room when Eliza had rushed out, and had seized her by the arms, and shook her gently, "good heavens! *Here!* You mustn't carry on like this! You mustn't take it this way! Why he's all right!" she cried out heartily and shook Eliza again. "Papa's going to be all right! Why, what are you crying for?" she laughed. "He's going to get well now — don't you know that?"

And Eliza could say nothing for a moment but kept smiling that false trembling and unnatural smile, shaking her head in a slight convulsive movement, her eyes blind with tears.

"I tell you what," she whispered, smiling tremulously again and shaking her head, "there was something about it — you know, the way he said it — says, 'There's no one who can come up to your mother' — there was

* Reproduced by permission of Charles Scribner's Sons. Copyright 1935 by Charles Scribner's Sons; renewal copyright 1963 by Paul Gitlin, Administrator C.T.A. Taken from *Of Time and the River*, pp 256-268.

something in the way he said it! Poor fellow, says, 'None of the rest of you can cook like her' — says, 'I tell you what, that was certainly a good chicken' — Poor fellow! It wasn't so much what he said as the way he said it — there was something about it that went through me like a knife — I tell you what it did!"

"Oh, here, here, here!" Helen cried again, laughing. But her own eyes were also wet, the bitter possessiveness that had dominated all her relations with her father, and that had thrust Eliza away from him, was suddenly vanquished. At that moment she began to feel an affection for her mother that she had never felt before, a deep and nameless pity and regret, and a sense of sombre satisfaction.

"Well," she thought, "I guess it's all she's had, but I'm glad she's got that much to remember. I'm glad he said it: she'll always have that now to hang on to."

And Gant lay looking up from that sunken depth of death and silence, his great hands of living power quiet with their immense and passive strength beside him on the bed.

XXXII

Towards one o'clock that night Gant fell asleep and dreamed that he was walking down the road that led to Spangler's Run. And although he had not been along that road for fifty years everything was as fresh, as green, as living and familiar as it had ever been to him. He came out on the road from Schaefer's farm, and on his left he passed by the little white frame church of the United Brethren, and the graveyard about the church where his friends and family had been buried. From the road he could see the line of family gravestones which he himself had carved and set up after he had returned from serving his apprenticeship in Baltimore. The stones were all alike: tall flat slabs of marble with plain rounded tops, and there was one for his sister Susan, who had died in infancy, and one for his sister Huldah, who had died in childbirth while the war was on, and one for Huldah's husband, a young farmer named Jake Lentz who had been killed at Chancellorsville, and one for the husband of his oldest sister, Augusta, a man named Martin, who had been an itinerant photographer and had died soon after the war, and finally one for Gant's own father. And since there were no stones for his brother George or for Elmer or for John, and none for his mother or Augusta, Gant knew that he was still a young man, and had just recently come home. The stones which he had put up were still white and new, and in the lower right hand corner of each stone, he had carved his own name: W. O. Gant.

It was a fine morning in early May and everything was sweet and green and as familiar as it had always been. The graveyard was carpeted with thick green grass, and all around the graveyard and the church there was the incomparable green velvet of young wheat. And the thought came back to Gant, as it had come to him a thousand times, that the wheat around the graveyard looked greener and richer than any other wheat that he had ever seen. And beside him on his right were the great fields of the Schaefer farm, some richly carpeted with young green wheat, and some ploughed, showing great bronze-red strips of fertile nobly swelling earth. And behind him on the great swell of the land, and commanding that sweet and casual scene with the majesty of its incomparable lay was Jacob Schaefer's great red barn and to the right the neat brick house with the white trimming of its windows, the white picket fence, the green yard with its rich tapestry of flowers and lilac bushes and the massed leafy spread of its big maple trees. And behind the house the hill rose, and all its woods were just greening into May, still smoky, tender and unfledged, gold-yellow with the magic of young green. And before the woods began there was the apple orchard halfway up the hill; the trees were heavy with the blossoms and stood there in all their dense still bloom incredible.

And from the greening trees the bird-song rose, the grass was thick with the dense gold glory of the dandelions, and all about him were a thousand magic things that came and went and never could be captured. Below the church, he passed the old frame house where Elly Spangler, who kept the church keys, lived, and there were apple trees behind the house, all dense with bloom, but the house was rickety, unpainted and dilapidated as it had always been, and he wondered if the kitchen was still buzzing with a million flies, and if Elly's half-wit brothers, Jim and Willy, were inside. And even as he shook his head and thought, as he had thought so many times "Poor Elly," the back door opened and Willy Spangler, a man past thirty wearing overalls, and with a fond, foolish witless face, came galloping down across the yard toward him, flinging his arms out in exuberant greeting, and shouting to him the same welcome that he shouted out to every one who passed, friends and strangers all alike — "I've been lookin' fer ye! I've been lookin' fer ye, Oll," using, as was the custom of the friends and kinsmen of his Pennsylvania boyhood, his second name — and then, anxiously, pleadingly, again the same words that he spoke to every one: "Ain't ye goin' to stay?"

And Gant, grinning, but touched by the indefinable sadness and pity which that kind and witless greeting had always stirred in him since his own childhood, shook his head, and said quietly:

"No, Willy. Not to-day. I'm meeting some one down the road" — and straightway felt, with thudding heart, a powerful and nameless excitement, the urgency of that impending meeting — why, where, with whom, he did not know — but all-compelling now, inevitable.

And Willy, still with wondering, foolish, kindly face followed along beside him now, saying eagerly, as he said to every one:

"Did ye bring anythin' for me? Have ye got a chew?"

And Gant, starting to shake his head in refusal, stopped suddenly, seeing the look of disappointment on the idiot's face, and putting his hand in the pocket of his coat, took out a plug of apple-tobacco, saying:

"Yes. Here you are, Willy. You can have this."

And Willy, grinning with foolish joy, had clutched the plug of tobacco and, still kind and foolish, had followed on a few steps more, saying anxiously:

"Are ye comin' back, Oll? Will ye be comin' back real soon?"

And Gant, feeling a strange and nameless sorrow, answered:

"I don't know, Willy" — for suddenly he saw that he might never come this way again.

But Willy, still happy, foolish, and contented, had turned and galloped away toward the house, flinging his arms out and shouting as he went:

"I'll be waitin' for ye. I'll be waitin' for ye, Oll."

And Gant went on then, down the road, and there was a nameless sorrow in him that he could not understand, and some of the brightness had gone out of the day.

When he got to the mill, he turned left along the road that went down by Spangler's run, crossed by the bridge below, and turned from the road into the wood-path on the other side. A child was standing in the path, and turned and went on ahead of him. In the wood the sunlight made swarming moths of light across the path, and through the leafy tangle of the trees: the sunlight kept shifting and swarming on the child's gold hair, and all around him were the sudden noises of the wood, the stir, the rustle, and the bullet thrum of wings, the cool broken sound of hidden water.

The wood got denser, darker as he went on and coming to a place where the path split away into two forks, Gant stopped, and turning to the child said, "Which one shall I take?" And the child did not answer him.

But some one was there in the wood before him. He heard footsteps on the path, and saw a footprint in the earth, and turning took the path where the footprint was, and where it seemed he could hear some one walking.

And then, with the bridgeless instancy of dreams, it seemed to him that all of the bright green-gold around him in the wood grew dark and sombre, the path grew darker, and suddenly he was walking in a strange and gloomy forest, haunted by the brown and tragic light of dreams. The forest shapes of great trees rose around him, he could hear no bird-song now, even his own feet on the path were soundless, but he always thought he heard the sound of some one walking in the wood before him. He stopped and listened: the steps were muffled, softly thunderous, they seemed so near that he thought that he must catch up with the one he followed in another second, and then they seemed immensely far away, receding in the dark mystery of that gloomy wood. And again he stopped and listened, the footsteps faded, vanished, he shouted, no one answered. And suddenly he knew that he had taken the wrong path, that he was lost. And in his heart there was an immense and quiet sadness, and the dark light of the enormous wood was all around him; no birds sang.

XXXIII

Gant awoke suddenly and found himself looking straight up at Eliza who was seated in a chair beside the bed.

60

"You were asleep," she said quietly with a grave smile, looking at him in her direct and almost accusing fashion.

"Yes," he said, breathing a little hoarsely, "what time is it?"

It was a few minutes before three o'clock in the morning. She looked at the clock and told him the time: he asked where Helen was.

"Why," said Eliza quickly, "she's right here in this hall room: I reckon she's asleep, too. Said she was tired, you know, but that if you woke up and needed her to call her. Do you want me to get her?"

"No," said Gant. "Don't bother her. I guess she needs the rest, poor child. Let her sleep."

"Yes," said Eliza, nodding, "and that's exactly what you must do, too, Mr. Gant. You try to go on back to sleep now," she said coaxingly, "for that's what we all need. There's no medicine like sleep — as the fellow says, it's Nature's sovereign remedy," said Eliza, with that form of sententiousness that she was very fond of — "so you go on, now, Mr. Gant, and get a good night's sleep, and when you wake up in the morning, you'll feel like a new man. That's half the battle — if you can get your sleep, you're already on the road to recovery."

"No," said Gant, "I've slept enough."

He was breathing rather hoarsely and heavily and she asked him if he was comfortable and needed anything. He made no answer for a moment, and then muttered something under his breath that she could not hear plainly, but that sounded like "little boy."

"Hah? What say? What is it, Mr. Gant?" Eliza said. "Little boy?" she said sharply, as he did not answer.

"Did you see him?" he said.

She looked at him for a moment with troubled eyes, then said:

"Pshaw, Mr. Gant, I guess you must have been dreaming."

He did not answer, and for a moment there was no sound in the room but his breathing, hoarse, a little heavy. Then he muttered:

"Did some one come into the house?"

She looked at him sharply, inquiringly again, with troubled eyes:

"Hah? What say? Why, no, I think not," she said doubtfully, "unless you may have heard Gilmer come in an' go up to his room."

And Gant was again silent for several moments, breathing a little heavily and hoarsely, his hands resting with an enormous passive strength, upon the bed. Presently he said quietly:

"Where's Bacchus?"

"Hah? Who's that?" Eliza said sharply, in a startled kind of tone. "Bacchus? You mean Uncle Bacchus?"

"Yes," said Gant.

"Why, pshaw, Mr. Gant!" cried Eliza laughing — for a startled moment she had wondered if "his mind was wanderin'," but one glance at his quiet eyes, the tranquil sanity of his quiet tone, reassured her —

"Pshaw!" she said, putting one finger up to her broad nose-wing and laughing slyly. "You must have been havin' queer dreams, for a fact!"

"Is he here?"

"Why, I'll vow, Mr. Gant!" she cried again. "What on earth is in your mind? You know that Uncle Bacchus is way out West in Oregon — it's been ten years since he came back home last — that summer of the reunion at Gettysburg."

"Yes, said Gant. "I remember now."

And again he fell silent, staring upward in the semi-darkness, his hands quietly at rest beside him, breathing a little hoarsely, but without pain. Eliza sat in the chair watching him, her hands clasped loosely at her waist, her lips pursed reflectively, and a puzzled look in her eyes: "Now I wonder what ever put that in his mind?" she thought. "I wonder what made him think of Bacchus. Now his mind's not wanderin' — that's one thing sure. He knows what he's doing just as well as I do — I reckon he must have dreamed it — that Bacchus was here — but that's certainly a strange thing, that he should bring it up like this."

He was so silent that she thought he might have gone to sleep again, he lay motionless with his eyes turned upward in the semi-darkness of the room, his hands immense and passive at his side. But suddenly he startled her again by speaking, a voice so quiet and low that he might have been talking to himself.

"Father died the year before the war," he said, "when I was nine years old. I never got to know him very well. I guess Mother had a hard time of it. There were seven of us — and nothing but that little place to live on — and some of us too young to help her much — and George away at war. She spoke pretty hard to us sometimes — but I guess she had a hard time of it. It was a tough time for all of us," he muttered, "I tell you what, it was."

"Yes," Eliza said, "I guess it was. I know she told me — I talked to her, you know, the time we went there on our honeymoon — whew! what about it?" she shrieked faintly, and put her finger up to her broad nose-wing with the same sly gesture — "it was all I could do to keep a straight face sometimes — why, you know, the way she had of talkin' — the expressions she used — oh! came right out with it, you know — sometimes I'd have to turn my head away so she wouldn't see me laughin' — says, you know, 'I was left a widow with seven children to bring up, but I never took charity from no one; as I told 'em all, I've crawled under the dog's belly all my life; now I guess I can get over its back.'"

"Yes," said Gant with a faint grin. "Many's the time I've heard her say that."

"But she told it then, you know," Eliza went on in explanatory fashion, "about your father and how he'd done hard labor on a farm all his life and died — well, I reckon you'd call it consumption."

"Yes," said Gant. "That was it."

"And," Eliza said reflectively, "I never asked — of course, I didn't want to embarrass her — but I reckon from what she said, he may have been — well, I suppose you might say he was a drinkin' man."

"Yes," said Gant, "I guess he was."

"And I know she told it on him," said Eliza, laughing again, and passing one finger slyly at the corner of her broad nose-wing, "how he went to town that time — to Grant's Mill, I guess it was — and how she was afraid he'd get to drinkin', and she sent you and Wes along to watch him to see he got home again — and how he met up with some fellers there and, sure enough, I guess he started drinkin' and stayed away too long — and then, I reckon he was afraid of what she'd say to him when he got back — and that was when he bought the clock — it's that very clock upon the mantel, Mr. Gant — but that was when he got the clock, all right — I guess he thought it would pacify her when she started out to scold him for gettin' drunk and bein' late."

"Yes," said Gant, who had listened without moving, staring at the ceiling, and with a faint grin printed at the corners of his mouth, "well do I remember: that was it, all right."

"And then," Eliza went on, "he lost the way comin' home — it had been snowin', and I reckon it was getting dark, and he had been drinkin' — and instead of turnin' in on the road that went down by your place he kept goin' on until he passed Jake Schaefer's farm — an' I guess Wes and you, poor child, kept follerin' where he led, thinkin' it was all right — and when he realized his mistake he said he was tired an' had to rest a while and — I'll vow! to think he'd go and do a thing like that," said Eliza, laughing again — "he lay right down in the snow, sir, with the clock beside him — and went sound to sleep."

"Yes," said Gant, "and the clock was broken."

"Yes," Eliza said, "she told me about that too — and how she heard you all come creepin' in real quiet an' easy-like about nine o'clock that night, when she and all the children were in bed — an' how she could hear him whisperin' to you and Wes to be quiet — an' how she heard you all come creepin' up the steps — and how he was tip-toein' in real easy-like an' laid the clock down on the bed — I reckon the glass had been broken out of it — hopin' she'd see it when she woke up in the morning an' wouldn't scold him then for stayin' out — "

"Yes," said Gant, still with the faint attentive grin, "and then the clock began to strike."

"Whew-w!" cried Eliza, putting her finger underneath her broad nose-wing — "I know she had to laugh about it when she told it to me — she said that all of you looked so sheepish when the clock began to strike that she didn't have the heart to scold him."

And Gant, grinning faintly again, emitted a faint rusty cackle that sounded like "E'God!" and said: "Yes, that was it. Poor fellow."

"But to think," Eliza went on, "that he would have no more sense than to do a thing like that — to lay right down there in the snow an' go to sleep with you two children watchin' him. And I know how she told it, how she questioned you and Wes next day, and I reckon started in to scold you for not takin' better care of him, and how you told her, 'Well, Mother, I thought that it would be all right. I kept steppin' where he stepped, I thought he knew the way.' And said she didn't have the heart to scold you after that — poor child, I reckon you were only eight or nine years old, and boy-like thought you'd follow in your father's footsteps and that everything would be all right."

"Yes," said Gant, with the faint grin again, "I kept stretchin' my legs to put my feet down in his tracks — it was all I could do to keep up with him...Ah, Lord," he said, and in a moment said in a faint low voice, "how well I can remember it. That was just the winter before he died."

"And you've had that old clock ever since," Eliza said. "That very clock upon the mantel, sir — at least, you've had it ever since I've known you, and I reckon you had it long before that — for I know you told me how you brought it South with you. And that clock must be all of sixty or seventy years old — if it's a day."

"Yes," said Gant, "it's all of that."

And again he was silent, and lay so still and motionless that there was no sound in the room except his faint and labored breathing, the languid stir of the curtains in the cool night breeze, and the punctual tocking of the old wooden clock. And presently, when she thought that he might have gone off to sleep again, he spoke, in the same remote and detached voice as before:

"Eliza," — he said — and at the sound of that unaccustomed word, a name he had spoken only twice in forty years — her white face and her worn brown eyes turned toward him with the quick and startled look of an animal — "Eliza," he said quietly, "you have had a hard life with me, a hard time. I want to tell you that I'm sorry."

And before she could move from her white stillness of shocked surprise, he lifted his great right hand and put it gently down across her own. And for a moment she sat there bolt upright, shaken, frozen, with a look of terror in her eyes, her heart drained of blood, a pale smile trembling uncertainly and foolishly on her lips. Then she tried to withdraw her hand with a clumsy movement, she began to stammer with an air of ludicrous embarrassment, she brindled, saying — "Aw-w, now, Mr. Gant. Well, now, I reckon," — and suddenly these few simple words of regret and affection did what all the violence, abuse, drunkenness and injury of forty years had failed to do. She wrenched her hand free like a wounded creature, her face was suddenly contorted by that grotesque and pitiable grimace of sorrow that women have had in moments of grief since the beginning of time, and digging her fist into her closed eye quickly with the pathetic gesture of a child, she lowered her head and wept bitterly:

"It was a hard time, Mr. Gant," she whispered, "a hard time, sure enough...It wasn't all the cursin' and the drinkin' — I got used to that...I reckon I was only an ignorant sort of girl when I met you and I guess," she went on with a pathetic and unconscious humor, "I didn't know what married life was like...but I could have stood the rest of it...the bad names an' all the things you called me when I was goin' to have another child...but it was what you said when Grover died...accusin' me of bein' responsible for his death because I took the children to St. Louis to the Fair — " and at the words as if an old and lacerated wound had been re-opened raw and bleeding, she wept hoarsely, harshly, bitterly — "that was the worst time that I had — sometimes I prayed to God that I would not wake up — he was a fine boy, Mr. Gant, the best I had — like the write-up in the paper said he had the sense an' judgment of one twice his age...an' somehow it had grown a part of me, I expected him to lead the others — when he died it seemed like everything was gone...an' then to have you say that I had — " her voice faltered to a whisper, stopped; with a pathetic gesture she wiped the sleeve of her old frayed sweater across her eyes and already ashamed of her tears, said hastily:

"Not that I'm blamin' you, Mr. Gant...I reckon we were both at fault...we were both to blame...if I had it to do all over I know I could do better...but I was so young and ignorant when I met you, Mr. Gant...knew nothing of the world...there was always something strange-like about you that I didn't understand."

Then, as he said nothing, but lay still and passive, looking at the ceiling, she said quickly, drying her eyes and speaking with a brisk and instant cheerfulness, the undaunted optimism of her ever-hopeful nature:

"Well, now Mr. Gant, that's all over, and the best thing we can do is to forget about it...We've both made our mistakes — we wouldn't be human if we didn't — but now we've got to profit by experience — the worst of all this trouble is all over — you've got to think of getting well now, that's the only thing you've got to do, sir," she said pursing her lips and winking briskly at him — "just set your mind on getting well — that's all you've got to do now, Mr. Gant — and the battle is half won. For half our ills and troubles are all imagination," she said sententiously, "and if you'll just make up your mind now that you're going to get well — why, sir, you'll do it," and she looked at him with a brisk nod. "And we've both got years before us, Mr. Gant — for all we know, the best years of our life are still ahead of us — so we'll both go on and profit by the mistakes of the past and make the most of what time's left," she said. "That's just exactly what we'll do!"

And quietly, kindly, without moving, and with the impassive and limitless regret of a man who knows that there is no return, he answered:

"Yes, Eliza. That is what we'll do."

"And now," she went on coaxingly, "why don't you go on back to sleep now, Mr. Gant? There's nothin' like sleep to restore a man to health — as the feller says, it's Nature's sovereign remedy, worth all the doctors and all the medicine on earth," she winked at him, and then concluded on a note of cheerful finality, "so you go on and get some sleep now, and tomorrow you will feel like a new man."

And again he shook his head in an almost imperceptible gesture of negation:

"No," he said, "not now. Can't sleep."

He was silent again, and presently, his breath coming somewhat hoarse and labored, he cleared his throat, and put one hand up to his throat, as if to relieve himself of some impediment.

Eliza looked at him with troubled eyes and said:

"What's the matter, Mr. Gant? There's nothing hurtin' you?"

"No," he said. "Just something in my throat. Could I have some water?"

"Why, yes, sir! That's the very thing!" She got up hastily, and looking about in a somewhat confused manner, saw behind her a pitcher of water and a glass upon his old walnut bureau, and saying "This very minute, sir!" started across the room.

And at the same moment, Gant was aware that some one had entered the house, was coming towards him through the hall, would soon be with him. Turning his head towards the door he was conscious of something approaching with the speed of light, the instancy of thought, and at that moment he was filled with a sense of inexpressible joy, a feeling of triumph and security he had never known. Something immensely bright and beautiful was converging in a flare of light, and at that instant, the whole room blurred around him, his sight was fixed upon that focal image in the door, and suddenly the child was standing there and looking towards him.

And even as he started from his pillows, and tried to call his wife he felt something thick and heavy in his throat that would not let him speak. He tried to call to her again but no sound came, then something wet and warm began to flow out of his mouth and nostrils, he lifted his hands up to his throat, the warm wet blood came pouring out across his fingers; he saw it and felt joy.

For now the child — or some one in the house — was speaking, calling to him; he heard great footsteps, soft but thunderous, imminent, yet immensely far, a voice well-known, never heard before. He called to it, and then it seemed to answer him; he called to it with faith and joy to give him rescue, strength, and life, and it answered him and told him that all the error, old age, pain and grief of life was nothing but an evil dream; that he who had been lost was found again, that his youth would be restored to him and that he would never die, and that he would find again the path he had not taken long ago in a dark wood.

And the child still smiled at him from the dark door; the great steps, soft and powerful, came ever closer, and as the instant imminent approach of that last meeting came intolerably near, he cried out through the lake of jetting blood, "Here, Father, here!" and heard a strong voice answer him, "My son!"

At that instant he was torn by a rending cough, something was wrenched loose in him, the death gasp rattled through his blood, and a mass of greenish matter foamed out through his lips. Then the world was blotted out, a blind black fog swam up and closed above his head, some one seized him, he was held, supported in two arms, he heard some one's voice saying in a low tone of terror and of pity, "Mr. Gant! Mr. Gant! Oh, poor man, poor man! He's gone!" And his brain faded into night. Even before she lowered him back upon the pillows, she knew that he was dead.

THE DEATH OF IVAN ILYCH   *

by

Leo Tolstoy

During an interval in the Melvinski trial in the large building of the Law Courts the members and public prosecutor met in Ivan Egorovich Shebek's private room, where the conversation turned on the celebrated Krasovski case. Fedor Vasilievich warmly maintained that it was not subject to their jurisdiction, Ivan Egorovich maintained the contrary, while Peter Ivanovich, not having entered into the discussion at the start, took no part in it but looked through the *Gazette* which had just been handed in.

'Gentlemen,' he said, 'Ivan Ilych has died!'

'You don't say so!'

'Here, read it yourself,' replied Peter Ivanovich, handing Fedor Vasilievich the paper still damp from the press. Surrounded by a black border were the words: 'Praskovya Fedorovna Golovina, with profound sorrow, informs relatives and friends of the demise of her beloved husband Ivan Ilych Golovin, Member of the Court of Justice, which occurred on February the 4th of this year 1882. The funeral will take place on Friday at one o'clock in the afternoon.'

Ivan Ilych had been a colleague of the gentlemen present and was liked by them all. He had been ill for some weeks with an illness said to be incurable. His post had been kept open for him, but there had been conjectures that in case of his death Alexeev might receive his appointment, and that either Vinnikov or Shtabel would succeed Alexeev. So on receiving the news of Ivan Ilych's death the first thought of each of the gentlemen in that private room was of the changes and promotions it might occasion among themselves or their acquaintances.

'I shall be sure to get Shtabel's place or Vinnikov's,' thought Fedor Vasilievich. 'I was promised that long ago, and the promotion means an extra eight hundred rubles a year for me besides the allowance.'

'Now I must apply for my brother-in-law's transfer from Kaluga,' thought Peter Ivanovich. 'My wife will be very glad, and then she won't be able to say that I never do anything for her relations.'

'I thought he would never leave his bed again,' said Peter Ivanovich aloud. 'It's very sad.'

'But what really was the matter with him?'

'The doctors couldn't say — at least they could, but each of them said something different. When last I saw him I thought he was getting better.'

'And I haven't been to see him since the holidays. I always meant to go.'

'Had he any property?'

'I think his wife had a little — but something quite trifling.'

'We shall have to go to see her, but they live so terribly far away.'

'Far away from you, you mean. Everything's far away from your place.'

'You see, he never can forgive my living on the other side of the river,' said Peter Ivanovich, smiling at Shebek. Then, still talking of the distances between different parts of the city, they returned to the Court.

Besides considerations as to the possible transfers and promotions likely to result from Ivan Ilych's death, the mere fact of the death of a near acquaintance aroused, as usual, in all who heard of it the complacent feeling that, 'it is he who is dead and not I.'

Each one thought or felt, 'Well, he's dead but I'm alive!' But the more intimate of Ivan Ilych's acquaintances, his so-called friends, could not help thinking also that they would now have to fulfil the very tiresome demands of propriety by attending the funeral service and paying a visit of condolence to the widow.

Fedor Vasilievich and Peter Ivanovich had been his nearest acquaintances. Peter Ivanovich had studied law with Ivan Ilych and had considered himself to be under obligations to him.

Having told his wife at dinner-time of Ivan Ilych's death, and of his conjecture that it might be possible to get her brother transferred to their circuit, Peter Ivanovich sacrificed his usual nap, put on his evening clothes, and drove to Ivan Ilych's house.

*   Reprinted from *Teller of Tales* edited by W. Somerset Maugham. Copyright 1939 by Doubleday and Company, Inc. Reprinted by permission of Doubleday & Company, Inc. pp 552-595.

At the entrance stood a carriage and two cabs. Leaning against the wall in the hall downstairs near the cloak-stand was a coffin-lid covered with cloth of gold, ornamented with gold cord and tassels, that had been polished up with metal powder. Two ladies in black were taking off their fur cloaks. Peter Ivanovich recognized one of them as Ivan Ilych's sister, but the other was a stranger to him. His colleague Schwartz was just coming downstairs, but on seeing Peter Ivanovich enter he stopped and winked at him, as if to say: 'Ivan Ilych has made a mess of things — not like you and me.'

Schwartz's face with his Piccadilly whiskers, and his slim figure in evening dress, had as usual an air of elegant solemnity which contrasted with the playfulness of his character and had a special piquancy here, or so it seemed to Peter Ivanovich.

Peter Ivanovich allowed the ladies to precede him and slowly followed them upstairs. Schwartz did not come down but remained where he was, and Peter Ivanovich understood that he wanted to arrange where they should play bridge that evening. The ladies went upstairs to the widow's room, and Schwartz with seriously compressed lips but a playful look in his eyes, indicated by a twist of his eyebrows the room to the right where the body lay.

Peter Ivanovich, like everyone else on such occasions, entered feeling uncertain what he would have to do. All he knew was that at such times it is always safe to cross oneself. But he was not quite sure whether one should make obeisances while doing so. He therefore adopted a middle course. On entering the room he began crossing himself and made a slight movement resembling a bow. At the same time, as far as the motion of his head and arm allowed, he surveyed the room.. Two young men — apparently nephews, one of whom was a high-school pupil — were leaving the room, crossing themselves as they did so. An old woman was standing motionless, and a lady with strangely arched eyebrows was saying something to her in a whisper. A vigorous, resolute Church Reader, in a frock-coat, was reading something in a loud voice with an expression that precluded any contradiction. The butler's assistant, Gerasim, stepping lightly in front of Peter Ivanovich, was strewing something on the floor. Noticing this, Peter Ivanovich was immediately aware of a faint odour of a decomposing body.

The last time he had called on Ivan Ilych, Peter Ivanovich had seen Gerasim in the study. Ivan Ilych had been particularly fond of him and he was performing the duty of a sick nurse.

Peter Ivanovich continued to make the sign of the cross slightly inclining his head in an intermediate direction between the coffin, the Reader, and the icons on the table in a corner of the room. Afterwards, when it seemed to him that this movement of his arm in crossing himself had gone on too long, he stopped and began to look at the corpse.

The dead man lay, as dead men always lie, in a specially heavy way, his rigid limbs sunk in the soft cushions of the coffin, with the head forever bowed on the pillow. His yellow waxen brow with bald patches over his sunken temples was thrust up in the way peculiar to the dead, the protruding nose seeming to press on the upper lip. He was much changed and had grown even thinner since Peter Ivanovich had last seen him, but, as is always the case with the dead, his face was handsomer and above all more dignified than when he was alive. The expression on the face said that what was necessary had been accomplished, and accomplished rightly. Besides this there was in that expression a reproach and a warning to the living. This warning seemed to Peter Ivanovich out of place, or at least not applicable to him. He felt a certain discomfort and so he hurriedly crossed himself once more and turned and went out of the door — too hurriedly and too regardless of propriety, as he himself was aware.

Schwartz was waiting for him in the adjoining room with legs spread wide apart and both hands toying with his top-hat behind his back. The mere sight of that playful, well-groomed, and elegant figure refreshed Peter Ivanovich. He felt that Schwartz was above all these happenings and would not surrender to any depressing influences. His very look said that this incident of a church service for Ivan Ilych could not be a sufficient reason for infringing the order of the session — in other words, that it would certainly not prevent his unwrapping a new pack of cards and shuffling them that evening while a footman placed four fresh candles on the table: in fact, there was no reason for supposing that this incident would hinder their spending the evening agreeably. Indeed he said this in a whisper as Peter Ivanovich passed him, proposing that they should meet for a game at Fedor Vasilievich's. But apparently Peter Ivanovich was not destined to play bridge that evening. Praskovya Fedorovna (a short, fat woman who despite all efforts to the contrary had continued to broaden steadily from her shoulders downwards and who had the same extraordinarily arched eyebrows as the lady who had been standing by the coffin), dressed all in black, her head covered with lace, came out of her own room with some other ladies, conducted them to the room where the dead body lay, and said: 'The service will begin immediately. Please go in.'

Schwartz, making an indefinite bow, stood still, evidently neither accepting nor declining this invitation. Praskovya Fedorovna, recognizing Peter Ivanovich, sighed, went close up to him, took his hand, and said: 'I know you were a true friend to Ivan Ilych...' and looked at him awaiting some suitable response. And Peter Ivanovich knew that, just as it had been the right thing to cross himself in that room, so what he had to do here was to press her hand, sigh, and say, 'Believe me...'. So he did all this and as he did it felt that the desired result had been achieved: that both he and she were touched.

'Come with me. I want to speak to you before it begins,' said the widow. 'Give me your arm.'

Peter Ivanovich gave her his arm and they went to the inner rooms, passing Schwartz who winked at Peter Ivanovich compassionately.

'That does for our bridge! Don't object if we find another player. Perhaps you can cut in when you do escape,' said his playful look.

Peter Ivanovich sighed still more deeply and despondently, and Praskovya Fedorovna pressed his arm gratefully. When they reached the drawing-room, upholstered in pink cretonne and lighted by a dim lamp, they sat down at the table — she on a sofa and Peter Ivanovich on a low pouffe, the springs of which yielded spasmodically under his weight. Praskovya Fedorovna had been on the point of warning him to take another seat, but felt that such a warning was out of keeping with her present condition and so changed her mind. As he sat down on the pouffe Peter Ivanovich recalled how Ivan Ilych had arranged this room and had consulted him regarding this pink cretonne with green leaves. The whole room was full of furniture and knick-knacks, and on her way to the sofa the lace of the widow's black shawl caught on the carved edge of the table. Peter Ivanovich rose to detach it, and the springs of the pouffe, relieved of his weight, rose also and gave him a push. The widow began detaching her shawl herself, and Peter Ivanovich again sat down, suppressing the rebellious springs of the pouffe under him. But the widow had not quite freed herself and Peter Ivanovich got up again, and again the pouffe rebelled and even creaked. When this was all over she took out a clean cambric handkerchief and began to weep. The episode with the shawl and the struggle with the pouffe had cooled Peter Ivanovich's emotions and he sat there with a sullen look on his face. This awkward situation was interrupted by Sokolov, Ivan Ilych's butler, who came to report that the plot in the cemetery that Praskovya Fedorovna had chosen would cost two hundred rubles. She stopped weeping and, looking at Peter Ivanovich with the air of a victim, remarked in French that it was very hard for her. Peter Ivanovich made a silent gesture signifying his full conviction that it must indeed be so.

'Please smoke,' she said in a magnanimous yet crushed voice, and turned to discuss with Sokolov the price of the plot for the grave.

Peter Ivanovich while lighting his cigarette heard her inquiring very circumstantially into the price of different plots in the cemetery and finally decide which she would take. When that was done she gave instructions about engaging the choir. Sokolov then left the room.

'I look after everything myself,' she told Peter Ivanovich, shifting the albums that lay on the table; and noticing that the table was endangered by his cigarette-ash, she immediately passed him an ash-tray, saying as she did so: 'I consider it an affectation to say that my grief prevents my attending to practical affairs. On the contrary, if anything can — I won't say console me, but — distract me, it is seeing to everything concerning him.' She again took out her handkerchief as if preparing to cry, but suddenly, as if mastering her feeling, she shook herself and began to speak calmly. 'But there is something I want to talk to you about.'

Peter Ivanovich bowed, keeping control of the springs of the pouffe, which immediately began quivering under him.

'He suffered terribly the last few days.'

'Did he?' said Peter Ivanovich.

'Oh, terribly! He screamed unceasingly, not for minutes but for hours. For the last three days he screamed incessantly. It was unendurable. I cannot understand how I bore it; you could hear him three rooms off. Oh, what I have suffered!'

'Is it possible that he was conscious all that time?' asked Peter Ivanovich.

'Yes,' she whispered. 'To the last moment. He took leave of us a quarter of an hour before he died, and asked us to take Volodya away.'

The thought of the sufferings of this man he had known so intimately, first as a merry little boy, then as a school-mate, and later as a grown-up colleague, suddenly struck Peter Ivanovich with horror, despite an unpleasant consciousness of his own and this woman's dissimulation. He again saw that brow, and that nose pressing down on the lip, and felt afraid for himself.

'Three days of frightful suffering and then death! Why, that might suddenly, at any time happen to me,' he thought, and for a moment felt terrified. But — he did not himself know how — the customary reflection at once occurred to him that this had happened to Ivan Ilych and not to him, and that it should not and could not happen to him, and that to think that it could would be yielding to depression which he ought not to do, as Schwartz's expression plainly showed. After which reflection Peter Ivanovich felt reassured, and began to ask with interest about the details of Ivan Ilych's death, as though death was an accident natural to Ivan Ilych but certainly not to himself.

After many details of the really dreadful physical sufferings Ivan Ilych had endured (which details he learnt only from the effect those sufferings had produced on Praskovya Fedorovna's nerves) the widow apparently found it necessary to get to business.

'Oh, Peter Ivanovich, how hard it is! How terribly, terribly hard!' and she again began to weep.

Peter Ivanovich sighed and waited for her to finish blowing her nose. When she had done so he said, 'Believe me...', and she again began talking and brought out what was evidently her chief concern with him — namely, to question him as to how she could obtain a grant of money from the government on the occasion of her husband's death. She made it appear that she was asking Peter Ivanovich's advice about her pension, but he soon saw that she already knew about that to the minutest detail, more even than he did himself. She knew how much could be got out of the government in consequence of her husband's death, but wanted to find out whether she could not possibly extract something more. Peter Ivanovich tried to think of some means of doing so, but after reflecting for a while and, out of propriety, condemning the government for its niggardliness, he said he thought that nothing more could be got. Then she sighed and evidently began to devise means of getting rid of her visitor. Noticing this, he put out his cigarette, rose, pressed her hand, and went out into the anteroom.

In the dining-room where the clock stood that Ivan Ilych had liked so much and had bought at an antique shop, Peter Ivanovich met a priest and a few acquaintances who had come to attend the service, and he recognized Ivan Ilych's daughter, a handsome young woman. She was in black and her slim figure appeared slimmer than ever. She had a gloomy, determined, almost angry expression, and bowed to Peter Ivanovich as though he were in some way to blame. Behind her, with the same offended look, stood a wealthy young man, an examining magistrate, whom Peter Ivanovich also knew and who was her fiance, as he had heard. He bowed mournfully to them and was about to pass into the death-chamber, when from under the stairs appeared the figure of Ivan Ilych's schoolboy son, who was extremely like his father. He seemed a little Ivan Ilych, such as Peter Ivanovich remembered when they studied law together. His tear-stained eyes had in them the look that is seen in the eyes of boys of thirteen or fourteen who are not pure-minded. When he saw Peter Ivanovich he scowled morosely and shame-facedly. Peter Ivanovich nodded to him and entered the death-chamber. The service began: candles, groans, incense, tears, and sobs. Peter Ivanovich stood looking gloomily down at his feet. He did not look once at the dead man, did not yield to any depressing influence, and was one of the first to leave the room. There was no one in the anteroom, but Gerasim darted out of the dead man's room, rummaged with his strong hands among the fur coats to find Peter Ivanovich's and helped him on with it.

'Well, friend Gerasim,' said Peter Ivanovich, so as to say something. 'It's a sad affair, isn't it?'

'It's God's will. We shall all come to it some day,' said Gerasim, displaying his teeth — the even, white teeth of a healthy peasant — and, like a man in the thick of urgent work, he briskly opened the front door, called the coachman, helped Peter Ivanovich into the sledge, and sprang back to the porch as if in readiness for what he had to do next.

Peter Ivanovich found the fresh air particularly pleasant after the smell of incense, the dead body, and carbolic acid.

'Where to, sir?' asked the coachman.

'It's not too late even now.... I'll call round on Fedor Vasilievich.'

He accordingly drove there and found them just finishing the first rubber, so that it was quite convenient for him to cut in.

II

Ivan Ilych's life had been most simple and most ordinary and therefore most terrible.

He had been a member of the Court of Justice, and died at the age of forty-five. His father had been an official who after serving in various ministries and departments in Petersburg had made the sort of career which brings men to positions from which by reason of their long service they cannot be dismissed, though they are obviously unfit to hold any responsible position, and for whom therefore posts are specially created, which though fictitious carry salaries of from six to ten thousand rubles that are not fictitious, and in receipt of which they live on to a great age.

Such was the Privy Councillor and superfluous member of various superfluous institutions, Ilya Epimovich Golovin.

He had three sons, of whom Ivan Ilych was the second. The eldest son was following in his father's footsteps only in another department, and was already approaching the stage in the service at which a similar sinecure would be reached. The third son was a failure. He had ruined his prospects in a number of positions and was now serving in the railway department. His father and brothers, and still more their wives, not merely disliked meeting him, but avoided remembering his existence unless compelled to do so. His sister had married Baron Greff, a Petersburg official of her father's type. Ivan Ilych was *le phenix de la famille* as people said. He was neither as cold and formal as his elder brother nor as wild as the younger, but was a happy mean between them — an intelligent, polished, lively and agreeable man. He had studied with his younger brother at the School of Law, but the latter had failed to complete the course and was expelled when he was in the fifth class. Ivan Ilych finished the course well. Even when he was at the School of Law he was just what he remained for the rest of his life: a capable, cheerful, good-natured, and sociable man, though strict in the fulfilment of what he considered to be his duty: and he considered his duty to be what was so consider. I by those in authority. Neither as a boy nor as a man was he a toady, but from early youth was by nature attracted to people of high station as a fly is drawn to the light, assimilating their ways and views of life and establishing friendly relations with them. All the enthusiasms of childhood and youth passed without leaving much trace on him; he succumbed to sensuality, to vanity, and latterly among the highest classes to liberalism, but always within limits which his instinct unfailingly indicated to him as correct.

At school he had done things which had formerly seemed to him very horrid and made him feel disgusted with himself when he did them; but when later on he saw that such actions were done by people of good position and that they did not regard them as wrong, he was able not exactly to regard them as right, but to forget about them entirely or not be at all troubled at remembering them.

Having graduated from the School of Law and qualified for the tenth rank of the civil service, and having received money from his father for his equipment, Ivan Ilych ordered himself clothes at Scharmer's, the fashionable tailor, hung a medallion inscribed *respice finen* on his watch-chain, took leave of his professor and the prince who was patron of the school, had a farewell dinner with his comrades at Donon's first-class restaurant, and with his new and fashionable portmanteau, linen, clothes, shaving and other toilet appliances, and a travelling rug, all purchased at the best shops, he set off for one of the provinces where, through his father's influence, he had been attached to the Governor as an official for special service.

In the province Ivan Ilych soon arranged as easy and agreeable a position for himself as he had had at the School of Law. He performed his official tasks, made his career, and at the same time amused himself pleasantly and decorously. Occasionally he paid official visits to country districts, where he behaved with dignity both to his superiors and inferiors, and performed the duties entrusted to him, which related chiefly to the sectarians, with an exactness and incorruptible honesty of which he could not but feel proud.

In official matters, despite his youth and taste for frivolous gaiety, he was exceedingly reserved, punctilious, and even severe; but in society he was often amusing and witty, and always good-natured, correct in his manner, and *bon enfant,* as the governor and his wife — with whom he was like one of the family — used to say of him.

In the provinces he had an affair with a lady who made advances to the elegant young lawyer, and there was also a milliner; and there were carousals with aides-de-camp who visited the district, and after-supper visits to a certain outlying street of doubtful reputation; and there was too some obsequiousness to his chief and even to his chief's wife, but all this was done with such a tone of good breeding that no hard names could be applied to it. It all came under the heading of the French saying: *'Il faut que jeunesse se passe.'*[1] It was all done with clean hands, in clean linen, with French phrases, and above all among people of the best society and consequently with the approval of people of rank.

So Ivan Ilych served for five years and then came a change in his official life. The new and reformed judicial institutions were introduced, and new men were needed. Ivan Ilych became such a new man. He was offered the post of Examining Magistrate, and he accepted it though the post was in another province and obliged him to give up the connexions he had formed and to make new ones. His friends met to give him a send-off; they had a group-photograph taken and presented him with a silver cigarette-case, and he set off to his new post.

As examining magistrate Ivan Ilych was just as *comme il faut* and decorous a man, inspiring general respect and capable of separating his official duties from his private life, as he had been when acting as an official on special service. His duties now as examining magistrate were far more interesting and attractive than before. In his former position it had been pleasant to wear an undress uniform made by Scharmer, and to pass through the crowd of petitioners and officials who were timorously awaiting an audience with the governor, and who envied him as with free and easy gait he went straight into his chief's private room to have a cup of tea and a cigarette with him. But not many people had then been directly dependent on him — only police officials and the sectarians when he went on special missions — and he liked to treat them politely, almost as comrades, as if he were letting them feel that he who had the power to crush them was treating them in this simple, friendly way. There were then but few such people. But now, as an examining magistrate, Ivan Ilych felt that everyone without exception, even the most important and self-satisfied, was in his power, and that he need only write a few words on a sheet of paper with a certain heading, and this or that important, self-satisfied person would be brought before him in the role of an accused person or a witness, and if he did not choose to allow him to sit down, would have to stand before him and answer his questions. Ivan Ilych never abused his power; he tried on the contrary to soften its expression, but the consciousness of it and of the possibility of softening its effect, supplied the chief interest and attraction of his office. In his work itself, especially in his examinations, he very soon acquired a method of eliminating all considerations irrelevant to the legal aspect of the case, and reducing even the most complicated case to a form in which it would be presented on paper only in its externals, completely excluding his personal opinion of the matter, while above all observing every prescribed formality. The work was new and Ivan Ilych was one of the first men to apply the new Code of 1864.

On taking up the post of examining magistrate in a new town, he made new acquaintances and connexions, placed himself on a new footing, and assumed a somewhat different tone. He took up an attitude of rather dignified aloofness towards the provincial authorities, but picked out the best circle of legal gentlemen and wealthy gentry living in the town and assumed a tone of slight dissatisfaction with the government, of moderate liberalism, and of enlightened citizenship. At the same time, without at all altering the elegance of his toilet, he ceased shaving his chin and allowed his beard to grow as it pleased.

Ivan Ilych settled down very pleasantly in this new town. The society there, which inclined towards opposition to the Governor, was friendly, his salary was larger, and he began to play *vint* [a form of bridge], which he found added not a little to the pleasure of life, for he had a capacity for cards, played good-humouredly, and calculated rapidly and astutely, so that he usually won.

After living there for two years he met his future wife, Praskovya Fedorovna Mikhel, who was the most attractive, clever, and brilliant girl of the set in which he moved, and among other amusements and relaxations from his labours as examining magistrate, Ivan Ilych established light and playful relations with her.

While he had been an official on special service he had been accustomed to dance, but now as an examining

---

[1] Youth must have its fling.

magistrate it was exceptional for him to do so. If he danced now, he did it as if to show that though he served under the reformed order of things, and had reached the fifth official rank, yet when it came to dancing he could do it better than most people. So at the end of an evening he sometimes danced with Praskovya Fedorovna, and it was chiefly during these dances that he captivated her. She fell in love with him. Ivan Ilych had at first no definite intention of marrying, but when the girl fell in love with him he said to himself: 'Really, why shouldn't I marry?'

Praskovya Fedorovna came of a good family, was not bad looking, and had some little property. Ivan Ilych might have aspired to a more brilliant match, but even this was good. He had his salary, and she, he hoped, would have an equal income. She was well connected, and was a sweet, pretty, and thoroughly correct young woman. To say that Ivan Ilych married because he fell in love with Praskovya Fedorovna and found that she sympathized with his views of life would be as incorrect as to say that he married because his social circle approved of the match. He was swayed by both these considerations: the marriage gave him personal satisfaction, and at the same time it was considered the right thing by the most highly placed of his associates.

So Ivan Ilych got married.

The preparations for marriage and the beginning of married life, with its conjugal caresses, the new furniture, new crockery, and new linen, were very pleasant until his wife became pregnant — so that Ivan Ilych had begun to think that marriage would not impair the easy, agreeable, gay and always decorous character of his life, approved of by society and regarded by himself as natural, but would even improve it. But from the first months of his wife's pregnancy, something new, unpleasant, depressing, and unseemly, and from which there was no way of escape, unexpectedly showed itself.

His wife, without any reason — *de gaiete de coeur* as Ivan Ilych expressed it to himself — began to disturb the pleasure and propriety of their life. She began to be jealous without any cause, expected him to devote his whole attention to her, found fault with everything, and made coarse and ill-mannered scenes.

At first Ivan Ilych hoped to escape from the unpleasantness of this state of affairs by the same easy and decorous relation to life that had served him heretofore: he tried to ignore his wife's disagreeable moods, continued to live in his usual easy and pleasant way, invited friends to his house for a game of cards, and also tried going out to his club or spending his evenings with friends. But one day his wife began upbraiding him so vigorously, using such coarse words, and continued to abuse him every time he did not fulfil her demands, so resolutely and with such evident determination not to give way till he submitted — that is, till he stayed at home and was bored just as she was — that he became alarmed. He now realized that matrimony — at any rate with Praskovya Fedorovna — was not always conducive to the pleasures and amenities of life but on the contrary often infringed both comfort and propriety, and that he must therefore entrench himself against such infringement. And Ivan Ilych began to seek for means of doing so. His official duties were the one thing that imposed upon Praskovya Fedorovna, and by means of his official work and the duties attached to it he began struggling with his wife to secure his own independence.

With the birth of their child, the attempts to feed it and the various failures in doing so, and with the real and imaginary illnesses of mother and child, in which Ivan Ilych's sympathy was demanded but about which he understood nothing, the need of securing for himself an existence outside his family life became still more imperative.

As his wife grew more irritable and exacting and Ivan Ilych transferred the centre of gravity of his life more and more to his official work, so did he grow to like his work better and became more ambitious than before.

Very soon, within a year of his wedding, Ivan Ilych had realized that marriage, though it may add some comforts to life, is in fact a very intricate and difficult affair towards which in order to perform one's duty, that is, to lead a decorous life approved of by society, one must adopt a definite attitude just as towards one's official duties.

And Ivan Ilych evolved such an attitude towards married life. He only required of it those conveniences — dinner at home, housewife, and bed — which it could give him, and above all that propriety of external forms required by public opinion. For the rest he looked for light-hearted pleasure and propriety, and was very thankful when he found them, but if he met with antagonism and querulousness he at once retired into his separate fenced-off world of official duties, where he found satisfaction.

Ivan Ilych was esteemed a good official, and after three years was made Assistant Public Prosecutor. His new duties, their importance, the possibility of indicting and imprisoning anyone he chose, the publicity his speeches received, and the success he had in all these things, made his work still more attractive.

More children came. His wife became more and more querulous and ill-tempered, but the attitude Ivan Ilych had adopted towards his home life rendered him almost impervious to her grumbling.

After seven years' service in that town he was transferred to another province as Public Prosecutor. They moved, but were short of money and his wife did not like the place they moved to. Though the salary was higher the cost of living was greater, besides which two of their children died and family life became still more unpleasant for him.

Praskovya Fedorovna blamed her husband for every inconvenience they encountered in their new home. Most of the conversations between husband and wife, especially as to the children's education, led to topics which recalled former disputes, and those disputes were apt to flare up again at any moment. There remained only those rare periods of amorousness which still came to them at times but did not last long. These were islets at which they anchored for a while and then again set out upon that ocean of veiled hostility which showed itself in their aloofness from one another. This aloofness might have grieved Ivan Ilych had he considered that it ought not to exist, but he now regarded the position as normal, and even made it the goal at which he aimed in family life. His aim was to free himself more and more from those unpleasantnesses and to give them a semblance of harmlessness and propriety. He attained this by spending less and less time with his family, and when obliged to be at home he tried to safeguard his position by the presence of outsiders. The chief thing however was that he had his official duties. The whole interest of his life now centred in the official world and that interest absorbed him. The consciousness of his power, being able to ruin anybody he wished to ruin, the importance, even the external dignity of his entry into court, or meetings with his subordinates, his success with superiors and inferiors, and above all his masterly handling of cases, of which he was conscious – all this gave him pleasure and filled his life, together with chats with his colleagues, dinners, and bridge. So that on the whole Ivan Ilych's life continued to flow as he considered it should do – pleasantly and properly.

So things continued for another seven years. His eldest daughter was already sixteen, another child had died, and only one son was left, a school-boy and a subject of dissension. Ivan Ilych wanted to put him in the School of Law, but to spite him Praskovya Fedorovna entered him at the High School. The daughter had been educated at home and had turned out well: the boy did not learn badly either.

III

So Ivan Ilych lived for seventeen years after his marriage. He was already a Public Prosecutor of long standing, and had declined several proposed transfers while awaiting a more desirable post, when an unanticipated and unpleasant occurrence quite upset the peaceful course of his life. He was expecting to be offered the post of presiding judge in a University town, but Happe somehow came to the front and obtained the appointment instead. Ivan Ilych became irritable, reproached Happe, and quarrelled both with him and with his immediate superiors – who became colder to him and again passed him over when other appointments were made.

This was in 1880, the hardest year of Ivan Ilych's life, It was then that it became evident on the one hand that his salary was insufficient for them to live on, and on the other that he had been forgotten, and not only this, but that what was for him the greatest and most cruel injustice appeared to others a quite ordinary occurrence. Even his father did not consider it his duty to help him. Ivan Ilych felt himself abandoned by everyone, and that they regarded his position with a salary of 3,500 rubles [about £350] as quite normal and even fortunate. He alone knew that with the consciousness of the injustices done him, with his wife's incessant nagging, and with the debts he had contracted by living beyond his means, his position was far from normal.

In order to save money that summer he obtained leave of absence and went with his wife to live in the country at her brother's place.

In the country, without his work, he experienced *ennui* for the first time in his life, and not only *ennui* but intolerable depression, and he decided that it was impossible to go on living like that, and that it was necessary to take energetic measures.

Having passed a sleepless night pacing up and down the veranda, he decided to go to Petersburg and bestir himself, in order to punish those who had failed to appreciate him and to get transferred to another ministry.

Next day, despite many protests from his wife and her brother, he started for Petersburg with the sole object of obtaining a post with a salary of five thousand rubles a year. He was no longer bent on any particular department, or tendency, or kind of activity. All he now wanted was an appointment to another post with a salary of five thousand rubles, either in the administration, in the banks, with the railways, in one of the Empress Marya's Institutions, or even in the customs – but it had to carry with it a salary of five thousand rubles and be in a ministry other than that in which they had failed to appreciate him.

And this quest of Ivan Ilych's was crowned with remarkable and unexpected success. At Kursk an acquaintance of his, F. I. Ilyin, got into the first-class carriage, sat down beside Ivan Ilych, and told him of a telegram just received by the Governor of Kursk announcing that a change was about to take place in the ministry: Peter Ivanovich was to be superseded by Ivan Semenovich.

The proposed change, apart from its significance for Russia, had a special significance for Ivan Ilych, because by bringing forward a new man, Peter Petrovich, and consequently his friend Zachar Ivanovich, it was highly favourable for Ivan Ilych, since Zachar Ivanovich was a friend and colleague of his.

In Moscow this news was confirmed, and on reaching Petersburg Ivan Ilych found Zachar Ivanovich and received a definite promise of an appointment in his former department of Justice.

A week later he telegraphed to his wife: 'Zachar in Miller's place. I shall receive appointment on presentation of report.'

Thanks to this change of personnel, Ivan Ilych had unexpectedly obtained an appointment in his former ministry which placed him two stages above his former colleagues besides giving him five thousand rubles salary and three thousand five hundred rubles for expenses connected with his removal. All his ill humour towards his former enemies and the whole department vanished, and Ivan Ilych was completely happy.

He returned to the country more cheerful and contented than he had been for a long time. Praskovya Fedorovna also cheered up and a truce was arranged between them. Ivan Ilych told of how he had been feted by everybody in Petersburg, how all those who had been his enemies were put to shame and now fawned on him, how envious they were of his appointment, and how much everybody in Petersburg had liked him.

Praskovya Fedorovna listened to all this and appeared to believe it. She did not contradict anything, but only made plans for their life in the town to which they were going. Ivan Ilych saw with delight that these plans were his plans, that he and his wife agreed, and that, after a stumble, his life was regaining its due and natural character of pleasant lightheartedness and decorum.

Ivan Ilych had come back for a short time only, for he had to take up his new duties on the 10th of September. Moreover, he needed time to settle into the new place, to move all his belongings from the province, and to buy and order many additional things: in a word, to make such arrangements as he had resolved on, which were almost exactly what Praskovya Fedorovna too had decided on.

Now that everything had happened so fortunately, and that he and his wife were at one in their aims and moreover saw so little of one another, they got on together better than they had done since the first years of marriage. Ivan Ilych had thought of taking his family away with him at once, but the insistence of his wife's brother and her sister-in-law, who had suddenly become particularly amiable and friendly to him and his family, induced him to depart alone.

So he departed, and the cheerful state of mind induced by his success and by the harmony between his wife and himself, the one intensifying the other, did not leave him. He found a delightful house, just the thing both he and his wife had dreamt of. Spacious, lofty reception rooms in the old style, a convenient and dignified study, rooms for his wife and daughter, a study for his son – it might have been specially built for them. Ivan Ilych himself superintended the arrangements, chose the wall-papers, supplemented the furniture (preferably with antiques which he considered particularly *comme il faut*), and supervised the upholstering. Everything progressed and progressed and approached the ideal he had set himself: even when things were only half completed they exceeded his expectations. He saw what a refined and elegant character, free from vulgarity, it would all have when it was ready. On falling asleep he pictured to himself how the reception-room would look.

Looking at the yet unfinished drawing-room he could see the fireplace, the screen, the what-not, the little chairs dotted here and there, the dishes and plates on the walls, and the bronzes, as they would be when everything was in place. He was pleased by the thought of how his wife and daughter, who shared his taste in this matter, would be impressed by it. They were certainly not expecting as much. He had been particularly successful in finding, and buying cheaply, antiques which gave a particularly aristocratic character to the whole place. But in his letters he intentionally understated everything in order to be able to surprise them. All this so absorbed him that his new duties — though he liked his official work — interested him less than he had expected. Sometimes he even had moments of absent-mindedness during the Court Sessions, and would consider whether he should have straight or curved cornices for his curtains. He was so interested in it all that he often did things himself, rearranging the furniture, or rehanging the curtains. Once when mounting a step-ladder to show the upholsterer, who did not understand, how he wanted the hangings draped, he made a false step and slipped, but being a strong and agile man he clung on and only knocked his side against the knob of the window frame. The bruised place was painful but the pain soon passed, and he felt particularly bright and well just then. He wrote: 'I feel fifteen years younger.' He thought he would have everything ready by September, but it dragged on till mid-October. But the result was charming not only in his eyes but to everyone who saw it.

In reality it was just what is usually seen in the houses of people of moderate means who want to appear rich, and therefore succeed only in resembling others like themselves: there were damasks, dark wood, plants, rugs, and dull and polished bronzes — all the things people of a certain class have in order to resemble other people of that class. His house was so like the others that it would never have been noticed, but to him it all seemed to be quite exceptional. He was very happy when he met his family at the station and brought them to the newly furnished house all lit up, where a footman in a white tie opened the door into the hall decorated with plants, and when they went on into the drawing-room and the study uttering exclamations of delight. He conducted them everywhere, drank in their praises eagerly, and beamed with pleasure. At tea that evening, when Praskovya Fedorovna among other things asked him about his fall, he laughed, and showed them how he had gone flying and had frightened the upholsterer.

'It's a good thing I'm a bit of an athlete. Another man might have been killed, but I merely knocked myself, just here; it hurts when it's touched, but it's passing off already — it's only a bruise.'

So they began living in their new home — in which, as always happens, when they got thoroughly settled in they found they were just one room short — and with the increased income, which as always was just a little (some five hundred rubles) too little, but it was all very nice.

Things went particularly well at first, before everything was finally arranged and while something had still to be done: this thing bought, that thing ordered, another thing moved, and something else adjusted. Though there were some disputes between husband and wife, they were both so well satisfied and had so much to do that it all passed off without any serious quarrels. When nothing was left to arrange it became rather dull and something seemed to be lacking, but they were then making acquaintances, forming habits, and life was growing fuller.

Ivan Ilych spent his mornings at the law court and came home to dinner, and at first he was generally in a good humour, though he occasionally became irritable just on account of his house. (Every spot on the tablecloth or the upholstery, and every broken window-blind string, irritated him. He had devoted so much trouble to arranging it all that every disturbance of it distressed him.) But on the whole his life ran its course as he believed life should do: easily, pleasantly, and decorously.

He got up at nine, drank his coffee, read the paper, and then put on his undress uniform and went to the law courts. There the harness in which he worked had already been stretched to fit him and he donned it without a hitch: petitioners, inquiries at the chancery, the chancery itself, and the sittings public and administrative. In all this the thing was to exclude everything fresh and vital, which always disturbs the regular course of official business, and to admit only official relations with people, and then only on official grounds. A man would come, for instance, wanting some information. Ivan Ilych, as one in whose sphere the matter did not lie, would have nothing to do with him: but if the man had some business with him in his official capacity, something that could be expressed on officially stamped paper, he would do everything, positively everything he could within the limits of such relations, and in doing so would maintain the semblance of friendly human relations, that is, would observe the courtesies of life. As soon as the official relations ended, so did everything else. Ivan Ilych possessed this capacity to separate his real life from the official side of affairs and not mix the two, in the highest degree, and by long practice and natural aptitude had brought it to such a pitch that sometimes, in the manner of a virtuoso, he would even allow himself to let the human and official relations mingle. He let himself do this just because he felt that he could at any time he chose resume the strictly official attitude again and drop the human relation. And he did it all easily, pleasantly, correctly, and even artistically. In the intervals between the sessions he smoked, drank tea, chatted a little about politics, a little about general topics, a little about cards, but most of all about official appointments. Tired, but with the feelings of a virtuoso — one of the first violins who had played his part in an orchestra with precision — he would return home to find that his wife and daughter had been out paying calls, or had a visitor, and that his son had been to school, had done his homework with his tutor, and was duly learning what is taught at High Schools. Everything was as it should be. After dinner, if they had no visitors, Ivan Ilych sometimes read a book that was being much discussed at the time, and in the evening settled down to work, that is, read official papers, compared the depositions of witnesses, and noted paragraphs of the Code applying to them. This was neither dull nor amusing. It was dull when he might have been playing bridge, but if no bridge was available it was at any rate better than doing nothing or sitting with his wife. Ivan Ilych's chief pleasure was giving little dinners to which he invited men and women of good social position, and just as his drawing-room resembled all other drawing-rooms so did his enjoyable little parties resemble all other such parties.

Once they even gave a dance. Ivan Ilych enjoyed it and everything went off well, except that it led to a violent quarrel with his wife about the cakes and sweets. Praskovya Fedorovna had made her own plans, but Ivan Ilych insisted on getting everything from an expensive confectioner and ordered too many cakes, and the quarrel occurred because some of those cakes were left over and the confectioner's bill came to forty-five rubles. It was a great and disagreeable quarrel. Praskovya Fedorovna called him 'a fool and an imbecile,' and he clutched at his head and made angry allusions to divorce.

But the dance itself had been enjoyable. The best people were there, and Ivan Ilych had danced with Princess Trufonova, a sister of the distinguished founder of the Society 'Bear my Burden.'

The pleasures connected with his work were pleasures of ambition; his social pleasures were those of vanity; but Ivan Ilych's greatest pleasure was playing bridge. He acknowledged that whatever disagreeable incident happened in his life, the pleasure that beamed like a ray of light above everything else was to sit down to bridge with good players, not noisy partners, and of course to four-handed bridge (with five players it was annoying to have to stand out, though one pretended not to mind), to play a clever and serious game (when the cards allowed it) and then to have supper and drink a glass of wine. After a game of bridge, especially if he had won a little (to win a large sum was unpleasant), Ivan Ilych went to bed in specially good humour.

So they lived. They formed a circle of acquaintances among the best people and were visited by people of importance and by young folk. In their views as to their acquaintances, husband, wife and daughter were entirely agreed, and tacitly and unanimously kept at arm's length and shook off the various shabby friends and relations who, with much show of affection, gushed into the drawing-room with its Japanese plates on the walls. Soon these shabby friends ceased to obtrude themselves and only the best people remained in the Golovins' set.

Young men made up to Lisa and Petrischhev, an examining magistrate and Dmitri Ivanovich Petrishchev's son and sole heir, began to be so attentive to her that Ivan Ilych had already spoken to Praskovya Fedorovna about it, and considered whether they should not arrange a party for them, or get up some private theatricals.

So they lived, and all went well, without change, and life flowed pleasantly.

IV

They were all in good health. It could not be called ill health if Ivan Ilych sometimes said that he had a queer taste in his mouth and felt some discomfort in his left side.

But this discomfort increased and, though not exactly painful, grew into a sense of pressure in his side accompanied by ill humour. And his irritability became worse and worse and began to mar the agreeable, easy, and correct life that had established itself in the Golovin family. Quarrels between husband and wife became more and more frequent, and soon the ease and amenity disappeared and even the decorum was barely maintained. Scenes again became frequent, and very few of those islets remained on which husband and wife could meet without an explosion. Praskovya Fedorovna now had good reason to say that her husband's temper was trying. With characteristic exaggeration she said he had always had a dreadful temper, and that it had needed all her good nature to put up with it for twenty years. It was true that now the quarrels were started by him. His bursts of temper always came just before dinner, often just as he began to eat his soup. Sometimes he noticed that a plate or dish was chipped, or the food was not right, or his son put his elbow on the table, or his daughter's hair was not done as he liked it, and for all this he blamed Praskovya Fedorovna. At first she retorted and said disagreeable things to him, but once or twice he fell into such a rage at the beginning of dinner that she realized it was due to some physical derangement brought on by taking food, and so she restrained herself and did not answer, but only hurried to get the dinner over. She regarded this self-restraint as highly praiseworthy. Having come to the conclusion that her husband had a dreadful temper and made her life miserable, she began to feel sorry for herself, and the more she pitied herself the more she hated her husband. She began to wish he would die; yet she did not want him to die because then his salary would cease. And this irritated her against him still more. She considered herself dreadfully unhappy just because not even his death could save her, and though she concealed her exasperation, the hidden exasperation of hers increased his irritation also.

After one scene in which Ivan Ilych had been particularly unfair and after which he had said in explanation that he certainly was irritable but that it was due to his not being well, she said that if he was ill it should be attended to, and insisted on his going to see a celebrated doctor.

He went. Everything took place as he had expected and as it always does. There was the usual waiting and the important air assumed by the doctor, with which he was so familiar (resembling that which he himself assumed in court), and the sounding and listening, and the questions which called for answers that were foregone conclusions and were evidently unnecessary, and the look of importance which implied that 'if only you put yourself in our hands we will arrange everything — we know indubitably how it has to be done, always in the same way for everybody alike.' It was all just as it was in the law courts. The doctor put on just the same air towards him as he himself put on towards an accused person.

The doctor said that so-and-so indicated that there was so-and-so inside the patient, but if the investigation of so-and-so did not confirm this, then he must assume that and that. If he assumed that and that, then... and so on. To Ivan Ilych only one question was important: was his case serious or not? But the doctor ignored that inappropriate question. From his point of view it was not the one under consideration, the real question was to decide between a floating kidney, chronic catarrh, or appendicitis. It was not a question of Ivan Ilych's life or death, but one between a floating kidney and appendicitis. And that question the doctor solved brilliantly, as it seemed to Ivan Ilych, in favour of the appendix, with the reservation that should an examination of the urine give fresh indications the matter would be reconsidered. All this was just what Ivan Ilych had himself brilliantly accomplished a thousand times in dealing with men on trial. The doctor summed up just as brilliantly, looking over his spectacles triumphantly and even gaily at the accused. From the doctor's summing up Ivan Ilych concluded that things were bad, but that for the doctor, and perhaps for everybody else, it was a matter of indifference, though for him it was bad. And this conclusion struck him painfully, arousing in him a great feeling of pity for himself and of bitterness towards the doctor's indifference to a matter of such importance.

He said nothing of this, but rose, placed the doctor's fee on the table, and remarked with a sigh: 'We sick people probably often put inappropriate questions. But tell me, in general, is this complaint dangerous, or not?...'

The doctor looked at him sternly over his spectacles with one eye, as if to say: 'Prisoner, if you will not keep to the questions put to you, I shall be obliged to have you removed from the court.'

'I have already told you what I consider necessary and proper. The analysis may show something more.' And the doctor bowed.

Ivan Ilych went out slowly, seated himself disconsolately in his sledge, and drove home. All the way home he was going over what the doctor had said, trying to translate those complicated, obscure, scientific phrases into plain language and find in them an answer to the question: 'Is my condition bad? Is it very bad? Or is there as yet nothing much wrong?' And it seemed to him that the meaning of what the doctor had said was that it was very bad. Everything in the streets seemed depressing. The cabmen, the houses, the passers-by, and the shops, were dismal. His ache, this dull gnawing ache that never ceased for a moment, seemed to have acquired a new and more serious significance from the doctor's dubious remarks. Ivan Ilych now watched it with a new and oppressive feeling.

He reached home and began to tell his wife about it. She listened, but in the middle of his account his daughter came in with her hat on, ready to go out with her mother. She sat down reluctantly to listen to this tedious story, but could not stand it long, and her mother too did not hear him to the end.

'Well, I am very glad,' she said. 'Mind now to take your medicine regularly. Give me the prescription and I'll send Gerasim to the chemist's.' And she went to get ready to go out.

While she was in the room Ivan Ilych had hardly taken time to breathe, but he sighed deeply when she left it.

'Well,' he thought, 'perhaps it isn't so bad after all.'

He began taking his medicine and following the doctor's directions, which had been altered after the examination of the urine. But then it happened that there was a contradiction between the indications drawn from the examination of the urine and the symptoms that showed themselves. It turned out that what was happening differed from what the doctor had told him, and that he had either forgotten, or blundered, or hidden something from him. He could not, however, be blamed for that, and Ivan Ilych still obeyed his orders implicitly and at first derived some comfort from doing so.

From the time of his visit to the doctor, Ivan Ilych's chief occupation was the exact fulfilment of the doctor's instructions regarding hygiene and the taking of medicine, and the observation of his pain and his excretions. His chief interests came to be people's ailments and people's health. When sickness, deaths, or recoveries, were mentioned in his presence, especially when the illness resembled his own, he listened with agitation which he tried to hide, asked questions, and applied what he heard to his own case.

The pain did not grow less, but Ivan Ilych made efforts to force himself to think that he was better. And he could do this so long as nothing agitated him. But as soon as he had any unpleasantness with his wife, any lack of success in his official work, or held bad cards at bridge, he was at once acutely sensible of his disease. He had formerly borne such mischances, hoping soon to adjust what was wrong, to master it and attain success, or make a grand slam. But now every mischance upset him and plunged him into despair. He would say to himself: 'There now, just as I was beginning to get better and the medicine had begun to take effect, comes this accursed misfortune, or unpleasantness...' And he was furious with the mishap, or with the people who were causing the unpleasantness and killing him, for he felt that this fury was killing him but could not restrain it. One would have thought that it should have been clear to him that this exasperation with circumstances and people aggravated his illness, and that he ought therefore to ignore unpleasant occurrences. But he drew the very opposite conclusion: he said that he needed peace, and he watched for everything that might disturb it and became irritable at the slightest infringement of it. His condition was rendered worse by the fact that he read medical books and consulted doctors. The progress of his disease was so gradual that he could deceive himself when comparing one day with another — the difference was so slight. But when he consulted the doctors it seemed to him that he was getting worse, and even very rapidly. Yet despite this he was continually consulting them.

That month he went to see another celebrity, who told him almost the same as the first had done but put his questions rather differently, and the interview with this celebrity only increased Ivan Ilych's doubts and fears. A friend of a friend of his, a very good doctor, diagnosed his illness again quite differently from the others, and though he predicted recovery, his questions and suppositions bewildered Ivan Ilych still more and increased his doubts. A homoeopathist diagnosed the disease in yet another way, and prescribed medicine which Ivan Ilych took secretly for a week. But after a week, not feeling any improvement and having lost confidence both in the former doctor's treatment and in this one's, he became still more despondent. One day a lady acquaintance mentioned a cure effected by a wonder-working icon. Ivan Ilych caught himself listening attentively and beginning to believe that it had occurred. This incident alarmed him. 'Has my mind really weakened to such an extent?' he asked himself. 'Nonsense! It's all rubbish. I mustn't give way to nervous fears but having chosen a doctor must keep strictly to his treatment. That is what I will do. Now it's all settled. I won't think about it, but will follow the treatment seriously till summer, and then we shall see. From now there must be no more of this wavering!' This was easy to say but impossible to carry out. The pain in his side oppressed him and seemed to grow worse and more incessant, while the taste in his mouth grew stranger and stranger. It seemed to him that his breath had a disgusting smell, and he was conscious of a loss of appetite and strength. There was no deceiving himself: something terrible, new, and more important than anything before in his life, was taking place within him of which he alone was aware. Those about him did not understand or would not understand it, but thought everything in the world was going on as usual. That tormented Ivan Ilych more than anything. He saw that his household, especially his wife and daughter who were in a perfect whirl of visiting, did not understand anything of it and were annoyed that he was so depressed and so exacting, as if he were to blame for it. Though they tried to disguise it he saw that he was an obstacle in their path, and that his wife had adopted a definite line in regard to his illness and kept to it regardless of anything he said or did. Her attitude was this: 'You know,' she would say to her friends, 'Ivan Ilych can't do as other people do, and keep to the treatment prescribed for him. One day he'll take his drops and keep strictly to his diet and go to bed in good time, but the next day unless I watch him he'll suddenly forget his medicine, eat sturgeon — which is forbidden — and sit up playing cards till one o'clock in the morning.'

'Oh, come, when was that?' Ivan Ilych would ask in vexation. 'Only once at Peter Ivanovich's.'

'And yesterday with Shebek.'

'Well, even if I hadn't stayed up, this pain would have kept me awake.'

'Be that as it may you'll never get well like that, but will always make us wretched.'

Praskovya Fedorovna's attitude to Ivan Ilych's illness, as she expressed it both to others and to him, was that it was his own fault and was another of the annoyances he caused her. Ivan Ilych felt that this opinion escaped her involuntarily — but that did not make it easier for him.

At the law courts too, Ivan Ilych noticed, or thought he noticed, a strange attitude towards himself. It sometimes seemed to him that people were watching him inquisitively as a man whose place might soon be vacant. Then again, his friends would suddenly begin to chaff him in a friendly way about his low spirits, as if the awful, horrible, and unheard-of thing that was going on within him, incessantly gnawing at him and irresistibly drawing him away, was a very agreeable subject for jests. Schwartz in particular irritated him by his jocularity, vivacity, and *savoir-faire,* which reminded him of what he himself had been ten years ago.

Friends came to make up a set and they sat down to cards. They dealt, bending the new cards to soften them, and he sorted the diamonds in his hand and found he had seven. His partner said 'No trumps' and supported him with two diamonds. What more could be wished for? It ought to be jolly and lively. They would make a grand slam. But suddenly Ivan Ilych was conscious of that gnawing pain, that taste in his mouth, and it seemed ridiculous that in such circumstances he should be pleased to make a grand slam.

He looked at his partner Mikhail Mikhaylovich, who rapped the table with his strong hand and instead of snatching up the tricks pushed the cards courteously and indulgently towards Ivan Ilych that he might have the pleasure of gathering them up without the trouble of stretching out his hand for them. 'Does he think I am too weak to stretch out my arm?' thought Ivan Ilych, and forgetting what he was doing he over-trumped his partner, missing the grand slam by three tricks. And what was most awful of all was that he saw how upset Mikhail Mikhaylovich was about it but did not himself care. And it was dreadful to realize why he did not care.

They all saw that he was suffering, and said : 'We can stop if you are tired. Take a rest.' Lie down? No, he was not at all tired, and he finished the rubber. All were gloomy and silent. Ivan Ilych felt that he had diffused this gloom over them and could not dispel it. They had supper and went away, and Ivan Ilych was left alone with the consciousness that his life was poisoned and was poisoning the lives of others, and that this poison did not weaken but penetrated more and more deeply into his whole being.

With this consciousness, and with physical pain besides the terror, he must go to bed, often to lie awake the greater part of the night. Next morning he had to get up again, dress, go to the law courts, speak, and write; or if he did not go out, spend at home those twenty-four hours a day each of which was a torture. And he had to live thus all alone on the brink of an abyss, with no one who understood or pitied him.

V

So one month passed and then another. Just before the New Year his brother-in-law came to town and stayed at their house. Ivan Ilych was at the law courts and Praskovya Fedorovna had gone shopping. When Ivan Ilych came home and entered his study he found his brother-in-law there — a healthy, florid man — unpacking his portmanteau himself. He raised his head on hearing Ivan Ilych's footsteps and looked up at him for a moment without a word. That stare told Ivan Ilych everything. His brother-in-law opened his mouth to utter an exclamation of surprise but checked himself, and that action confirmed it all.

'I have changed, eh?'

'Yes, there is a change.'

And after that, try as he would to get his brother-in-law to return to the subject of his looks, the latter would say nothing about it. Praskovya Fedorovna came home and her brother went out to her. Ivan Ilych locked the door and began to examine himself in the glass, first full face, then in profile. He took up a portrait of himself taken with his wife, and compared it with what he saw in the glass. The change in him was immense. Then he bared his arms to the elbow, looked at them, drew the sleeves down again, sat down on an ottoman, and grew blacker than night.

'No, no, this won't do!' he said to himself, and jumped up, went to the table, took up some law papers and began to read them, but could not continue. He unlocked the door and went into the reception-room. The door leading to the drawing-room was shut. He approached it on tiptoe and listened.

'No, you are exaggerating!' Praskovya Fedorovna was saying.

'Exaggerating! Don't you see it? Why, he's a dead man! Look at his eyes — there's no light in them. But what is it that is wrong with him?'

'No one knows. Nikolaevich [that was another doctor] said something, but I don't know what. And Leshchetitsky [this was the celebrated specialist] said quite the contrary...'

Ivan Ilych walked away, went to his own room, lay down, and began musing: 'The kidney, a floating kidney.' He recalled all the doctors had told him of how it detached itself and swayed about. And by an effort of imagination he tried to catch that kidney and arrest it and support it. So little was needed for this, it seemed to him. 'No, I'll go to see Peter Ivanovich again.' [That was the friend whose friend was a doctor.] He rang, ordered the carriage, and got ready to go.

'Where are you going, Jean?' asked his wife, with a specially sad and exceptionally kind look....

This exceptionally kind look irritated him. He looked morosely at her.

'I must go to see Peter Ivanovich.'

He went to see Peter Ivanovich, and together they went to see his friend, the doctor. He was in, and Ivan Ilych had a long talk with him.

Reviewing the anatomical and physiological details of what in the doctor's opinion was going on inside him, he understood it all.

There was something, a small thing, in the vermiform appendix. It might all come right. Only stimulate the energy of one organ and check the activity of another, then absorption would take place and everything would come right. He got home rather late for dinner, ate his dinner, and conversed cheerfully, but could not for a long time bring himself to go back to work in his room. At last, however, he went to his study and did what was necessary, but the consciousness that he had put something aside — an important, intimate matter which he would revert to when his work was done — never left him. When he had finished his work he remembered that this intimate matter was the thought of his vermiform appendix. But he did not give himself up to it, and went to the drawing-room for tea. There were callers there, including the examining magistrate who was a desirable match for his daughter, and they were conversing, playing the piano, and singing. Ivan Ilych, as Praskovya Fedorovna remarked, spent that evening more cheerfully than usual, but he never for a moment forgot that he had postponed the important matter of the appendix. At eleven o'clock he said good-night and went to his bedroom. Since his illness he had slept alone in a small room next to his study. He undressed and took up a novel by Zola, but instead of reading it he fell into thought, and in his imagination that desired improvement in the vermiform appendix occurred. There was the absorption and evacuation and the re-establishment of normal activity. 'Yes, that's it!' he said to himself. 'One need only assist nature, that's all.' He remembered his medicine, rose, took it, and lay down on his back watching for the beneficent action of the medicine and for it to lessen the pain. 'I need only take it regularly and avoid all injurious influences. I am already feeling better, much better.' He began touching his side: it was not painful to the touch. 'There, I really don't feel it. It's much better already.' He put out the light and turned on his side... 'The appendix is getting better, absorption is occurring.' Suddenly he felt the old, familiar, dull, gnawing pain, stubborn and serious. There was the same familiar loathsome taste in his mouth. His heart sank and he felt dazed. 'My God! My God!' he muttered. 'Again, again! And it will never cease.' And suddenly the matter presented itself in a quite different aspect. 'Vermiform appendix! Kidney!' He said to himself. 'It's not a question of appendix or kidney, but of life and ... death. Yes, life was there and now it is going, going and I cannot stop it. Yes. Why deceive myself? Isn't it obvious to everyone but me that I'm dying, and that it's only a question of weeks, days ... it may happen this moment. There was light and now there is darkness. I was here and now I'm going there! Where?' A chill came over him, his breathing ceased, and he felt only the throbbing of his heart.

'When I am not, what will there be? There will be nothing. Then where shall I be when I am no more? Can this be dying? No, I don't want to!' He jumped up and tried to light the candle, felt for it with trembling hands, dropped candle and candlestick on the floor, and fell back on his pillow.

'What's the use? It makes no difference,' he said to himself, staring with wide-open eyes into the darkness. 'Death. Yes, death. And none of them know or wish to know it, and they have no pity for me. Now they are playing.' (He heard through the door the distant sound of a song and its accompaniment.) 'It's all the same to them, but they will die too! Fools! I first, and they later, but it will be the same for them. And now they are merry ... the beasts!'

Anger choked him and he was agonizingly, unbearably miserable. 'It is impossible that all men have been doomed to suffer this awful horror!' He raised himself.

'Something must be wrong. I must calm myself — must think it all over from the beginning.' And he again began thinking. 'Yes, the beginning of my illness: I knocked my side, but I was still quite well that day and the next. It hurt a little, then rather more. I saw the doctors, then followed despondency and anguish, more doctors, and I drew nearer to the abyss. My strength grew less and I kept coming nearer and nearer, and now I have wasted away and there is no light in my eyes. I think of the appendix — but this is death! I think of mending the appendix, and all the while here is death! Can it really be death?' Again terror seized him and he gasped for breath. He leant down and began feeling for the matches, pressing with his elbow on the stand beside the bed. It was in his way and hurt him, he grew furious with it, pressed on it still harder, and upset it. Breathless and in despair he fell on his back, expecting death to come immediately.

Meanwhile the visitors were leaving. Praskovya Fedorovna was seeing them off. She heard something fall and came in.

'What has happened?'

'Nothing. I knocked it over accidentally.'

She went out and returned with a candle. He lay there panting heavily, like a man who has run a thousand yards, and stared upwards at her with a fixed look.

'What is it, Jean?'

'No...o...thing. I upset it.' ('Why speak of it? She won't understand,' he thought.)

And in truth she did not understand. She picked up the stand, lit his candle, and hurried away to see another visitor off. When she came back he still lay on his back, looking upwards.

'What is it? Do you feel worse?'

'Yes.'

She shook her head and sat down.

'Do you know, Jean, I think we must ask Leshchetitsky to come and see you here.'

This meant calling in the famous specialist, regardless of expense. He smiled malignantly and said 'No.' She remained a little longer and then went up to him and kissed his forehead.

While she was kissing him he hated her from the bottom of his soul and with difficulty refrained from pushing her away.

'Good-night. Please God you'll sleep.'

'Yes.'

VI

Ivan Ilych saw that he was dying, and he was in continual despair.

In the depth of his heart he knew he was dying, but not only was he not accustomed to the thought, he simply did not and could not grasp it.

The syllogism he had learnt from Kiezewetter's Logic: 'Caius is a man, men are mortal, therefore Caius is mortal,' had always seemed to him correct as applied to Caius, but certainly not as applied to himself. That Caius — man in the abstract — was mortal, was perfectly correct, but he was not Caius, not an abstract man, but a creature quite quite separate from all others. He had been little Vanya, with a mamma and a papa, with Mitya and Volodya, with the toys, a coachman and a nurse, afterwards with Katenka and with all the joys, griefs, and delights of childhood, boyhood, and youth. What did Caius know of the smell of that striped leather ball Vanya has been so fond of? Had Caius kissed his mother's hand like that, and did the silk of her dress rustle so for Caius? Had he rioted like that at school when the pastry was bad? Had Caius been in love like that? Could Caius preside at a session as he did? 'Caius really was mortal, and it was right for him to die; but for me, little Vanya, Ivan Ilych, with all my thoughts and emotions, it's altogether a different matter. It cannot be that I ought to die. That would be too terrible.'

Such was his feeling.

'If I had to die like Caius I should have known it was so. An inner voice would have told me so, but there was nothing of the sort in me and I and all my friends felt that our case was quite different from that of Caius. And now here it is!' he said to himself. 'It can't be. It's impossible! But here it is. How is this? How is one to understand it?'

He could not understand it, and tried to drive this false, incorrect, morbid thought away and to replace it by other proper and healthy thoughts. But that thought, and not the thought only but the reality itself, seemed to come and confront him.

And to replace that thought he called up a succession of others, hoping to find in them some support. He tried to get back into the former current of thoughts that had once screened the thought of death from him. But strange to say, all that had formerly shut off, hidden, and destroyed, his consciousness of death, no longer had that effect. Ivan Ilych now spent most of his time in attempting to re-establish that old current. He would say to himself: 'I will take up my duties again — after all I used to live by them.' And banishing all doubts he would go to the law courts, enter into conversation with his colleagues, and sit carelessly as was his wont, scanning the crowd with a thoughtful look and leaning both his emaciated arms on the arms of his oak chair; bending over as usual to a colleague and drawing his papers nearer he would interchange whispers with him, and then suddenly raising his eyes and sitting erect would pronounce certain words and open the proceedings. But suddenly in the midst of those proceedings the pain in his side, regardless of the stage the proceedings had reached, would begin its own gnawing work. Ivan Ilych would turn his attention to it and try to drive the thought of it away, but without success. *It* would come and stand before him and look at him, and he would be petrified and the light would die out of his eyes, and he would again begin asking himself whether *It* alone was true. And his colleagues and subordinates would see with surprise and distress that he, the brilliant and subtle judge, was becoming confused and making mistakes. He would shake himself, try to pull himself together, manage somehow to bring the sitting to a close, and return home with the sorrowful consciousness that his judicial labours could not as formerly hide from him what he wanted them to hide, and could not deliver him from *It*. And what was worst of all was that *It* drew his attention to itself not in order to make him take some action but only that he should look at *It*, look it straight in the face: look at it and without doing anything, suffer inexpressibly.

And to save himself from this condition Ivan Ilych looked for consolations — new screens — and new screens were found and for a while seemed to save him, but then they immediately fell to pieces or rather became transparent, as if *It* penetrated them and nothing could veil *It*.

In these latter days he would go into the drawing-room he had arranged — that drawing-room where he had fallen and for the sake of which (how bitterly ridiculous it seemed) he had sacrificed his life — for he knew that his illness originated with that knock. He would enter and see that something had scratched the polished table. He would look for the cause of this and find that it was the bronze ornamentation of an album, that had got bent. He would take up the expensive album which he had lovingly arranged, and feel vexed with his daughter and her friends for their untidiness — for the album was torn here and there and some of the photographs turned upside down. He would put it carefully in order and bend the ornamentation back into position. Then it would occur to him to place all those things in another corner of the room, near the plants. He would call the footman, but his daughter or wife would come to help him. They would not agree, and his wife would contradict him, and he would dispute and grow angry. But that was all right, for then he did not think about *It. It* was invisible.

But then, when he was moving something himself, his wife would say: 'Let the servants do it. You will hurt yourself again.' And suddenly *It* would flash through the screen and he would see it. It was just a flash, and he hoped it would disappear, but he would involuntarily pay attention to his side. 'It sits there as before, gnawing just the same!' And he could no longer forget *It,* but could distinctly see it looking at him from behind the flowers. 'What is it all for?'

'It really is so I lost my life over that curtain as I might have done when storming a fort. Is that possible? How terrible and how stupid. It can't be true! It can't, but it is.'

He would go to his study, lie down, and again be alone with *It:* face to face with *It.* And nothing could be done with *It* except to look at it and shudder.

VII

How it happened it is impossible to say because it came about step by step, unnoticed, but in the third month of Ivan Ilych's illness, his wife, his daughter, his son, his acquaintances, the doctors, the servants, and above all he himself, were aware that the whole interest he had for other people was whether he would soon vacate his place, and at last release the living from the discomfort caused by his presence and be himself released from his sufferings.

He slept less and less. He was given opium and hypodermic injections of morphine, but this did not relieve him. The dull depression he experienced in a somnolent condition at first gave him a little relief, but only as something new, afterwards it became as distressing as the pain itself or even more so.

Special foods were prepared for him by the doctors' orders, but all those foods became increasingly distasteful and disgusting to him.

For his excretions also special arrangements had to be made, and this was a torment to him every time — a torment from the uncleanliness, the unseemliness, and the smell, and from knowing that another person had to take part in it.

But just through this most unpleasant matter, Ivan Ilych obtained comfort. Gerasim, the butler's young assistant, always came in to carry the things out. Gerasim was a clean, fresh peasant lad, grown stout on town food and always cheerful and bright. At the first the sight of him, in his clean Russian peasant costume, engaged on that disgusting task embarrassed Ivan Ilych.

Once when he got up from the commode too weak to draw up his trousers, he dropped into a soft armchair and looked with horror at his bare, enfeebled thighs with the muscles so sharply marked on them.

Gerasim with a firm light tread, his heavy boots emitting a pleasant smell of tar and fresh winter air, came in wearing a clean Hessian apron, the sleeves of his print shirt tucked up over his strong bare young arms; and refraining from looking at his sick master out of consideration for his feelings, and restraining the joy of life that beamed from his face, he went up to the commode.

'Gerasim!' said Ivan Ilych in a weak voice.

Gerasim started, evidently afraid he might have committed some blunder, and with a rapid movement turned his fresh, kind, simple young face which just showed the first downy signs of a beard.

'Yes, sir?'

'That must be very unpleasant for you. You must forgive me. I am helpless.'

'Oh, why, sir,' and Gerasim's eyes beamed and he showed his glistening white teeth, 'what's a little trouble? It's a case of illness with you, sir.'

And his deft strong hands did their accustomed task, and he went out of the room stepping lightly. Five minutes later he as lightly returned.

Ivan Ilych was still sitting in the same position in the armchair.

'Gerasim,' he said when the latter had replaced the freshly-washed utensil. 'Please come here and help me.' Gerasim went up to him. 'Lift me up. It is hard for me to get up, and I have sent Dmitri away.'

Gerasim went up to him, grasped his master with his strong arms deftly but gently, in the same way that he stepped — lifted him, supported him with one hand, and with the other drew up his trousers and would have set him down again, but Ivan Ilych asked to be led to the sofa. Gerasim, without an effort and without apparent pressure, led him, almost lifting him, to the sofa and placed him on it.

'Thank you. How easily and well you do it all!'

Gerasim smiled again and turned to leave the room. But Ivan Ilych felt his presence such a comfort that he did not want to let him go.

'One thing more, please move up that chair. No, the other one — under my feet. It is easier for me when my feet are raised.'

Gerasim brought the chair, set it down gently in place, and raised Ivan Ilych's legs on to it. It seemed to Ivan Ilych that he felt better while Gerasim was holding up his legs.

'It's better when my legs are higher,' he said. 'Place that cushion under them.'

Gerasim did so. He again lifted the legs and placed them, and again Ivan Ilych felt better while Gerasim held his legs. When he set them down Ivan Ilych fancied he felt worse.

'Gerasim,' he said. 'Are you busy now?'

'Not at all, sir,' said Gerasim, who had learnt from the townsfolk how to speak to gentlefolk.

'What have you still to do?'

'What have I to do? I've done everything except chopping the logs for to-morrow.'

'Then hold my legs up a bit higher, can you?'

'Of course I can. Why not?' And Gerasim raised his master's legs higher and Ivan Ilych thought that in that position he did not feel any pain at all.

'And how about the logs?'

'Don't trouble about that, sir. There's plenty of time.'

Ivan Ilych told Gerasim to sit down and hold his legs, and began to talk to him. And strange to say it seemed to him that he felt better while Gerasim held his legs up.

After that Ivan Ilych would sometimes call Gerasim and get him to hold his legs on his shoulders, and he liked talking to him. Gerasim did it all easily, willingly, simply, and with a good nature that touched Ivan Ilych. Health, strength, and vitality in other people were offensive to him, but Gerasim's strength and vitality did not mortify but soothed him.

What tormented Ivan Ilych most was the deception, the lie, which for some reason they all accepted, that he was not dying but was simply ill, and that he only need keep quiet and undergo a treatment and then something very good would result. He however knew that do what they would nothing would come of it, only still more agonizing suffering and death. This deception tortured him — their not wishing to admit what they all knew and what he knew, but wanting to lie to him concerning his terrible condition, and wishing and forcing him to participate in that lie. Those lies — lies enacted over him on the eve of his death and destined to degrade this awful, solemn act to the level of their visitings, their curtains, their sturgeon for dinner — were a terrible agony for Ivan Ilych. And strangely enough, many times when they were going through their antics over him he had been within a hairbreadth of calling out to them: 'Stop lying! You know and I know that I am dying. Then at least stop lying about it!' But he had never had the spirit to do it. The awful, terrible act of his dying was, he could see, reduced by those about him to the level of a casual, unpleasant, and almost indecorous incident (as if someone entered a drawing-room diffusing an unpleasant odour) and this was done by that very decorum which he had served all his life long. He saw that no one felt for him, because no one even wished to grasp his position. Only Gerasim recognized it and pitied him. And so Ivan Ilych felt at ease only with him. He felt comforted when Gerasim supported his legs (sometimes all night long) and refused to go to bed, saying: 'Don't you worry, Ivan Ilych. I'll get sleep enough later on,' or when he suddenly became familiar and exclaimed: 'If you weren't sick it would be another matter, but as it is, why should I grudge a little trouble?' Gerasim alone did not lie; everything showed that he alone understood the facts of the case and did not consider it necessary to disguise them, but simply felt sorry for his emaciated and enfeebled master. Once when Ivan Ilych was sending him away he even said straight out: 'We shall all of us die, so why should I grudge a little trouble?' — expressing the fact that he did not think his work burdensome, because he was doing it for a dying man and hoped someone would do the same for him when his time came.

Apart from this lying, or because of it, what most tormented Ivan Ilych was that no one pitied him as he wished to be pitied. At certain moments after prolonged suffering he wished most of all (though he would have been ashamed to confess it) for someone to pity him as a sick child is pitied. He longed to be petted and comforted. He knew he was an important functionary, that he had a beard turning grey, and that therefore what he longed for was impossible, but still he longed for it. And in Gerasim's attitude towards him there was something akin to what he wished for, and so that attitude comforted him. Ivan Ilych wanted to weep, wanted to be petted and cried over, and then his colleague Shebek would come, and instead of weeping and being petted, Ivan Ilych would assume a serious, severe, and profound air, and by force of habit would express his opinion on a decision of the Court of Cassation and would stubbornly insist on that view. This falsity around him and within him did more than anything else to poison his last days.

VIII

It was morning. He knew it was morning because Gerasim had gone, and Peter the footman had come and put out the candles, drawn back one of the curtains, and begun quietly to tidy up. Whether it was morning or evening, Friday or Sunday, made no difference, it was all just the same: the gnawing, unmitigated, agonizing pain, never ceasing for an instant, the consciousness of life inexorably waning but not yet extinguished, the approach of that ever dreaded and hateful Death which was the only reality, and always the same falsity. What were days, weeks, hours, in such a case?

'Will you have some tea, sir?'

'He wants things to be regular, and wishes the gentlefolk to drink tea in the morning,' thought Ivan Ilych, and only said 'No'.

'Wouldn't you like to move onto the sofa, sir?'

'He wants to tidy up the room, and I'm in the way. I am uncleanliness and disorder,' he thought, and said only:

'No, leave me alone.'

The man went on bustling about. Ivan Ilych stretched out his hand. Peter came up, ready to help.

'What is it, sir?'

'My watch.'

Peter took the watch which was close at hand and gave it to his master.

'Half-past eight. Are they up?'

'No, sir, except Vladimir Ivanich' (the son) 'who has gone to school. Praskovya Fedorovna ordered me to wake her if you asked for her. Shall I do so?'

'No, there's no need to.' 'Perhaps I'd better have some tea,' he thought, and added aloud: 'Yes, bring me some tea.'

Peter went to the door but Ivan Ilych dreaded being left along. 'How can I keep him here? Oh yes, my medicine.' 'Peter, give me my medicine.' 'Why not? Perhaps it may still do me some good.' He took a spoonful and swallowed it. 'No, it won't help. It's all tomfoolery, all deception,' he decided as soon as he became aware of the familiar, sickly, hopeless taste. 'No, I can't believe in it any longer. But the pain, why this pain? If it would only cease just for a moment!' And he moaned. Peter turned towards him. 'It's all right. Go and fetch me some tea.'

Peter went out. Left alone Ivan Ilych groaned not so much with pain, terrible though that was, as from mental anguish. Always and for ever the same, always these endless days and nights. If only it would come quicker! If only *what* would come quicker? Death, darkness? ...No, no! Anything rather than death!

When Peter returned with the tea on a tray, Ivan Ilych stared at him for a time in perplexity, not realizing who and what he was. Peter was disconcerted by that look and his embarrassment brought Ivan Ilych to himself.

'Oh, tea! All right, put it down. Only help me to wash and put on a clean shirt.'

And Ivan Ilych began to wash. With pauses for rest, he washed his hands and then his face, cleaned his teeth, brushed his hair, and looked in the glass. He was terrified by what he saw, especially by the limp way in which his hair clung to his pallid forehead.

While his shirt was being changed he knew that he would be still more frightened at the sight of his body, so he avoided looking at it. Finally he was ready. He drew on a dressing-gown, wrapped himself in a plaid, and sat down in the armchair to take his tea. For a moment he felt refreshed, but as soon as he began to drink the tea he was aware of the same taste, and the pain also returned. He finished it with an effort, and then lay down stretching out his legs, and dismissed Peter.

Always the same. Now a spark of hope flashes up, then a sea of despair rages, and always pain; always pain, always despair, and always the same. When alone he had a dreadful and distressing desire to call someone, but he knew beforehand that with others present it would be still worse. 'Another dose of morphine — to lose consciousness. I will tell him, the doctor, that he must think of something else. It's impossible, impossible, to go on like this.'

An hour and another pass like that. But now there is a ring at the door bell. Perhaps it's the doctor? It is. He comes in fresh, hearty, plump, and cheerful, with that look on his face that seems to say: 'There now, you're in a panic about something, but we'll arrange it all for you directly!' The doctor knows this expression is out of place here, but he has put it on once for all and can't take it off — like a man who has put on a frock-coat in the morning to pay a round of calls.

The doctor rubs his hands vigorously and reassuringly.

'Brr! How cold it is! There's such a sharp frost; just let me warm myself!' he says, as if it were only a matter of waiting till he was warm, and then he would put everything right.

'Well now, how are you?'

Ivan Ilych feels that the doctor would like to say: 'Well, how are our affairs?' but that even he feels that this would not do, and says instead: 'What sort of a night have you had?'

Ivan Ilych looks at him as much as to say: 'Are you really never ashamed of lying?' But the doctor does not wish to understand this question, and Ivan Ilych says: 'Just as terrible as ever. The pain never leaves me and never subsides. If only something...'

'Yes, you sick people are always like that.... There, now I think I am warm enough. Even Praskovya Fedorovna, who is so particular, could find no fault with my temperature. Well, now I can say good-morning,' and the doctor presses his patient's hand.

Then, dropping his former playfulness, he begins with a most serious face to examine the patient, feeling his pulse and taking his temperature, and then begins the sounding and auscultation.

Ivan Ilych knows quite well and definitely that all this is nonsense and pure deception, but when the doctor, getting down on his knee, leans over him, putting his ear first higher then lower, and performs various gymnastic movements over him with a significant expression on his face, Ivan Ilych submits to it all as he used to submit to the speeches of the lawyers, though he knew very well that they were all lying and why they were lying.

The doctor, kneeling on the sofa, is still sounding him when Praskovya Fedorovna's silk dress rustles at the door and she is heard scolding Peter for not having let her know of the doctor's arrival.

She comes in, kisses her husband, and at once proceeds to prove that she has been up a long time already, and only owing to a misunderstanding failed to be there when the doctor arrived.

Ivan Ilych looks at her, scans her all over, sets against her the whiteness and plumpness and cleanness of her hands and neck, the gloss of her hair, and the sparkle of her vivacious eyes. He hates her with his whole soul. And the thrill of hatred he feels for her makes him suffer from her touch.

Her attitude towards him and his disease is still the same. Just as the doctor had adopted a certain relation to his patient which he could not abandon, so had she formed one towards him — that he was not doing something he ought to do and was himself to blame, and that she reproached him lovingly for this — and she could not now change that attitude.

'You see he doesn't listen to me and doesn't take his medicine at the proper time. And above all he lies in a position that is no doubt bad for him — with his legs up.'

She described how he made Gerasim hold his legs up.

The doctor smiled with a contemptuous affability that said: 'What's to be done? These sick people do have foolish fancies of that kind, but we must forgive them.'

When the examination was over the doctor looked at his watch, and then Praskovya Fedorovna announced to Ivan Ilych that it was of course as he pleased, but she had sent to-day for a celebrated specialist who would examine him and have a consultation with Michael Danilovich (their regular doctor).

'Please don't raise any objections. I am doing this for my own sake,' she said ironically, letting it be felt that she was doing it all for his sake and only said this to leave him no right to refuse. He remained silent, knitting his brows. He felt that he was so surrounded and involved in a mesh of falsity that it was hard to unravel anything.

Everything she did for him was entirely for her own sake, and she told him she was doing for herself what she actually was doing for herself, as if that was so incredible that he must understand the opposite.

At half-past eleven the celebrated specialist arrived. Again the sounding began and the significant conversations in his presence and in another room, about the kidneys and the appendix, and the questions and answers, with such an air of importance that again, instead of the real question of life and death which now alone confronted him, the question arose of the kidney and appendix which were not behaving as they ought to and would now be attacked by Michael Danilovich and the specialist and forced to amend their ways.

The celebrated specialist took leave of him with a serious though not hopeless look, and in reply to the timid question Ivan Ilych, with eyes glistening with fear and hope, put to him as to whether there was a chance of recovery, said that he could not vouch for it but there was a possibility. The look of hope with which Ivan Ilych watched the doctor out was so pathetic that Praskovya Fedorovna, seeing it, even wept as she left the room to hand the doctor his fee.

The gleam of hope kindled by the doctor's encouragement did not last long. The same room, the same pictures, curtains, wall-paper, medicine bottles, were all there, and the same aching suffering body, and Ivan Ilych began to moan. They gave him a subcutaneous injection and he sank into oblivion.

It was twilight when he came to. They brought him his dinner and he swallowed some beef tea with difficulty, and then everything was the same again and night was coming on.

After dinner, at seven o'clock, Praskovya Fedorovna came into the room in evening dress, her full bosom pushed up by her corset, and with traces of powder on her face. She had reminded him in the morning that they were going to the theatre. Sarah Bernhardt was visiting the town and they had a box, which he had insisted on their taking. Now he had forgotten about it and her toilet offended him, but he concealed his vexation when he remembered that he had himself insisted on their securing a box and going because it would be an instructive and aesthetic pleasure for the children.

Praskovya Fedorovna came in, self-satisfied but yet with a rather guilty air. She sat down and asked how he was but, as he saw, only for the sake of asking and not in order to learn about it, knowing that there was nothing to learn — and then went on to what she really wanted to say: that she would not on any account have gone but that the box had been taken and Helen and their daughter were going, as well as Petrishchev (the examining magistrate, their daughter's fiance) and that it was out of the question to let them go alone; but that she would have much preferred to sit with him for a while; and he must be sure to follow the doctor's orders while she was away.

'Oh, and Fedor Petrovich' (the fiance) 'would like to come in. May he? And Lisa?'

'All right.'

Their daughter came in in full evening dress, her fresh young flesh exposed (making a show of that very flesh which in his own case caused so much suffering), strong, healthy, evidently in love, and impatient with illness, suffering, and death, because they interfered with her happiness.

Fedor Petrovich came in too, in evening dress, his hair curled *a la Capoul*, a tight still collar round his long sinewy neck, and enormous white shirtfront and narrow black trousers tightly stretched over his strong thighs. He had one white glove tightly drawn on, and was holding his opera hat in his hand.

Following him the schoolboy crept in unnoticed, in a new uniform, poor little fellow, and wearing gloves. Terribly dark shadows showed under his eyes, the meaning of which Ivan Ilych knew well.

His son had always seemed pathetic to him, and now it was dreadful to see the boy's frightened look of pity. It seemed to Ivan Ilych that Vasya was the only one besides Gerasim who understood and pitied him.

They all sat down and again asked how he was. A silence followed. Lisa asked her mother about the opera-glasses, and there was an altercation between mother and daughter as to who had taken them and where they had been put. This occasioned some unpleasantness.

Fedor Petrovich inquired of Ivan Ilych whether he had ever seen Sarah Bernhardt. Ivan Ilych did not at first catch the question, but then replied: 'No, have you seen her before?'

'Yes, in *Adrienne Lecouvreur.*'

Praskovya Fedorovna mentioned some roles in which Sarah Bernhardt was particularly good. Her daughter disagreed. Conversation sprang up as to the elegance and realism of her acting — the sort of conversation that is always repeated and is always the same.

In the midst of the conversation Fedor Petrovich glanced at Ivan Ilych and became silent. The others also looked at him and grew silent. Ivan Ilych was staring with glittering eyes straight before him, evidently indignant with them. This had to be rectified, but it was impossible to do so. The silence had to be broken, but for a time no one dared to break it and they all became afraid that the conventional deception would suddenly become obvious and the truth become plain to all. Lisa was the first to pluck up courage and break that silence, but by trying to hide what everybody was feeling, she betrayed it.

'Well, if we are going it's time to start,' she said, looking at her watch, a present from her father, and with a faint and significant smile at Fedor Petrovich relating to something known only to them. She got up with a rustle of her dress.

They all rose, said good-night, and went away.

When they had gone it seemed to Ivan Ilych that he felt better; the falsity had gone with them. But the pain remained — that same pain and that same fear that made everything monotonously alike, nothing harder and nothing easier. Everything was worse.

Again minute followed minute and hour followed hour. Everything remained the same and there was no cessation. And the inevitable end of it all became more and more terrible .

'Yes, send Gerasim here,' he replied to a question Peter asked.

IX

His wife returned late at night. She came in on tiptoe, but he heard her, opened his eyes, and made haste to close them again. She wished to send Gerasim away and to sit with him herself, but he opened his eyes and said: 'No, go away.'

'Are you in great pain?'

'Always the same.'

'Take some opium.'

He agreed and took some. She went away.

Till about three in the morning he was in a state of stupefied misery. It seemed to him that he and his pain were being thrust into a narrow, deep black sack, but though they were pushed further and further in they could not be pushed to the bottom. And this, terrible enough in itself, was accompanied by suffering. He was frightened yet wanted to fall through the sack, he struggled but yet co-operated. And suddenly he broke through, fell, and regained consciousness. Gerasim was sitting at the foot of the bed dozing quietly and patiently, while he himself lay with his emaciated stockinged legs resting on Gerasim's shoulders; the same shaded candle was there and the same unceasing pain.

'Go away, Gerasim,' he whispered.

'It's all right, sir. I'll stay a while.'

'No. Go away.'

He removed his legs from Gerasim's shoulders, turned sideways onto his arm, and felt sorry for himself. He only waited until Gerasim had gone into the next room and then restrained himself no longer but wept like a child. He wept on account of his helplessness, his terrible loneliness, the cruelty of man, the cruelty of God, and the absence of God.

'Why hast Thou done all this? Why hast Thou brought me here? Why, why dost Thou torment me so terribly?'

He did not expect an answer and yet wept because there was no answer and could be none. The pain again grew more acute, but he did not stir and did not call. He said to himself: 'Go on! Strike me! But what is it for? What have I done to Thee? What is it for?'

Then he grew quiet and not only ceased weeping but even held his breath and became all attention. It was as though he were listening not to an audible voice but to the voice of his soul, to the current of thoughts arising within him.

'What is it you want?' was the first clear conception capable of expression in words, that he heard.

'What do you want? What do you want?' he repeated to himself.

'What do I want? To live and not to suffer,' he answered.

And again he listened with such concentrated attention that even his pain did not distract him.

'To live? How?' asked his inner voice.

'Why, to live as I used to — well and pleasantly.'

'As you lived before, well and pleasantly?' the voice repeated.

And in imagination he began to recall the best moments of his pleasant life. But strange to say none of these best moments of his pleasant life now seemed at all what they had then seemed — none of them except the first recollections of childhood. There, in childhood, there had been something really pleasant with which it would be possible to live if it could return. But the child who had experienced that happiness existed no longer, it was like a reminiscence of somebody else.

As soon as the period began which had produced the present Ivan Ilych, all that had then seemed joys now melted before his sight and turned into something trivial and often nasty.

And the further he departed from childhood and the nearer he came to the present the more worthless and doubtful were the joys. This began with the School of Law. A little that was really good was still found there — there was light-heartedness, friendship, and hope. But in the upper classes there had already been fewer of such good moments. Then during the first years of his official career, when he was in the service of the Governor, some pleasant moments again occurred: they were the memories of love for a woman. Then all became confused and there was still less of what was good; later on again there was still less that was good, and the further he went the less there was. His marriage, a mere accident, then the disenchantment that followed it, his wife's bad breath and the sensuality and hypocrisy: then the deadly official life and those preoccupations about money, a year of it, and two, and ten, and twenty, and always the same thing. And the longer it lasted the more deadly it became. 'It is as if I had been going downhill while I imagined I was going up. And that is really what it was. I was going up in public opinion, but to the same extent life was ebbing away from me. And now it is all done and there is only death.'

'Then what does it mean? Why? It can't be that life is so senseless and horrible. But if it really has been so horrible and senseless, why must I die and die in agony? There is something wrong!'

'Maybe I did not live as I ought to have done,' it suddenly occurred to him. 'But how could that be, when I did everything properly?' he replied, and immediately dismissed from his mind this, the sole solution of all the riddles of life and death, as something quite impossible.

'Then what do you want now? To live? Live how? Live as you lived in the law courts when the usher proclaimed "The judge is coming!" 'The judge is coming, the judge!' he repeated to himself. 'Here he is, the judge. But I am not guilty!' he exclaimed angrily. 'What is it for?' And he ceased crying, but turning his face to the wall continued to ponder on the same question: Why, and for what purpose, is there all this horror? But however much he pondered he found no answer. And whenever the thought occurred to him, as it often did, that it all resulted from his not having lived as he ought to have done, he at once recalled the correctness of his whole life and dismissed so strange an idea.

X

Another fortnight passed. Ivan Ilych now no longer left his sofa. He would not lie in bed but lay on the sofa, facing the wall nearly all the time. He suffered even the same unceasing agonies and in his loneliness pondered always on the same insoluble question: 'What is this? Can it be that it is Death?' And the inner voice answered: 'Yes, it is Death.'

'Why these sufferings?' And the voice answered, 'For no reason — they just are so.' Beyond and besides this there was nothing.

From the very beginning of his illness, ever since he had first been to see the doctor, Ivan Ilych's life had been divided between two contrary and alternating moods: now it was despair and the expectation of this uncomprehended and terrible death, and now hope and an intently interested observation of the functioning of his organs. Now before his eyes there was only a kidney or an intestine that temporarily evaded its duty, and now only that incomprehensible and dreadful death from which it was impossible to escape.

These two states of mind had alternated from the very beginning of his illness, but the further it progressed the more doubtful and fantastic became the conception of the kidney, and the more real the sense of impending death.

He had but to call to mind what he had been three months before and what he was now, to call to mind with what regularity he had been going downhill, for every possibility of hope to be shattered.

Latterly during that loneliness in which he found himself as he lay facing the back of the sofa, a loneliness in the midst of a populous town and surrounded by numerous acquaintances and relations but that yet could not have been more complete anywhere — either at the bottom of the sea or under the earth — during that terrible loneliness Ivan Ilych had lived only in memories of the past. Pictures of his past rose before him one after another. They always began with what was nearest in time and then went back to what was most remote — to his childhood — and rested there. If he thought of the stewed prunes that had been offered him that day, his mind went back to the raw shrivelled French plums of his childhood, their peculiar flavour and the flow of saliva when he sucked their stones, and along with the memory of that taste came a whole series of memories of those days: his nurse, his brother, and their toys. 'No, I mustn't think of that .... It is too painful,' Ivan Ilych said to himself, and brought himself back to the present — to the button on the back of the sofa and the creases in its morocco. 'Morocco is expensive, but it does not wear well: there had been a quarrel about it. It was a different kind of quarrel and a different kind of morocco that time when we tore father's portfolio and were punished, and mamma brought us some tarts....' And again his thoughts dwelt on his childhood, and again it was painful and he tried to banish them and fix his mind on something else.

Then again together with that chain of memories another series passed through his mind — of how his illness had progressed and grown worse. There also the further back he looked the more life there had been. There had been more of what was good in life and more of life itself. The two merged together. 'Just as the pain went on getting worse and worse so my life grew worse and worse,' he thought. 'There is one bright spot there at the back, at the beginning of life, and afterwards all becomes blacker and blacker and proceeds more and more rapidly — in inverse ratio — to the square of the distance from death,' thought Ivan Ilych. And the example of a stone falling downwards with increasing velocity entered his mind. Life, a series of increasing sufferings, flies further and further towards its end — the most terrible suffering. 'I am flying....' He shuddered, shifted himself, and tried to resist, but was already aware that resistance was impossible, and again with eyes weary of gazing but unable to cease seeing what was before them, he stared at the back of the sofa and waited — awaiting that dreadful fall and shock and destruction.

'Resistance is impossible!' he said to himself. 'If I could only understand what it is all for! But that too is impossible. An explanation would be possible if it could be said that I have not lived as I ought to. But it is impossible to say that,' and he remembered all the legality, correctitude, and propriety of his life. 'That at any rate can certainly not be admitted,' he thought, and his lips smiled ironically as if someone could see that smile and be taken in by it. 'There is no explanation! Agony, death.... What for?'

XI

Another two weeks went by in this way and during that fortnight an event occurred that Ivan Ilych and his wife had desired. Petrishchev formally proposed. It happened in the evening. The next day Praskovya Fedorovna came into her husband's room considering how best to inform him of it, but that very night there had been a fresh change for the worse in his condition. She found him still lying on the sofa but in a different position. He lay on his back, groaning and staring fixedly straight in front of him.

She began to remind him of his medicines, but he turned his eyes towards her with such a look that she did not finish what she was saying; so great an animosity, to her in particular, did that look express.

'For Christ's sake let me die in peace!' he said.

She would have gone away, but just then their daughter came in and went up to say good morning. He looked at her as he had done at his wife, and in reply to her inquiry about his health said dryly that he would soon free them all of himself. They were both silent and after sitting with him for a while went away.

'Is it our fault?' Lisa said to her mother. 'It's as if we were to blame! I am sorry for papa, but why should we be tortured?'

The doctor came at his usual time. Ivan Ilych answered 'Yes' and 'No', never taking his angry eyes from him, and at last said: 'You know you can do nothing for me, so leave me alone.'

'We can ease your sufferings.'

'You can't even do that. Let me be.'

The doctor went into the drawing-room and told Praskovya Fedorovna that the case was very serious and that the only resource left was opium to allay her husband's sufferings, which must be terrible.

It was true, as the doctor said, that Ivan Ilych's physical sufferings were terrible, but worse than the physical sufferings were his mental sufferings which were his chief torture.

His mental sufferings were due to the fact that that night, as he looked at Gerasim's sleepy, good-natured face with its prominent cheek-bones, the question suddenly occurred to him: 'What if my whole life had really been wrong?'

It occurred to him that what had appeared perfectly impossible before, namely that he had not spent his life as he should have done, might after all be true. It occurred to him that his scarcely perceptible attempts to struggle against what was considered good by the most highly placed people, those scarcely noticeable impulses which he had immediately suppressed, might have been the real thing, and all the rest false. And his professional duties and the whole arrangement of his life and of his family, and all his social and official interests, might all have been false. He tried to defend all those things to himself and suddenly felt the weakness of what he was defending. There was nothing to defend.

'But if that is so,' he said to himself, 'and I am leaving this life with the consciousness that I have lost all that was given me and it is impossible to rectify it — what then?'

He lay on his back and began to pass his life in review in quite a new way. In the morning when he saw first his footman, then his wife, then his daughter, and then the doctor, their every word and movement confirmed to him the awful truth that had been revealed to him during the night. In them he saw himself — all that for which he had lived — and saw clearly that it was not real at all, but a terrible and huge deception which had hidden both life and death. This consciousness intensified his physical suffering tenfold. He groaned and tossed about, and pulled at his clothing which choked and stifled him. And he hated them on that account.

He was given a large dose of opium and became unconscious, but at noon his sufferings began again. He drove everybody away and tossed from side to side.

His wife came to him and said:

'Jean, my dear, do this for me. It can't do any harm and often helps. Healthy people often do it.'

He opened his eyes wide.

'What? Take communion? Why? It's unnecessary! However....'

She began to cry.

'Yes, do, my dear. I'll send for our priest. He is such a nice man.'

'All right. Very well,' he muttered.

When the priest came and heard his confession, Ivan Ilych was softened and seemed to feel a relief from his doubts and consequently from his sufferings, and for a moment there came a ray of hope. He again began to think of the vermiform appendix and the possibility of correcting it. He received the sacrament with tears in his eyes.

When they laid him down again afterwards he felt a moment's ease, and the hope that he might live awoke in him again. He began to think of the operation that had been suggested to him. 'To live! I want to live!' he said to himself.

His wife came in to congratulate him after his communion, and when uttering the usual conventional words she added:

'You feel better, don't you?'

Without looking at her he said 'Yes'.

Her dress, her figure, the expression of her face, the tone of her voice, all revealed the same thing. 'This is wrong, it is not as it should be. All you have lived for and still live for is falsehood and deception, hiding life and death from you.' And as soon as he admitted that thought, his hatred and his agonizing physical suffering again sprang up, and with that suffering a consciousness of the unavoidable, approaching end. And to this was added a new sensation of grinding shooting pain and a feeling of suffocation.

The expression of his face when he uttered that 'yes' was dreadful. Having uttered it, he looked her straight in the eyes, turned on his face with a rapidity extraordinary in his weak state and shouted:

'Go away! Go away and leave me alone!'

XII

From that moment the screaming began that continued for three days, and was so terrible that one could not hear it through two closed doors without horror. At the moment he answered his wife he realized that he was lost, that there was no return, that the end had come, the very end, and his doubts were still unsolved and remained doubts.

'Oh! Oh! Oh!' he cried in various intonations. He had begun by screaming 'I won't!' and continued screaming on the letter 'o'.

For three whole days, during which time did not exist for him, he struggled in that black sack into which he was being thrust by an invisible, resistless force. He struggled as a man condemned to death struggles in the hands of the executioner, knowing that he cannot save himself. And every moment he felt that despite all his efforts he was drawing nearer and nearer to what terrified him. He felt that his agony was due to his being thrust into that black hole and still more to his not being able to get right into it. He was hindered from getting into it by his conviction that his life had been a good one. That very justification of his life held him fast and prevented his moving forward, and it caused him most torment of all.

Suddenly some force struck him in the chest and side, making it still harder to breathe, and he fell through the hole and there at the bottom was a light. What had happened to him was like the sensation one sometimes experiences in a railway carriage when one thinks one is going backwards while one is really going forwards and suddenly becomes aware of the real direction.

'Yes, it was all not the right thing,' he said to himself, 'but that's no matter. It can be done. But what *is* the right thing?' he asked himself, and suddenly grew quiet.

This occurred at the end of the third day, two hours before his death. Just then his schoolboy son had crept softly in and gone up to the bedside. The dying man was still screaming desperately and waving his arms. His hand fell on the boy's head, and the boy caught it, pressed it to his lips, and began to cry.

At that very moment Ivan Ilych fell through and caught sight of the light, and it was revealed to him that though his life had not been what it should have been, this could still be rectified. He asked himself, 'What *is* the right thing? and grew still, listening. Then he felt that someone was kissing his hand. He opened his eyes, looked at his son, and felt sorry for him. His wife came up to him and he glanced at her. She was gazing at him open-mouthed, with undried tears on her nose and cheek and a despairing look on her face. He felt sorry for her too.

'Yes, I am making them wretched,' he thought. 'They are sorry, but it will be better for them when I die.' He wished to say this but had not the strength to utter it. 'Besides, why speak? I must act,' he thought. With a look at his wife he indicated his son and said: 'Take him away...sorry for him...sorry for you too....' He tried to add, 'forgive me', but said 'forego' and waved his hand, knowing that He whose understanding mattered would understand.

And suddenly it grew clear to him that what had been oppressing him and would not leave him was all dropping away at once from two sides, from ten sides, and from all sides. He was sorry for them, he must act so as not to hurt them: release them and free himself from these sufferings. 'How good and how simple!' he thought. 'And the pain?' he asked himself. 'What has become of it? Where are you, pain?'

He turned his attention to it.

'Yes, here it is. Well, what of it? Let the pain be.

'And death...where is it?'

He sought his former accustomed fear of death and did not find it. 'Where is it? What death?' There was no fear because there was no death.

In place of death there was light.

'So that's what it is!' he suddenly exclaimed aloud. 'What joy!'

To him all this happened in a single instant, and the meaning of that instant did not change. For those present his agony continued for another two hours. Something rattled in his throat, his emaciated body twitched, then the gasping and rattle became less and less frequent.

'It is finished!' said someone near him.

He heard these words and repeated them in his soul.

'Death is finished,' he said to himself. 'It is no more!'

He drew in a breath, stopped in the midst of a sigh, stretched out, and died.

DO NOT GO GENTLE INTO THAT GOOD NIGHT   *

Do not go gentle into that good night,
Old age should burn and rave at close of day
Rage, rage against the dying of the light.

Though wise men at their end know dark is right
Because their words had forked no lightning they
Do not go gentle into that good night.

Good men, the last wave by, crying how bright
Their frail deeds might have danced in a green bay,
Rage, rage against the dying of the light.

Wild men who caught and sang the sun in flight,
And learn, too late, they grieved it on its way,
Do not go gentle into that good night.

Grave men, near death, who see with blinding sight
Blind eyes could blaze like meteors and be gay,
Rage, rage against the dying of the light.

And you, my father, there on the sad height,
Curse, bless, me now with your fierce tears, I pray.
Do not go gentle into that good night.
Rage, rage against the dying of the light.

Dylan Thomas

* Reprinted from *The Collected Poems of Dylan Thomas*. Copyright 1952 by Dylan Thomas, used by
permission of New Directions Publishing Corporation, New York.

FATHER, ONCE YOU SAID THAT IN THE GRACE OF GOD *

Father, once you said that in the grace of God you might,
As did Hokusai, live to the age of eighty-nine;
I thought my own thoughts about the prophecy:
Take your time leaving this life,
Go slowly, not for your, but for our sake.

Father, when you went away finally,
The striped lily, waiting to bloom, bloomed,
Taking up your going breath,
Standing among other-colored lilies and crimson dahlias
In the old garden's morning fog.

I was not there, but the others told me
Of your favorite nurse, the beautiful Negro, Mrs. Green,
Putting Chopin on the record player a few evenings before
And bringing you a Magnolia Grandiflora flower,
White-petaled and a foot across, as was her custom,
From the great tree outside your balcony,
And how you were sleeping and night began coming on
And the room became like a cup brimming over
With that music and the heavy lemon scent of the
  enormous flower
And how everyone then somehow felt better
And more able to endure your inevitable leaving.

Father, when they told me to come, I could not weep
And arrived serious and went to look at your room,
Where the magnolia bloom, now brown and sculptured,
Still was upon the white mantel near where the high bed,
Now removed along with the wheelchair, had been.
When I had helped to carry the trays away,
That held the bottles and spoons and glasses and pills,
And threw them all away and changed the room
So chairs and lamps and tables were patterned anew,
And fresh dahlias and zinnias and lilies were brought in
From the gardens of my mother which hem the house,
I said, "I am going to look at him," and went.

Father, you wore the suit they had picked with care,
One of your old double-breasted ones, the tie broad
And red and black, and your hands resting quiet, familiar,

*   Reprinted by permission of the author Helga Sandburg. The poem appeared in McCall's Magazine, October 1968, p 96.

And your face not you, but your shell, so I let you go
For the first time and went unweeping into the sun.
Flowers and relations kept coming into the house:
Chrysanthemums and carnations and arranged red roses,
The bearded brother of my mother, son, daughter-in-law,
  daughter,
Alien never-seen cousins and aunts, children become adults,
Placed helter-skelter about the house's rooms,
Settling themselves here and there, pulling from pockets
Photographs and notebooks implicating you with their lives.

Father, it was a celebration and everyone laughed
And kept watching my mother to see if she stayed strong,
Which would make them so.
The table's three unused leaves were brought from the cellar
And the long yellow damask cloth unfolded.
Chairs and plates were placed for most of us,
Some overflowing into window seats.
A roasted rare beef was sliced and a chocolate cake,
Creamy yellow iced, which some neighbor had sent.
My bearded uncle, who loves flowers the way my mother does,
Declared that he had dug and pirated roots
From her old garden to take back with him,
Not knowing they came from the same striped lily
Which had bloomed in recognition of you.
My mother remembered that when you came in towns to lecture,
You went to libraries to find how many books were stolen
Of yours, pleased when the number exceeded other authors.
And still outside the sun was blazing on the pines
And someone was sitting in your chair at the table's head.

The breeze and the yellow ball above behaved,
The green trees' needles became inordinantly green,
And no rain dared to rain.
As the family and invited nurses and maids
Stood on your white porch waiting to be told to go,
Pulling on gloves and relating what you said to them and when,
And Mrs. Green asked to see your rooms,
Where the position of everything was now changed.

The cars were driving down your driveway,
Myself in the second one, recollecting other days,
When we broke speed limits making trains and planes.
The car ahead, which held my mother and sister and uncle,
Halted, and he clambered out, cane in hand,
And went to break a green pine branch for love.
And the white police car with the red flashing on its roof
Was guiding us to where your shell would come.

Father, the row of candles on each of the candelabra wavered.
Burning down thinly beyond the altar,
To which your closed coffin lay perpendicular,
Your feet toward it within your pale satin bed.
My uncle placed his green branch over your head,
And I gazed upon the church's pearl-colored pall
While the minister read words from your books
And, for the second time, now weeping, I let you go.

That night most of the relatives went away,
The flowers in your rooms were growing old,
Alone I held your worn guitar and sang your songs
And wondered if you'd gone now from our lives.
Then all at once I heard from another room
My children's and my mother's voices laugh.
I felt the essence of yourself in them
And thank you for the way you chose to go.

                    Helga Sandburg

CHAPTER V

DOCTORS AND DYING PATIENTS

Introduction

Most of us die in hospitals. What can we expect of these institutions when we enter them to die? While recent research findings have publicized the sometimes dehumanized, isolated circumstances under which hospitals allow us to die—and hence have started a trend toward self-examination of terminal care on the part of many hospitals—there is no systematic provision for confronting one's own attitudes about death in the educational processes of doctors and nurses. Young nurses usually encounter for the first time the death of a patient with little or no preparation for the emotional impact this event will have upon them. Expressed grief is considered unprofessional. The staff is likely to be caught up in a process of denial much like that described by Kazzaz and Vickers: "...it was clear that they could not accept the fact that the patient was dead." However, Glaser and Strauss show us that when a patient does not die "on time," or when the staff had expected him to, the nurse's composure is even more threatened; any outcome, even death, is viewed as preferable to the tense waiting.

In the selection, "A Person's Right to Die," a physician considers the ability of modern medicine to prolong life far beyond "ordinary" or "reasonable" limits. Dr. Lasagna's plea is: "...that we all stop trying to hide from the highly complex questions involved (in justifying euthanasia), and that serious attention be given to them by our most competent jurists, legislators, moral philosophers, religious leaders, and physicians."

We cannot leave you with only the dark side of the picture. While hospitals indeed have their cold, fearsome, dehumanizing aspects, there are individual staff members who have the warmth and humanity to try to put the dying patient at the center of attention and concern because he is "the person who matters." Dr. Saunders is one such warm, understanding physician and she describes vividly the "moment of truth" as she has helped several of her dying patients encounter it. Her case history approach is like a conversation with a wondrously wise colleague.

GERIATRIC STAFF ATTITUDES TOWARD DEATH *

by

David S. Kazzaz and Raymond Vickers

Abstract: Multiple educational approaches to the subject of hospital staff attitudes toward death were tested. It was not known which approaches, if any, would work, and it is still not known if one is better than another. The staff's resistance to discussing the topic of death seemed connected with a culturally-induced denial. Attempts to promote academic discussion failed. Not until situations occurred which provoked emotional involvement — an actual death, the staging of psychodrama involving death, seminars on religion and psychiatry, and attendance at an autopsy — could the staff members begin to understand their own feelings and open the way for true communication with their patients.

Several factors in our culture have tended to move members of society farther and farther away from facing and understanding death. The increase in urbanization and the technological revolution have produced compelling reasons for the denial of aging and death. The family structure now rarely includes aged parents or grandparents (1); instead, our elder family members are isolated in lonely apartments or nursing homes. Because youth is greatly emphasized and age devalued, aged people must maintain youthful appearances to be accepted in social and economic spheres (2). Advancements in general health services have reduced markedly the number of deaths among children and young adults (3). All these factors feed the fantasy that life is eternal and death is nonexistent (4). Morticians, too, have turned burial rites into elaborate ceremonies which convey the message that death has not really taken place (5). Perhaps most important of all, religious leaders often strengthen the denial of death by focusing on the "hereafter" to the exclusion of helping the living with the problems surrounding bereavement (6).

Gitelson's statement (7), "to die with one's boots on is the keynote of mental health in old age," succinctly reflects the current thinking of the community. At Fort Logan Mental Health Center, we also embrace a "progressive" type of geriatric program which lays heavy emphasis on such activities as hair styling, fashion shows, tiring bus trips, prodigally joyful games, and strident music (8), all in the service of denial of aging and death.

Only recently has the medical and general literature begun to focus on attitudes toward death in the American society (9). To an increasing degree, the literature of philosophy, theology and psychology (10) has become the vehicle for the existentialist concern with the anxieties of living and with the anxieties of dying. Donahue and Stoll (11) point out that death is a significant emotional and spiritual concern of the aged that deserves the attention of the geriatrician. Feifel (12), in describing the prevalent unhealthy type of defense mechanism, says, "Denial and avoidance of the countenance of death characterizes much of the American outlook." He urges a more concerted effort to understand and cope with the problem.

Staff Attitudes Toward Death

The senescence of the patients and their failing health keep the thought of death ever present in a geriatric ward, just as the thought of birth is always present in an obstetric unit. Because many staff members in our geriatric units at Fort Logan seemed unable to resolve their feelings adequately about death and the dying patient, we undertook to study their attitudes and reactions, how much their fears and uneasiness affected the level of care for the patients, and whether their attitude-sets regarding death were also reflected in their handling of problems of loss through separation.

* Reprinted by permission of the publisher American Geriatrics Society, Vol. XVI, No.12 (Dec. 1968.) pp 1364-1371.

Our Geriatric Division consists of two units, known as Team I and Team II. Each 25-bed unit has its own treatment program, but leisure and sleeping facilities are shared. Both resident and day patients are admitted on the basis of psychiatric need, but many kinds of physical disability co-exist in this population of men and women over the age of 65 (13). The observations and work described here were carried out primarily with the unit known as Team II.

When Team II was being organized, two orientation sessions dealt with feelings the staff had about possible forthcoming encounters with dying patients. Some of the group who had a prior theoretical background and experience in geriatrics recognized that death was a significant area of concern for the patients. At the time, it was expected that death would be rather frequent, and the nurses expressed some anxiety. However, during the first year of operation, there were no deaths among the patients assigned to this unit. To what extent there was a cause-and-effect relationship between the lack of deaths and the type of patients admitted is unknown. Strong efforts may have been made to refuse admissions of patients who were judged to be moribund. This would be easily justified, since such patients are not very good candidates for our vigorous psychiatric program.

The first death in the Geriatric Division occurred in March 1966. A Team-I patient who had progressive cardiac disability for many years, died in the arms of his roommate, a Team-II patient. No staff members of either team witnessed the death, and the roommate's call for help was met with confusion among the nurses of both teams. Although the nurses knew the procedures to be followed in such cases, they felt compelled to consult other members of the medical staff, asking essentially the same questions of each person. From their emotional reactions and their extensive efforts to revive the patient, it was clear that they could not accept the fact that the patient was dead.

So engrossed with their own emotions were the staff that they all but ignored the roommate of the patient who died. Who was this "roommate". A 76-year-old man who had been admitted five weeks previously because of depression, preoccupation with thoughts of death, and a serious suicidal attempt! He also had a respiratory disease, and his recurrent attacks of severe dyspnea always made him feel that he was dying.

Failure to recognize how strongly the Team-I patient's death might reinforce his roommate's fear of dying pointed up the team's lack of insight into their own reactions, and those of aged patients, toward death (14). Because of the group's reluctance to pursue the problem, we re-introduced the subject for discussion in a series of patient-staff community meetings. However, those early discussions stagnated in dependent silence or, at best, polite agreement by the group, without real involvement.

The staff's disabling conflicts about death were brought into sharper focus about a month later, when the chairman of the community meeting (a patient) announced the death of a relative of a Team-II patient. The grieving Team-II member was a spinster whose reaction to death was typical of the emotionally unstable personality described by Wolff (15). During the meeting, intermittent screams came from her room, and to every scream the staff reacted with visible discomfort. In spite of the staff's obvious concern, the patient's plight was not mentioned except by the doctor, who joined the meeting late and explained that he had been helping the patient to handle her grief. The meeting went on more or less at the insistence of the patients but the agitation among the staff led one staff member to suggest early adjournment, saying, "We have had a tense meeting; we are all upset." The staff members *were* upset, but the patients weren't and they seemed well able to accept the unabashed expression of grief.

As we considered our staff's attitude to these problems and looked for ways to alleviate them, we noted one incident in staff-to-staff relationships that seemed to bear out our assumption that basic fears of death influenced their ability to handle losses through separation: A well-liked staff member told some of his co-workers that his future plans included the possibility of leaving the Center. He was surprised at the tumultuous reaction — the other staff members first expressed denial and disbelief. Next came a period in which they were apathetic and uninterested in their work. When asked about this, they referred to their friend's announcement of termination. Puzzled by their behavior, the staff member discussed the issue with us. When asked to recall as accurately as he could just what he had said, he remembered it this way, "I'll be moving out one day to a different place. I don't have any plans right now, but I can't be sure that tomorrow something might not turn up and I'd have to leave." The staff seemed to see an oblique reference to death in these casual remarks, and their reactions were certainly intense enough to cause us concern.

Approaches to the Problem.

It was clear that more intensive efforts would have to be made to help staff members resolve their conflicts, which were severely inhibiting their growth and effectiveness as therapists. The first step was taken in early June 1966, with a two-day "think session" to explore the meaning of death as a subjective encounter. The highlight of the session was the first of a series of psychodramas developed under the guidance of Carl E. Hollander, Psychodramatist at Fort Logan.

Psychodrama (16) has two primary foci at the Center: to treat patients and to train staff. The method with which psychodrama is applied begins with a "warm-up," a period in which spontaneous interaction is encouraged. It proceeds into an enactment of a problem of experience and concludes with a group interaction centering around the theme of the drama.

The contrast between staff attitudes and patients' attitudes toward death may be seen in these examples:

1.   In a "staff only" session, the group began by talking about patients in a general abstract way, using the editorial "we." They said that when a patient died they felt paralyzed and, when a death occurred on another shift, they didn't want to know about it. Each one felt that painful personal experience made it difficult to talk about death. The younger members took refuge in their youth, but the older people admitted to greater apprehension. Moving into the dramatization, each participant was instructed to select anyone he wished who had passed away and to project that person into a designated empty chair. Each individual was to approach the empty chair and speak as though the person he had selected were actually sitting there. The first few speakers were diffident about expressing very deep feelings. It was only when Dr. Vickers, the team leader, shared his personal feelings about death that other members of the group felt freer to express their reactions. Dr. Vickers related that although initially he projected the deceased patient into the chair, he suddenly realized as he began to speak that he was talking to his grandmother, whom he had greatly loved and admired. As he became emotionally involved in expressing his sense of loss at her death, an older staff member began to cry and, one by one, the others also wept. Now each member of the group spoke more openly and with more realistic feelings, to his chosen person. Those who projected the deceased patient were able to express feelings of anger — not at the person who died, but at the relatives who put him there to die, thereby forcing the staff's encounter with death. At the close of the session, the group seemed comforted by their greater awareness that no one is immune to encounters with death, and that such experiences need not be faced alone.

2.   In one of the primarily patient-oriented sessions, one group's feelings about death were expressed in this vignette: The patients arranged chairs to represent a bus; the driver's seat, a lone chair out front, was taken by a male patient. The seats behind him were occupied by the other patients, with two or three staff members to fill in. The "bus driver" announced that he would take his passengers on a tour of Paris. He went through the motions of driving the bus, with comments on the sights, such as, "Ladies and gentlemen, on your right is a classical engineering structure symbolic of all Paris and France — the Eiffel Tower." Throughout the drive, the "passengers" paid no attention to the driver and talked only with their seat-mates. Then the driver announced that they would go to the mountains. "Ladies and gentlemen, we are now 75 miles from anywhere. My God! Our road is slipping away!" Every passenger stopped talking and began to look around. One said, "Let's get

out and go back!" Then other reactions came, "It isn't slipping away; he's lying!" "Let somebody else get out and fix it." Finally, one patient said, "Hey, you know, we might die here." And someone's reply was,"C'est la vie!"

In this psychodrama, the patients portrayed the gamut of responses from denial, projection, and wishful thinking to final acceptance of the inevitable. This is the kind of understanding we would like the staff to have.

Because we considered religious belief (or nonbelief) to be a prime factor in the evolution of attitudes toward death, our next step was the assignment of a chaplain to the team. The young chaplain resident who was appointed first asked for a period of orientation in which he could get to know the team members by sharing in their daily tasks. When meetings ultimately were held in which the staff's concerns about death could have been discussed, great reluctance was again observed — time had passed, the team had undergone changes of staff, and denial had built up to the point that discussions were desultory and unmotivated. The only heated discussion was evoked by mutual misunderstandings of religious beliefs, and even this animosity was extinguished when the chaplain stated categorically that "there is no systematic explicit doctrine of death within Christian theology." Because of his own conflicts on the subject of death, the chaplain limited his involvement to an area with which he could cope intellectually. He emphasized that his role was to help the team determine whether or not patients used their religious thoughts on death in constructive or constrictive ways. Although his contribution fell considerably short of the hoped-for assistance, he did present a study paper reviewing the pertinent literature, which served as a baseline for some team discussions during the fall of 1966. (17).

The next resource we tapped was assistance from an outside consultant. In January 1967, Dr. Seward Hiltner[1] (18) came to the Center to present a series of seminars which dealt with the interface of religion and psychiatry and their mutual concerns. Though not focused primarily on death, this was discussed among other things. These seminars established religious and ethical concerns as a legitimate area of thought and action in psychotherapy.

Later, in a seminar with Team II in which the stated topic was "concerns about death," Dr. Hiltner pointed out that the medical profession regards death as a defeat. He felt that this was so because we fail to separate our own feelings and existential concern from the expectations of our scientific techniques. In the discussion which followed a physician and several nurses expressed their frustration and anger over patients who unexpectedly died after "everything possible had been done" for them. In this way our feelings were contrary to our expressed philosophy of "adding life to years rather than years to life." We identified with the patient despite our therapeutic goal not to; yet we suffered grief and damage by his death while preserving our immunity from it. By insisting we were here to "help the patient get the most out of life," we were prohibiting him from contemplating death. In considering what our role should be, one staff member expressed her belief that "by helping people to feel more fulfilled at any given time... then we help them to die more easily." This is the antithesis of Freud's (19), "If you would endure life, be prepared for death."

At this time, previous staff conflicts over interpretations of Judeo-Christian teachings about death and resurrection again came to the fore. It was concluded that shifts in religious interpretations of the basic Biblical teachings had occurred during the centuries. The essential change was from one of trust in the unknown God to one of institutional fantasies about the hereafter. This ' discovery" by the group was one of the key steps in which the team members, with their variety of social and religious backgrounds, were able to accept each others' beliefs.

[1]Professor of Theology and Personality, Princeton Theological Seminary, Princeton, New Jersey.

It seemed to us by this time that the Team-II staff and patients had made significant progress toward resolution of their conflicts over the specter of death, and we looked hopefully toward an ongoing effort to come to terms with the fears with which they had been plagued. It had been decided to hold regular meetings with the chaplain to continue discussion, but the battle was not quite won — the first such meeting was cancelled. In its place a busy administrative meeting was held, and someone added to the notes, "If I rest, I rust." In other evasive tactics during the next few weeks, the projected meeting was moved about during the week, often cancelled, and finally assigned to a time when fewest of the group could attend. It continued then quite regularly for several months, but supported only by a loyal group of nurses and psychiatric technicians.

Whereas the original team members who had shared in all the experiences described here had developed a considerable degree of insight into their own feelings regarding death and could approach the patients on their own terms, the status of new members was more comparable to that which prevailed in the days before the problem was recognized. This contrast could be seen most significantly in group therapy; the patients seemed frequently to wish to discuss death if the older team members were present, but never if only the newer members were there. By what verbal or nonverbal cues the newer staff conveyed their reluctance to discuss death was not always clear, but communication did occur. However, the older team members gradually were able to evoke in the new members a desire for deeper insight. A heightened emotional experience which was strong enough to break through the resistances of the new members presented itself when one of the patients died from a postoperative complication, and postmortem examination was scheduled. When Dr. Vickers, as ward physician, indicated his intention to attend the examination, a social worker and two psychiatric technicians on the team asked to be present also. Unlike the nurses, these staff members had no conditioning for such an experience and had little involvement with the physical care of patients. Nevertheless, their interest seemed genuine and apparently had arisen from prior group discussions on death, so they were allowed to attend.

At the autopsy, both the neurosurgeon and the pathologist explained the physical findings. The three staff members afterward displayed rather forced cheerfulness but no great amount of affect. But just before the group split up, one said in a very intense manner how much the contact with real death was making her think of her spiritual beliefs. Encouraged to talk more about this, the level of frankness and intimacy of the group increased suddenly to the point of tears being shed. Each of the three felt that this was a turning point in his understanding of patients. Further discussion was held later, and the experience was recounted to a number of other staff members. Subsequently, other group members who had expressed dislike of being near a dead person stated that they believed that attending an autopsy would be of significant benefit.

As a result of efforts to increase their knowledge and to work out their feelings toward death, the staff seem to have attained considerable ease in working with patients. Interest in their work has been more evident, and one staff member commented recently that she no longer felt the need to use further education as an escape, because her work no longer seemed empty.

Discussion

As we faced the inhibition and limitation of the staff for working with geriatric patients, we turned our attention to the education they had had. It was evident that preparation to understand and cope with death has been uniformly lacking in all disciplines. Nurses' education in recent years has tended to concentrate on the nurse's role in caring for the moribund patient (20), but in this painful transaction there is no acknowledgement of the existence of the nurse's feelings; she is invariably left very much to her own resources.

Equally lacking in preparation is the medical graduate. The shock which many students experience with the usual method used by medical schools to introduce courses in anatomy and pathology is regarded as an idiosyncrasy and often is ridiculed. It is the rare teacher of these subjects who devotes any time to discussion of students' feelings about death (21); the student is expected to "brave it out." In his later professional career he may or may not be able to cope with his feelings in a way which can help his patients (22).

One looks in vain among the trainings in other professional disciplines for any significant preparation for the problems of death as they relate to the individual. There is a remarkable lack of consistency and relevance in studies of the subject (23). Only by ongoing programs aimed at realistic understanding and acceptance can we overcome the trend in society toward denial of death.

References:

1. Nimkoff, M. F., "Changing Family Relationships of Older People in the United States During the Last Forty Years," *Gerontologist* 1:92, 1961.
2. Linden, M. E., "Effects of Social Attitudes on the Mental Health of the Aging," *Geriatrics,* 12:109, 1957.
3. Gordon, N. B., and Kutner, B., "Long Term and Fatal Illness and the Family," *J. Health Hum. Behav.* 6:190, 1965.
4. Wahl, C. W., "The Fear of Death," *Bull. Menninger Clin.* 22:214, 1958.
5. Mitford, J., *The American Way of Death.* New York, Simon and Schuster, 1963.
6. Rheingold, J. C., *The Mother, Anxiety and Death; the Catastrophic Death Complex,* Boston, Little, Brown & Co., 1967.
7. Gitelson, M., "The Emotional Problems of Older People," *Geriatrics,* 3:135, 1948.
8. Chandler, R., Eslinger, E., Mackler, M., and Selkin, J. "A Geriatric Treatment Philosophy," *J. Fort Logan Mental Health Center,* 3:99, 1965.
9. Hoffman, F. J., "Grace, Violence and Self," *Virginia Quart Rev.,* 34:439, 1958.
10. Choron, J., *Modern Man and Mortality.* New York, Macmillan Co., 1964,
11. Donahue, W., and Stoll, M. R., "Psychological Aspects of Geriatric Care," in E. V. Cowdry (Ed.), *The Care of the Geriatric Patient,* Ed. 2. St. Louis, C. V. Mosby, 1963.
12. Feifel, H., *The Meaning of Death.* New York, McGraw-Hill, 1959.
13. Chandler, R., Fort Logan Mental Health Center Geriatric Service, *Denver Med. Bull.,* 57:44, 1967.
14. Swenson, W. M., "The Psychology of Aging: Its Significance in the Practice of Geriatric Medicine," *Postgrad. Med.,* 34:89, 1963.
15. Wolff, L., "Personality type and Reaction Toward Aging and Death," *Geriatrics,* 21:189, 1966.
16. Ossorio, A. G., and Fine, L., "Psychodrama as a Catalyst for Social Change in a Mental Hospital," *Progr. in Psychother.,* 5:122, 1960.
17. Plummer, A., "Thoughts Regarding the Meaning of Death," *J. Pastoral Care,* 21:24, 1967.
18. Hiltner, S., *Pastoral Counseling,* New York, Abingdon Press, 1949.
19. Freud, S., Thoughts for the Times on War and Death, in Collected Papers, Vol. 4, Chapter 17. London, Hogarth Press, Ltd., 1948.
20. Quint, J. C., *The Nurse and the Dying Patient.* New York, Macmillan Co., 1967.
21. Worcester, A., Care of the Aged, the Dying and the Dead (ed. 2, vol. 1), Springfield, Ill., Charles C. Thomas, Publisher, 1940.
22. Norton, J., Treatment of a Dying Patient, *Psychoanal. Stud. Child,* 18:541, 1963.
23. Lester, D., "Experimental and Correctional Studies of the Fear of Death," *Psychol. Bull.,* 67:27, 1967.

DYING ON TIME: ARRANGING THE FINAL HOURS OF LIFE IN A HOSPITAL   *

by

Barney G. Glaser and Anselm L. Strauss

Most American death takes place in hospitals. But dying, unlike meals or laundry, cannot be precisely scheduled; and in a bureaucratic institution uncertain scheduling upsets proper routine and staff functions.

Consider the following situations:

A head nurse in pediatrics, noting the disturbance that weeping nurses made when a favorite child died, forbade further tears in the ward. Crying had to be saved for the coffee room, away from the children.

A nurse tried to maintain her composure and efficiency with a dying young patient she liked by avoiding any contact with him not dictated by treatment. But he demanded that she spend more time with him. When she refused he accused her of deserting him, saying, "You hate me." In the end she had to give in and spend his final days in close association.

A doctor faced a difficult decision about a patient he had predicted would die in four days, but who lingered a month-and-a-half. The hospital had originally accepted him as a charity case, supplying a very expensive machine to ease his dying; relatives had prepared themselves for his death. But then expenses began to mount, along with the baseless hope that he might somehow survive. The doctor finally felt compelled to keep reassuring both family and hospital administration that the patient would indeed, without fail, soon die.

What are the tactics developed by hospital personnel to cope with dying patients? How do they preserve their own emotional health when surrounded by death? To see if there are distinctive patterns of behavior, we conducted a study in a number of hospitals in San Francisco and Oakland, California. Since nurses work most closely and frequently with the dying, we concentrated on analyzing their activities and responses.

Nurses' tactics vary with situations, wards, and individuals. Most importantly, they vary with the way nurses interpret the situation from whatever information they can get. Is there still some hope for the patient? When can we be sure there is no hope? If the patient is certain to die – when?

In a situation with so much uncertainty, nurses try to establish *expectations* on which they can rely, and build their responses and actions accordingly. Expectations have two major components – *certainty* and *time*: (1) there is still hope that the patient will survive; (2) he is certain to die, but no ones knows precisely when; or (3) both death and the time of its onset are established.

It is extremely difficult to establish correct expectations; and they can change as the nurses' perceptions change, and they can vary from one nurse to another. The nurses have two primary sources of information: definite word from the physician (which they much prefer) and the cues and clues they can pick up indirectly – from the behavior of the physician, the treatment prescribed, the charts, or the way the patient looks and acts.

Certain to Die

So long as hope is real, and nurses feel they are working to save a life, they are apt to become intensely involved. High involvement is also likely when it seems especially tragic that the patient should die – he is young, has great promise, has an important job, has a devoted family dependent upon him. A gifted or beautiful patient has great appeal and the threat of death distresses nurses and drives them harder.

Working on the evening shift also increases involvement. The bulk of the day's work is over, the patient is awake and relaxed, the families are visiting, fewer doctors and duties interfere, and a cooperative, casual, talkative atmosphere results. It is easier then to recognize the patient as a person rather than a case.

As long as the nurses do not know if the patient will die, nor when they will find out, they are unsettled, and search for clues. But when they know that information will soon be available, whatever the outcome, this mood is relieved. What to do becomes clear. Such hospital units as intensive care rooms, wards for premature infants, emergency rooms, and operating suites are devoted to the crisis stage of care, and they contain good talent and the best available equipment. They limit uncertainty: an operation will be over in a few hours; chances for a "preemie" can be determined in two to three days; and if an emergency patient does not die on the first day he will be dispatched to a medical ward (if expected to recover) or to an intensive care unit (if there is still doubt). At this stage nurses become totally engaged in the fight for life. As one doctor said, "Intensive care makes for intense nurses." Keeping busy, working hard, helps them maintain composure, no matter how involved they are with the patient. Even during a lull they will find work to do while awaiting the outcome.

Failure becomes a great threat. But staff people feel differently about the seriously ill and the terminal patients. They might save the seriously ill, so they feel worse if they didn't. They want to believe that "no stone was left unturned," that no one believes "they could have done more." In case of failure they switch attention to the patients who can still be saved, or to the "poor doctor" who tried so hard; they lean on each other with mutual assurances that "we did all we could," and "there is nothing more to do." They try to minimize the loss — "Even if he had lived he would have had brain damage."

Losing composure because of excessive involvement is a particular hazard to nurses in premature-infant wards. They tend to become very involved trying to save a baby when they know the mother wants it; but they can become equally involved with one that nobody seems to want — the poor little thing is alone and helpless but for the staff. They "adopt" the babies, give them names, and watch over them closely to the end. Nurses off duty may call in to see how "their" babies are doing; and if they become upset when "their" babies fail, other nurses understand and adjust. They try to limit involvement, however, by only rarely following cases on which they are not immediately working.

Generally, nurses must be careful of what they say around critical patients; the emotional breakdown of such a patient can be as hard on the nurse as his actual dying. But with "preemies" they can let themselves go and often do, indulging in a kind of running catharsis. They can tell their "adopted" infants anything: scold them for lack of cooperation, talk of love, joke, or act possessive.

When Will We Know?

When a patient seems to swing back and forth between death and life, nurses seek the relief of any outcome. They may become optimistic: "She's looking better, she really is," or, "We would like her to die and get it over with; yet is she getting better, maybe...." Pessimism is an important way to maintain composure — then if the patient dies the shock will not be as great. However, this can cause a nurse to "pull away" prematurely, and may be very hard on a patient not really as close to dying as believed.

In the absence of definite word, sudden shifting of clues can become very important to nurses. When the doctor stops blood transfusions, indicating imminent death, the nurses are alerted but still not sure, and may continue trying to save the patient. "If he comes out of it we'll work on him. He had only to give us the slightest cue." If the doctor flatly states the patient will die that day, the nurses can shift from life-saving to easing the way out. In sum, what doctors tell nurses, apart from orders, can considerably affect the care of the dying patient and the atmosphere around him.

The doctor is the ultimate authority on the whether and when of death, and he will not make — or communicate — his decision lightly, knowing he must face the consequences of an error. Usually he will tell the nurses first, but he may deem it safest not to tell anyone; we have seen cases where a patient knew he was going to die but the nurse did not, and kept urging him not to be so gloomy. "The doctor may or may not tell us a patient is critical," one nurse said. "We decide. They expect us to use our beans." Nurses seldom ask doctors directly. But they drop hints to the doctor to drop hints; and by this oblique method — often becoming more direct as death approaches — the nurses get their information and make their adjustments. "There is no formal declaration that a patient is terminal," said one. "Usually you just pick it up."

Some hospitals require doctors to commit themselves to the extent of putting the patient's name on a list of critically, dangerously, or seriously ill. Since this often initiates many difficult-to-reverse consequences (telegrams to relatives who may come from great distances and stay around the clock, unpleasant conferences with the family, and involvement with social workers and the chaplain), the doctor may wait until the very last minute. This imposes an added burden on the nurse: she may have to rely exclusively on clues, and she may even be forced to remind the physician that he should "get that name on the list before it's too late."

If a patient makes a sudden unexpected change for the worse, there may be a searching of symptoms and consciences to see what went wrong or was missed. Could we have foreseen it? Were we negligent? A sudden death with no apparent warning, as on the operating-table, can have tremendous impact, and detailed examination, including autopsy, may be undertaken immediately not only for medical reasons but to fix blame and provide reassurance. Nurses may blame the doctors for not telling them, and thus gain some excuse for themselves. Another, extreme, tactic is to blame oneself first, and thereby become an object of sympathy rather than criticism. In one very dramatic case a mother hemorrhaged on the delivery table and both she and the baby died. The husband "absolutely lost his mind." The nurses were terribly upset and the doctor broke down and cried. His tears were genuine and heartfelt; but they also served to forestall accusations of negligence and incompetence. Having to support him also helped the nurses regain composure.

Whether a patient will die usually becomes evident after a while; *when* is much more difficult to say. Nurses tend to evade the question with ultimate generalities: he will die "sometime" (as we all do), or may die "anytime," meaning probably soon. Once the patient is sure to die, the problems of maintaining composure, of what-to-tell the patient, of controlling family involvement, all multiply rapidly. Expectations can change at any time and have broad consequences.

Patients expected to die soon can seem to linger indefinitely and upset arrangements. Perhaps most nerve-wracking is the "vacillating pattern." The patient, after several false alarms, starts to fade; the nurses again call the family ("If you don't call the family and the patient dies, that's wrong"); the family gathers; but the patient lingers. After some hours the family leaves, begging personnel to "be sure to call immediately" at any change; and in a few hours or more the cycle may be repeated. When the end, formerly dreaded, finally comes, all are relieved. "He's better off."

Expectations of death change not only with new developments, but from person to person, according to the information and training each has. Laymen may feel that a cancer patient who has been sent home cannot be in serious danger; but the doctor may know that he was sent home precisely because nothing further could be done in the hospital except to relieve his dying days when he comes back. (Or they may not want terminal cases in that hospital and may, in effect, as long as he can ambulate, turn him loose to die somewhere else.) Different degrees of awareness will often be managed by the medical team for its purposes. Doctors may hold back knowledge of certainty of death to keep the nurses working harder; and keeping families uncertain can often be a convenient technique for avoiding physician involvement in emotional and "time-wasting" family scenes, as Fred Davis points out in "Uncertainty in Medical Prognosis." (*The American Journal of Sociology*, July 1960)

Open Awareness

Sometimes a doctor will choose to tell everyone the facts, including the patient (if he has to be told). This "open awareness" allows as much free discussion as anyone can reasonably take. Families can get relatively reliable information. Patients can talk to nurses about their closing lives. They can focus their dwindling time on getting ready for death rather than wasting it in the vain attempt to get well. One cancer patient we observed held off sedation as much as possible to keep his head clear while he wound up his affairs; another instructed his son on his duties as new head of the house; one young man even tried to arrange a future marriage between his wife and a hospital employee.

In short, all have a chance to prepare realistically for the future. Nurses do not have to walk on eggs; if they can manage their own feelings they can devote themselves to the real needs of the patient. Of course patients who know they are doomed will sometimes withdraw, become uncooperative, or attempt suicide. But more often, after an initial depression, they become fairly cheerful and cooperative, making the nurses grateful and cheerful too. The patient can then arrange his affairs and prepare himself, and be master of the mood and dignity with which he dies.

More often the doctors will not tell everyone—especially the patient himself; so, frequently, the patient is the only one who doesn't know. Therefore, he may not understand the reasons for treatment, and may refuse a medicine, an awkward position, an inconvenient diet. The nurse cannot tell him openly; but to get her job done she may have to let him know, by cues, hoping that he will get the point long enough (and quietly enough) so that she can do what is necessary. This is a very delicate and difficult undertaking—who wants to recognize that he is dying, especially through hints? To the extent that the tactic does work it usually brings on demands for answers that the nurse is not supposed to give. She tries to manipulate her cues so that the patient gets the idea strongly enough to take the treatment; but then, through other cues, she tries to retract or indicate that he misunderstood. "Where did you get the idea you were dying?"

Can the hospital personnel ever really be sure the patient *doesn't* know? They often can't; and an elaborate mutual charade and game of scanning and spying goes on. A nurse who doesn't know herself may speak blithely and hopefully of the future—does the patient intend taking his girl to the graduation dance? If she is informed but the patient is not she tends to confine her remarks to the immediate and the material—"Is that pillow comfortable?"—and to dodge questions about the future and especially about death. Often the best way to avoid questions is to avoid the patient himself, popping in and out of the room often and long enough to keep tabs and give him treatment, but moving and talking too fast to answer questions. At the same time, however, she must keep a watchful eye on him, pick up all clues she can, interpret and report on them. Does he know he is going to die or doesn't he? The debate among the bedside watchers may go on even after death, without resolution. Did he or didn't he know?

It becomes clear sometimes that the patient does know; but the show must go on. For instance, one young man slated to die within a year found his marriage blocked by his family. He started to "live it up" to a degree that indicated awareness of more than a balked marriage. Strong hints also come when a patient is suddenly moved nearer the nursing station, or screened off from the other patients, or placed in a single room or the intensive care unit. The nurses may suspect that further pretense is futile or worse. But if still under obligation to hide the truth, they will fall back on reassuring statements like: "The intensive care unit is really not a place to die, only a place for more intensive, better care."

The Refuge of Subterfuge

Some nurses find refuge in the professional stance. They do not want to lie, but they do not want to commit themselves either, so they become bland, neutral, vague, and given to ultimate statements: "*I* don't know—nobody does." "We all have to die sometime." They refuse to respond to hints or testing questions; patients are quite capable of interpreting even a denial into its opposite. One nurse said, "You go back to your professional dignity, your professional bearing, your professional attitudes. This is what the patient needs at this time."

Dissembling may impose almost intolerable strains. In one instance a nurse felt impotent to avert family difficulties because she couldn't tell an unaware patient the father about his fate. The wife had already been informed by the doctor; she had told friends, whose daughter told the patient's son. The son developed a strong distrust of the physician. He felt socially disinherited by his father because they held no conversations about the son's future rights and responsibilities. But the father could not will these rights and duties to the son because he did not yet know he was going to die.

Sometimes a nurse will break the rule of silence—even though she can get into serious trouble (military hospital personnel can be court-martialed). She may feel forced to tell because the doctor is inaccessible; or she may want to help the patient with family problems; or she may believe that to keep silent longer is to violate nursing ethics, which require that she give her patient what comfort she can—he may be fearful because of radical symptoms and feel isolated and betrayed. Further, she may feel that she cannot retain the trust of a patient when trust is essential to doing the job properly. A patient complained bitterly to us of being lied to, "strung along," and, when he rebelled, neglected. He was right; but, though he became uncooperative and increasingly ornery, the nurses couldn't change the situation.

One simple—and usually unwitting—way of disclosing the truth to a patient is to call the chaplain or priest. Few patients can deny such a cue. And once the patients know, the nurses can feel relieved of the strain and concentrate on being helpful.

Generally a nurse confronted with a hopeless case finds it easiest to maintain her composure when the patient can be made comfortable with sedation and a minimum of talk. Nurses will often ask doctors for flexible sedation orders so they can control the dosage; and occasionally may even give the patient more sedation then either he or the doctor wants. They can be considerate and attentive, and yet confine themselves only to the patient's existence as a medical problem, a body (that is, socially dead).

Nurses do have standard tactics for avoiding upset when a patient—especially one with strong appeal, like an attractive child—dies or is dying. They "switch objects" if they can—concentrate intensely on some other patient for whom there is still hope, and let someone else, a chaplain perhaps, take over the death watch. They try to minimize the loss—the patient could not have led a normal life, death stopped his suffering, he died easy of mind because he left his family well fixed. They speak of God's will. They try to absolve themselves of negligence and believe they did all they could. They try various kinds of catharses—crying, talking, keeping busy. Most important they try to forget—or at least block the memory off: "We talk over death here, get our feelings out, then forget it and go home."

Are these methods always desirable? Perhaps not—no methods are always desirable. But maintaining composure and efficiency are more than matters of personal comfort or expressions of hard-heartedness. Death takes no holiday. The next patient coming up from emergency may also need competent, steady care and solace on the passage out.

A PERSON'S RIGHT TO DIE *

by

Louis Lasagna

A growing aged population, crowded hospitals, and modern medicine's ability to prolong life signal the need for serious debate of an issue too long ignored, says the author.

One of the most difficult problems facing a physician is the prolonged existence of terminally ill patients. All doctors sooner or later are charged with the care of an individual — most often an aged patient — in a coma, with dilated and fixed pupils, incapable of spontaneous respiration and kept "alive" by a mechanical respirator. Fluids and nutrition are being pumped into the patient day and night. But the patient is really dead physiologically, and he's dead legally the moment the respirator is turned off. Such patients do not regain the ability to breathe spontaneously or to think clearly. (Autopsies almost always show advanced degeneration of the brain.) Is there any point in maintaining life in such an individual? If not, is there a difference between not starting the respirator at the very beginning and stopping it once it has started? Historically, the shortening of a person's life under any circumstances has been considered undesirable and illegal. However, even in the 16th and 17th centuries ecclesiastical opinion made a distinction between "ordinary" and "extraordinary" means of preserving life. These authorities stated that individuals were required to utilize ordinary means of avoiding death, but not extraordinary ones. At the time, the amputation of a leg or the incision of an abdomen was considered extraordinary. With the coming of modern anesthesia and surgery such procedures became "ordinary," and what was immoral in the 17th century, would, by that century's definition, be moral today.

Some Catholic authorities believe that persons are bound to use only "natural" aids — a position which in its literal sense is difficult to defend, for if it is carried to its logical conclusion it might exclude the use of certain modern antibiotics, which are artificially produced and administered.

How is the ending of a life preferable to its continuation? Can we make such decisions without coming to grips with the meaning of human life itself, and why it must be preserved? Is it the sort of thing that can be handled by law? Shouldn't it be a highly individualistic and flexible decision involving philosophy and religion as well as science?

The Reverend Joseph Fletcher in a lecture at the Yale Medical School has suggested a new term called "antidysthanasia," or indirect euthanasia. Direct euthanasia, according to Fletcher, would be an act specifically intended to end life, such as introducing air into a patient's blood to cause a fatal embolism, or administering a fatal dose of morphine. Indirect euthanasia amounts to "mercifully hastening death or at least mercifully refusing to prolong it." Death is permitted, but not induced. By this definition, withholding treatment or stopping it would be allowable, whereas administering an overdose of drug would not.

Legally, there is no way for the physician to hasten death, even if the patient requests it and the family approves of it. Yet, the physician is duty bound and morally justified to relieve suffering. Two recent Swedish cases involving the same physician illustrate the confusion. In the first instance, an 80-year-old woman died when the physician stopped intravenous therapy that had been keeping her alive for five weeks following a massive cerebral hemorrhage. The relatives had consented to stop the treatment. In the second case, the doctor had told the relatives of a 65-year-old woman in a coma that her condition was hopeless, and he had asked for the right to end treatment that was sustaining life. Both cases came to public attention when the son of the second patient accused the doctor of planning to kill his mother. Sweden's Central Medical Board found the physician guilty in both cases; but in court, the judge ruled that the physician had acted properly both times, and that relatives had the moral right to make decisions as to prolongation of life in such hopeless cases. The decision has been termed a big step toward legalizing euthanasia.

The ambivalence of society itself is manifest in certain public treatments of the problem. In the early 1950's a New Hampshire physician injected air into one of his dying patients, but his only punishment was the

*   Reprinted by permission of the author and the Johns Hopkins Magazine, (Spring 1968.) Baltimore, Md. pp 34-41.

temporary suspension of his license. In 1963 a physician was tried on a murder charge in Liege for complicity with a mother in destroying a thalidomide baby, but was acquitted. A bill was actually introduced (passage failed) in the New York legislature which would have permitted a patient to apply for euthanasia. It required certification from a physician, and aproval by a committee set up to consider such petitions.

Most people who are opposed to any form of euthanasia are unwilling to allow the patient to have any say in the matter. It is true that many patients are incapable of giving permission because they are in a coma or otherwise unresponsive, but what about the situation where a patient has indicated his desire? Ingemar Hedenius, a Swedish philosophy professor, has proposed that healthy people be given the right to sign up for "dodshjalp" (death help) on their health insurance cards. He divides death help into passive and active categories. An example of "passive" death help would be the physician's refraining from undertaking treatment vital to maintain life or discontinuing such treatment (Fletcher's "antidysthanasia"). "Active" death help is equated with giving pain-killing drugs in such amounts as to shorten life, or giving such drugs so that death occurs immediately. Professor Hedenius had indicated that he would rather die than suffer immeasurable pain or become a helpless wreck without any prospect of a decent human existence, that he would rather die than usurp a hospital bed with his own meaningless suffering when others might be nursed back to health in that bed, and that he would rather die than have relatives wish him dead in vain and remember him as a distasteful wreck.

It is of interest that surveys of American physicians have shown that approximately a third of all doctors feel that euthanasia is justified in the case of a patient in great pain without hope of relief or recovery. (This figure is close to 40 per cent for Protestants and Jews, but only 7 per cent for Roman Catholic physicians.) Similar figures apply to the case of infants born with serious abnormalities and with no chance of a normal life. Indeed, many physicians practice at least indirect euthanasia without admitting it, such as making little or no effort at resuscitation of a child born with the grossest of congenital anomalies.

Those physicians who oppose euthanasia cite a number of reasons for their stand. One is the possibility that a new cure may be discovered at any moment, a notion which is impossible to dismiss even if it is unlikely statistically. On the other hand, there are more cogent reasons, such as the knowledge that the physician is fallible, and that his diagnosis and prognosis may be incorrect. No one is keen to place himself in that difficult position where he must judge whether the quality of a given life is worth maintaining. The taking of a life is a grievous burden to bear, even when the motives are beyond reproach.

Yet, whether he likes it or not, the physician cannot avoid this judgment. He is in essence making a decision about euthanasia whenever he has to order a life-sustaining medication for a terminally ill patient. When different treatments of potentially fatal illnesses are available, such as surgery or radiotherapy or drugs for malignant cancer, the physician has to decide whether one form of treatment is to be preferred to another. He may have to choose between a treatment that provides less physical and mental distress but shortens life and one that prolongs life, but at the cost of great suffering. There is no place for the physician to hide.

It is time, in fact, that we all stop trying to hide from the highly complex questions involved, and that serious attention be given to them by our most competent jurists, legislators, moral philosophers, religious leaders, and physicians.

THE MOMENT OF TRUTH: CARE OF THE DYING PERSON   *

by

Cicely Saunders

The title I have chosen, "The Moment of Truth," includes far more than the question "Who should tell—or should you tell—a patient that his death is near?" I think that the title includes many more of the realities and challenges of the situation. It is a situation that concerns all of us, whether we are doctors, nurses, psychiatrists, psychologists, social workers, or theologians. (I have deliberately made the list alphabetical, because all are of equal importance.) Perhaps most of all, the situation concerns us when a member of our family or a friend is dying. This is, or should be, a "moment of truth." It is not a matter of mere words, of who says what; it is a moment with many implications, not only for research and treatment, but implications for the whole of life, and its meaning, implications for us as well as for the patient. But it is the patient who is, or who should be, in the center. The question is *his* because it is his situation and he is the person who matters. This is why the second part of my title is "Care of the Dying *Person*" and not simply "Care of the Dying." I think that with the increased interest in this problem there is a danger that the dying may, in a sense, be put in quotes, and I believe it is very important that they should not be. The expression, "moment of truth," was taken by Boros, a philosopher and theologian, for a book about death. But apparently the phrase comes originally from the Spanish, and is a technical term referring to the moment at the end of a bullfight when the matador is alone with the bull. The whole audience, and everybody else in the ring, are secondary. It is just these two together, and the person is absolutely in the center. This is what I want to do now—put the patient in the center. This is why I am going to tell about people I have known in my seven years at St. Joseph's. I am not going to describe my work there very much—I think it will describe itself.

When I arrived at St. Joseph's, I had the good fortune to be given responsibility for some forty or forty-five patients (out of their total capacity of 150) who came with malignant disease, and with a prognosis of three months or less to live. They were sent to us by other centers when the stage of active treatment was over. They were having pain or distress, or had no family to look after them, or had some other complication that made home care impossible. This hospice had a link with the National Health Service and so did the patient, so there was no charge for their stay, and no "parking meter," as it were, ticking away beside the bed. Once a patient came, this was his bed and he could stay. What I must try to do as we proceed is distill the many teaching sessions we have had during these seven years with various groups of students; to try to encourage you, as I encouraged them, just to look at the patients and listen to them to learn from them what they had to teach us. It was far more important that the students should go alone and informally round the wards, and be able to talk to people than to have the usual formal rounds, and then afterwards to sit down over tea discussing the questions that arose. After these informal visits, often they would see the patients in a totally different way, be concerned with the individual people they had been meeting, learn respect and regard for them, and the beginnings of understanding.

Though I do not consider training in psychotherapy a necessity for this kind of work, I do believe that we need all the understanding we can acquire of the patients, who are, after all, people similar to ourselves. Of course, we cannot understand exactly how a dying person feels; death is totally unknown until a person comes to it. But I do think that we can talk of the implications of what individual patients say or do. Moreover, we do not need to have had the same experience as another person in order to enter into it to some extent. We just need to have *had* our own experiences and not to have slid past or, as it were, ducked out from under any hard fact of reality that happens to have hit us. Having had these, we can begin to look at this "moment," which is as much a part of life as any other part, and, for very many, the most important, it is a time of summing-up, a time of final decisions for this person who is the patient. Since our work at St. Joseph's is completely person centered, the criterion of success is not how our treatment is working, but how the patient

* Reprinted from *Death and Dying: Current Issues in the Treatment of the Dying Person.* Ed. Leonard Pearson. Copyright 1969 by the Press of Case Western Reserve University, Cleveland.

is; what he is doing; or, still more important, what he is *being* in the face of his physical deterioration. Our attitude toward the dying patient betrays a good deal of our attitude toward people in general, and, of course, of our interpretation of the meaning of life. So often, it is *we* who need rehabilitation, not the patient, just as it is the psychology of the seeing rather than the psychology of the blind that is the problem.

I speak from a special viewpoint, but, because this is such a very personal part of caring, I do not think it will be too difficult for you to find relevance to your own situations. What I want to discuss concerns attitudes much more than details. I want to somehow to convey the sort of atmosphere that I have seen as being very helpful to these dying patients—the attention, the security, the hospitality of St. Joseph's. St. Joseph's is a sectarian religious foundation, but welcomes patients of all sorts and kinds, and welcomed me as a staff member of a different denomination. All are welcomed with a confident sense of strength and peace, with the immense strength of a recognized shared purpose—full-time concern for the patient.

Prolonging Living and Prolonging Dying

I want to talk about the personal achievement of the dying. It is people and the look on their faces that matters, because from the look on their faces we learn both their needs and their achievements. I think we must learn to recognize the moment when our treatment turns into "care of the dying person." To go on pressing for acute, active treatment at a stage when a patient has gone too far and should not be made to return is not good medicine. *There is a difference between prolonging living and what can really only be called prolonging dying.* Because something is possible does not mean that it is necessarily either right or kind to do it. One often sees a great weariness with the sort of pain and illness that brings our patients to us such as that of Sir William Osler who, when he was dying, said, "I'm too far across the river now to want to come back and have it all over again." I do not think he would have given a "thank you" to someone who pulled him back at that stage. Recognition of this stage is not defeatism either on the part of the patient or on that of the doctor. Rather it is respect and awareness of the individual person and his dignity. When one patient came to us, she described her situation by saying, "It was *all* pain." Another patient said to me, "Well, doctor, it began in my back, but now it seems that all of me is wrong." And she went on to describe the physical pain, her feeling that nobody understood how she felt, that the world was against her, that she could have cried for pills and injections but knew that she should not; that her husband and son were having to stay off work to look after her—and that it was wonderful to come to St. Joseph's and begin to feel safe again. She began by talking about her physical problems and her many symptoms but went on to describe mental pain, emotional distress, financial problems, and this need for security. They are all interwoven, tied together, so that you cannot say at one moment that you are treating one problem and not the other. The treatment at St. Joseph's is designed to relieve the pain. Yes, one *can* do that, to enable the patient not only to die peacefully but to live fully until he dies, living as himself, neither swamped with distress nor smothered by treatments and drugs and the things that we are doing; nor yet enduring in sterile isolation. Now, this is the very opposite of doing nothing, and one *can* do it.

The patient who had described her world as "*all* pain" showed a remarkable difference just a few months later when she was relieved and relaxed; when she had given up her flat and organized all her affairs and when she had really forgotten that the medicine she was taking was for pain, because, as she said, "Now it's gone and I'm free," adding, "Doctor, do you think I could leave off the medicine because I really don't much like the taste of gin?" (Our normal pain medication does have gin in it—a good mild sedative.) She did not even remember that it was for that purpose. This was two weeks before her death.

Family Considerations

If we could, we would want to look after a patient at home. But many patients have so much distress that this is not possible. I have two photographs of a patient, photographs that tell a story. In the first, taken in his ward at St. Joseph's with his wife soon after he arrived, he is sitting up with tense alertness; his face betrays his anxiety, and his wife's face, her despair and guilty feeling of inadequacy. In the second photograph, taken after he had been under our care for a time and was on a diamorphine mixture, he looks as I think a patient ought to look: peaceful and comfortable. He is filling in his football pools (a mild English form of gambing) while his wife sits nearby, her relief at *his* relief showing in her face. I remember the wife of another patient stopping outside the ward and saying to me, "Oh doctor, I won't hurry in. I'll just stay here and look at him. I haven't seen him look like this for weeks!"

If we can give this kind of comfort to the patient and his family, then we have given them back something in this last time. It is of great importance to both of them. A patient can still be part of his family when he has to be admitted—and he can also fail to be part of his family while he is still at home. Wherever we are looking after these patients we have a tremendous responsibility to help them know they are still part of life and still a part of their own family. We have a photograph of a patient and his wife taken for their golden wedding anniversary only forty-eight hours before he died. Though he did not have the energy to smile, the picture shows his peacefulness and his feeling of closeness to his wife. I recall that when he came to St. Joseph's he was confused and did not recognize his wife or anything else. But after a short while with us he was himself once more. When his wife visited they were as close as they had been at any time during their fifty years of marriage. It is very important to share this "moment of truth" in whatever way one can. It is very important to say "Good-bye." Good-byes matter. We all give importance to saying "Good-bye" when we go on a journey—how much more meaning "Good-bye" has now. We can do a lot to create this sort of quiet togetherness for a couple by telling the patient that we can help him cope with the pain as it comes and letting him know in advance that the moment of death itself is quiet. Then he can, as far as possible, have this moment alone with a relative, shielded from the things that the staff can do something about. You cannot take away parting and its hardness, but you can help it.

Dr. Lawrence LeShan has spoken of "the wall of glass between the patient and other people." My thought is more of a vacuum around the patient, in part created by the anxious family who keep pulling themselves up and wondering, "Have I let something out?" Then all communication ceases and they are just not able to relax and talk about "something else," let alone real things. This can be a vastly important time, and often family members bitterly regret afterwards that they were not in touch. To get them to talk together, we may first have to do a lot of listening to both sides. We find it easier to do this separately, and we say to the family, who are usually the ones who are concealing their awareness, "You know, he really does realize." We point out that they must not come in being too cheerful and say, "You know, you're going to get better," because the patient is saying, "They won't even let me say 'Good-bye' to them." Usually, this sharing of awareness happens quietly, without fuss, and in its own time. I sound as if I take the line of least resistance all the time, but we have found that in our atmosphere at St. Joseph's, this problem resolves itself spontaneously, especially after pain and distress are relieved and we have listened to the anxiety. Sometimes a family member will say, "I can't talk to him. I just can't. I can only keep going without." Then perhaps the patient can talk to us, and then at least he is sharing it with someone. The nuns listen to the families more than I do, for they are always available. They do not have a day off and they are always there, or on call. There is a strong feeling of "Sister's there and I can always talk to her." They often do. But we share together as a group. Conditions in the typical general hospital do not apply in the same way here.

I think it is particularly important to try to help a dying parent say "Good-bye" to the children. I have seen mothers with quite young children saying "Good-bye" not in so many words, but deeply all the same. I have seen mothers doing something special for a daughter. I remember going out to buy a copy of *The Messiah* for a patient of mine to give her daughter as a last present—a gift which obviously is going to be unusually precious. Sometimes, when patients are failing, they have said to me, "Oh, there's nothing I can do now." You can say to them, "You know, she isn't ever going to forget how you were loving, how you were patient, how you did this, that, or the other while you were so ill."

I know this is true from my own memories, and I have two tape recordings of patients, one in her forties leaving two children who had both been problems, and another separated from her husband, leaving a son about sixteen. They both say the same words, repeating before they died, "I've done what I can." One went on, "I've said what I wanted done, and I have written it all down in my will." The other dictated a letter to me for her children. This was of immense help to them, to feel that they had done all that they could. They could then trust that their children would be cared for, just as they trusted that they would be cared for at St. Joseph's. It is a long way to come, to this place, and as soon as a young patient with a young family comes in, we know that this is going to take special time. We know we are going to feel awed by having to try to help this person face something much harder than anything we ever had to cope with. The fact is that while this is, indeed, sad work, yet when you come to the bedside you are not saying, "How can *I* help Mrs. So-and-so?" but rather, "This is St. Joseph's and I just happen to be the one here at the moment. And it will be all right."

Communicating With the Dying

At St. Joseph's, there is one nun in charge of each ward, but the rest of our nurses are not nuns. Most of them are young Irish girls who come over and do apprentice nursing with us before they go and get further training elsewhere. Since they have not yet been taught to hurry, as many a trained nurse will, they are well suited to work with dying patients. You cannot hurry the dying. You cannot hurry them to realize what is happening; you cannot hurry them to turn over in bed quickly; you cannot hurry them to eat faster than they can manage. Within this slow speed, their own speed, they often make a great deal of improvement. Certainly they are quieter and easier.

I recall being with a patient with a cerebral tumor about two weeks before he died. He had been blind for about six months and was very slow now. His wife tried to get him to look up as I got ready to take their photograph, but he could not manage it and sank back again. She looked up at me and the picture shows the tremendous grace and maturity that I have seen again and again, both in patients and in their families. You might ask, "What is the point of looking after a man for fifteen months since he's going to die at the end?" But there are no short cuts to this kind of maturity. Though there may not be a long time available for a couple to be together, time is a matter of depth and quality rather than length. At this period I remember asking his wife, "Does he always know you?" And she said, "Oh, yes, he does." Then she added, "The other day when I came in I said to him, 'Who's here?' and he said, 'I don't know.' When I said, 'It's me,' he just said, 'Ah, but you're always there!'" It was marvelous how she had gotten across to him the sense that she always was there with him, by her faithfulness, by coming whenever she could, even though she was working at the time. And he, who was a gentle and courteous person by nature, was giving her this absolutely perfect "thanks," and still responding in his own character to the reduced information that his senses were now giving him. He was still much the same person, unique and irreplaceable.

I remember another patient, who, like so many, showed that her heart was still loving though her mind could no longer grasp much at all. A picture of her shows her loving response to an unsophisticated little nurse who is just enjoying her as she is, demonstrating her pleasure in just meeting her, somehow still the same person as ever. Now, this simplicity is a quality we too often lose, but I notice that the young seem to have it almost by nature, if they choose to come into this kind of work. This quality is, I think, important for a relative to observe and feel—to see this person as himself, indefinably the same, still with his own worth until the moment he dies.

Awareness of Dying and "Telling"

Now I have to consider the old question of what to tell the patient. In the first place, I am sure I have to make a distinction between telling somebody his diagnosis (that it is a malignant disease) and his prognosis (that he is not going to get better as far as we can see). I think we have to remember that the degree of insight a patient has into his condition is not under our control. It does not depend just on what we tell him. There are many other factors in the situation—his intelligence, his courage, what is happening in his own body and what this is saying to him, what he overhears. *I know that some fifty per cent of my patients not only knew that they were dying but talked about it with me.* Of the remaining fifty per cent, there were some who were senile, some who had cerebral tumors, and some who were just not able to have insight. There were others who, I think, recognized but did not choose to talk about it—at least not with me. The choice should be theirs. The real question is not, "What do you tell your patients?" but rather, "What do you let your patients tell you?" Learn to hear what they are saying; what they are not saying; what is hidden underneath; what *is* going on. Incidentally, only a very few of our patients did know at first that they had been sent to St. Joseph's as the last stage of their journey. Usually they had been told something such as "You need specialized treatment for pain," or "You need longer-term nursing than we can provide in a general ward." Later some of them told me that they had a pretty shrewd idea that it was something like this when they came in. They do not often discuss their diagnosis, which seems often to be irrelevant at this age, but they do talk about their prognosis, about what is happening, and they all do it differently. Since giving a general description is difficult, all I can do is describe a group of people and tell you what happened to each one of them.

I recall one young woman who had been with us for two months. She and I were quite friendly. I thought she "knew" and that she had chosen never to mention it. She just kept her own counsel until one day she suddenly looked up at me and said, with courage and determination in her voice, "Doctor, where did all this begin?" I pulled the curtains round and sat on her bed (as an ex-nurse, rejoicing in the fact that I was no longer bound by the rule that nurses do not sit on beds!). This is important for communicating: standing at the bedside, I would tower over a patient. In this two-way traffic, I want to be on the same level. Then she went on, talking about her family, and soon got to her real question: "Is it wrong for me to let my children come up and visit me now that I'm getting so thin?" She said that she had "known" since her operation six months before, adding, "I haven't talked to my husband about it and I think it would be so hard for him when he realized that I've been carrying this on my own all this time. I just don't know quite how to begin." I told her, "Well, you know, it will just happen, quite easily, and you've been sharing it together anyway." And, of course, having talked to someone else she found herself talking with him the next day. At last it was possible for them to share openly. About a week later she died, but in her face she showed a quietness and acceptance that upheld her whole family.

Other patients are quiet and objective and unworried. I remember one old man saying, quite unexpectedly, "Of course, doctor, I realize this isn't a question of cure now, is it? It's just a matter of jogging along." He was quite sure that it would be all right, that it was his family who needed reassuring. But there are common questions and common fears that lie beyond the one big question that we seem to talk of as if it were the only one. Many are concerned about their families. Many ask, "Will it be very long?" "Will I have pain?" "What will it be like in the end?" Or, "I hope it will be in my sleep." Now, we can be reassuring about it all. If we refuse to discuss it openly, or smother their questions in a kind of blanket of reassurance, they still know very well what is happening. What we have said to them, in effect, is, "I'm afraid to discuss it." They want to talk about the other questions, and they will do it when they are ready if only we will let them. We can also help them without doing so in every word. Effective communicaton can take place indirectly. Discussing symptoms with a patient, often a way out of having to talk openly, can also be a way to begin. It can give reassurance, understanding, a feeling of "I will be here."

It can be a great release to be frank. I remember one man saying to me, "You know, I've had it all out with my wife and now we can relax and talk about something else." I think that is important too.

Rather unusually, one family took complete control and told a young woman patient so that she could share her knowledge of dying with her husband all the way through. For the two months or so that she was with us, she maintained an air of serenity until the end. Of course, this would not work for every family. With another family and another patient the situation is completely different.

I remember one old woman telling me, very firmly, "And when I'm going downhill, doctor, I don't intend you to tell me!" (That reminds me of another patient who, looking at me rather sideways, said, "I know you know how much chance I've got, doctor, but I'm not going to ask you.") Such feelings are to be respected; it is the patient's choice and we should honor it. When the woman was beginning to go downhill I saw her sitting pensively with her great-grandchild on her knee, realizing — but not telling. At St. Joseph's we certainly admit, allow, and welcome children into the ward. They are very important to *all* our patients, not just the ones they are visiting. The patients need to have this sense of continuity, to know that life is going on. A child, just because it is a child, should be welcomed in this sort of ward.

We all know the very anxious patient who has, as it were, an invisible extra pillow: she can never rest her head right back on her pillow, she is constantly in some kind of tension. Such a person will tend to deny what is happening, will talk only about her symptoms, and has to be reassured by practical things — being given this or that drug or treatment. Not only is every patient different from every other patient, but the same patient will have a different face on a different day. One particular patient made her will with a fair amount of drama one day, and then a week or two later confided to me, "Doctor, you know what I *really* need is a new set of false teeth." Care of the dying person is a changing situation, and we have to time the help we give to the right moment. Patients will reach out to us on two levels at the same time. And they, too, want a day off! Mankind cannot bear too much reality. There is a day when you think you see a crisis coming and think, "Ah, now we're going to talk about it." Not at all — the patient only wants to talk about the weather, and naturally should be allowed to. The rule is that there are no general rules here except that you must listen. You must be ready to listen; you must be ready to be silent; and you must just be committed.

Sometimes one gets a very direct question. One man asked me a direct question at a stage when I knew him very well and when it would have been an insult not to have fully answered him. Often I give a rather open or perhaps two-way answer and the person can pick up whichever one he really wants. But when this man asked, "Am I going to die?" I just said "Yes." And he said "Long?" and I said "No." He said, "Was it hard for you to tell me that?" "Yes, it was." He just said, "Thank you. It's hard to be told, but it's hard to tell too." His comment was, I think, truly significant. In the first place, it shows how extremely courteous and outward-looking these patients are. And secondly, it should be hard to tell. You just should not be doing this easily. It *should* be hard because you are trying to bring everything you have of understanding to hear what this patient is really asking you. Then you should be concerned that he does well with what you give him, and that you really are committing yourself to helping him in everyway you can, helping him right up to the end. I remember also asking him, "What do you look for most of all in the people who are looking after you?" He thought and said, "Well, for someone to look as if they are trying to understand me. I'm hard to understand." He asks not for success but for somebody who looks as if he cares enough to try. I think that is the fundamental thing. Of course, when you are a student, and when you are a nurse, the patient must know that you really do not know the answer, but this gives you all the more opportunity to try to learn by listening, to ask yourself, "What does the patient really want to know? What is it he's worried about?"

Pain

A great deal of my time has been spent with patients who have severe intractable pain. This is really where my interest in this work began. I remember one patient who, when she was admitted, simply could not think of anything but pain. In a tape recording made at the time she said, "I love my family but I couldn't bear to have them in the room because I couldn't think of anything else, and they would have seen the pain in my face." That sort of pain we can control, nearly always without rendering the patient sleepy. Later in her stay at St. Joseph's I looked in on her and found her peacefully writing a letter.

Chronic pain of this kind is a very complicated condition, different from acute pain. One woman had a whole variety of symptoms and problems including a very large, open wound. She was restless and in severe pain. Upon admission the referring doctor had written on her form, "Mainly stuporous now." But that was due to drugs, and not her mental condition. Three months later, she was sitting up in a chair, organizing the ward and so on. When she was finally dying it was she who told me at what stage she thought she really ought to take to bed. I think that to be in such control can be a psychologically healthy and reassuring situation.

I recall a girl newly admitted. When I went in to talk to her she just burst into tears because she expected to be hurt so much the moment anybody came near her. She had chronic pain that went on the whole time but also was exacerbated by movement. The situation held her, as it were, in a vise. As she described it, "The pain was all around me." This is so different from the protective, warning pain of a kitchen burn or of the symptom that brings a patient for diagnosis or the postoperative pain which has a reason and which you know is not going to go on for very long. This is a *chronic* pain which seems to be timeless and endless as well as meaningless. Now, it is important to realize that many patients make their pain worse by anticipating it.

Consequently *we* should do the anticipating. At St. Joseph's we use our drugs to prevent the pain from ever happening rather than trying to get on top of it once it has occurred. This means a careful analysis of the total situation — the other symptoms, attention to details, a lot of careful nursing, and just listening so that we know what their sensation is like, and so that they know we are interested. I had a patient say to me, "And then I came here and *you listened*. The pain seemed to go by just talking." She was not just trying to be polite; her perception of pain had really been influenced by our attention and time.

I stopped to talk with a girl about six weeks before she died, and she had the rather "yonderly" look of someone who is beginning to let go. Preparation for dying seems to begin in the subconscious. How much was conscious for her at any stage I do not really know. I had hoped we might get her home again, but when I saw her face that day I knew it would not be possible. The surgeon came up to consult again and told us that nothing more could be done. She had been in our ward for five and a half months, and when she died she was on the same dose of narcotic at which we stabilized her when she first came in. This can be done. The problems of tolerance and dependence can be almost eliminated by the way in which the administration of drugs is managed. It should be part of the whole process of caring for the patient. The aim is that the patient should be alert — alert and himself, and that he should be independent. If every time the patient has a pain he must ask somebody else for something to relieve it, it reminds him that he is dependent on the drug, dependent on another person. But, if instead, the staff can anticipate the occurrence of pain, at St. Joseph's by a system of regular giving of adequate medication to cover the chosen routine time, the patient does not continually have to ask for relief. He can stay alert, thinking of other things, and "forgetting" the pain.

Relief from pain should be given all the way to the end. If it is, the patient can remain himself. I remember talking to one woman who clearly demonstrated the capacity for meeting person-to-person that we so often see in the very ill. This was five days before her death. This woman was Jewish: she was deaf and dumb and she had lived in the east end of London all her life. She could not have had an easy life. But just by looking at her, we knew a great deal about her as she truly was. Our job was to control her distress and pain so that she could be herself until the end.

After this patient died, I remember the woman in the next bed confiding to me, "She didn't suffer. They don't here. I think the motto of this place is 'There shall be no pain.' It makes you feel very safe." This is a safety which gives independence, not dependence.

Balancing Clarity and Reduction of Pain

To give enough help up to the end without making a patient sleepy is a problem of delicate balance. If you balance your drugs for the control of incipient confusion, anxiety, and depression the patient will not be sleepy and confused. It is often more difficult to get the balance of the tranquilizers and sedatives than of the analgesics but all the more rewarding for that.

Alcohol remains our best sedative, especially for the elderly. Most of us feel better after a drink; why should the patient be any different? We are allowed to give alcohol in the National Health Service and we are allowed to give gin as part of our favorite pain-relief cocktail, and "it's on the house." Also we encourage relatives to bring in alcohol if they know the patient would enjoy it. I mean quite honestly that a bottle of whiskey may be more valuable than a whole great basket of oranges. A little of what the patient likes does him good. I know you have a problem with alcoholism in the United States as well as with addiction, and perhaps you feel differently, but I have not noticed that Americans feel any differently about serving drinks. I am not suggesting that I have my patients high on alcohol. I am not trying to produce a high positive euphoria. But they come in with a heavy burden, which makes them feel lower than the next person, and we are trying to reduce their burden to manageable proportions. As visitors often remark, our patients look like ordinary, relaxed, serene, cheerful people. I heard one of the students explain the atmosphere this way: "It's the kind of atmosphere that makes one feel that death really isn't anything to be frightened of, but a sort of homecoming." I think she summed it up very well. You just go on. You go on trying something different. You go on listening. You keep coming in, day after day, trying to get the balance right. With some patients you have to keep on trying. With others, you get them balanced and it remains perfect for them to the end.

Personal, caring contact is the most important comfort we can give. It is not necessary always to pay a long visit. Often we are very busy, but there is always time for a brief word. Above all, we must never let the patients down. Never just go by. The dying will lie with their eyes shut just out of tiredness when they are waiting for you. If you then fly past the end of the bed, rather pleased to find them asleep, they have lost that precious moment for which they were waiting. In a Chinese poem of the ninth century A.D. are the lines: "Tranquil talk was better than any medicine. Gradually the feelings came back to my numbed heart." Once a patient knows that you are really interested, he also knows well enough when you are in a hurry. Some of the things to which you listen are not particularly fine, maybe, and some are jolly good grumbles. But I think it is essential that the aggressive person who wants to grumble should be able to do it to you and not to other patients. Somebody who is basically a "doing" sort of person, such as one old patient I remember, a former flyweight boxer, finds it very hard having things done for him. If he is going to let his frustration out and blow some of it off by grumbling away about it, then he should be allowed — not indulged — but allowed to do so.

The Importance of Choice

If a patient chooses to be out and about, as far as possible we let him. If he says, "Oh, I really must take to bed," we usually find that he is right. He knows what he can manage. On the whole, we really do let him make the choice. I think this is valuable, but it is usually difficult to do in a general ward, where the whole process is geared to getting the patient out, getting him going, and so on. You may see some poor old man propped up in a wheelchair when you know he is just longing, "Please put me back." When a patient does not have much energy, he may want to save it for talking to relatives at visiting time, and not use it being gotten in and out of bed. As far as the control of physical symptoms and the control of pain are concerned, some of our patients say, "I don't want to get used to it." We can always reassure them that what we are using will go on being effective. I find that patients are more often fearful about taking something for sleep than about taking something for pain. I say to my patients, "Now, I'm going to give you something for your restlessness and something for this and something for the other." I do not tell them exactly what the drugs are—they would not remember, anyway. But I do tell them what I am trying to do, and I try to involve them in the situation. I also try to change only one drug at a time, because if you change three drugs and the patient feels sick, which one is responsible? As the guides to public speaking advise, "Tell them what's going on." There is a paper written by a patient who says that he had received many pills and many medicines in his various visits to hospitals and nobody had ever told him what any one of them was for. He said, "I could have at least added one minim of faith if I'd been told in what direction to project my faith."

The Issue of Euthanasia

I am in the happy position of not being able to carry out drastic life-prolonging measures because we just do not have the facilities at St. Joseph's. Other people have made the decision, at a prior stage, that this is a patient for whom such procedures are not suitable or right or kind. This makes it very much easier for us than for the staff of a busy general ward. I think that it is extremely important that the decision be made by a person who has learned all he can about the family, about the patient himself, and about the whole situation. The further we go in having special means at our disposal, the more important it is that we stop and think what we are doing. Of course we must consider the facilities available in the particular institution and the demands on them, but the most crucial consideration is the welfare of the individual patient. In England there is a society that works to get euthanasia legalized. They are specially concerned with the problem of the patients that I work with, those with terminal malignant disease. Though these are not necessarily the most difficult patients to look after, I will stick to them because they are the ones I know best. I have had much correspondence with the former chairman of the Euthanasia Society in Great Britain, and I took him round St. Joseph's after I had been working there some eighteen months. He came away saying, "I didn't know you could do it. If all patients died something like this, we could disband the Society." And he added, "I'd like to come and die in your Home." I do not believe in taking a deliberate step to end a patient's life—but then, I do not get asked. If you relieve a patient's pain and if you can make him feel like a wanted person, which he is, then you are not going to be asked about euthanasia. It is sad that so many patients still do not die in this condition. However, there is no situation in which you cannot get across to a patient that he is a person you care about. Even if you are in a hurry, you can do it; I have seen it happening again and again. This is the positive side of the issue. The idea of euthanasia, legalized killing, is to me morally wrong. But if my own standard of morals, or code of ethics, does not make sense for the other person, I am not going to change his mind by saying that. I think that euthanasia is an admission of defeat, and a totally negative approach. One should be working to see that it is not needed. The great responsibility that we have, those of us who think it is wrong to relieve all pains by euthanasia, is to see that the pains *are* relieved. After all, this is no more than the total responsibility that you take on with any patient under your care.

Ward Dynamics: Death of a Patient

The patient who is upset when another patient dies is usually the one who has just come in, and who does not yet know us or trust us. The patient who has been with us for some time, and knows that the other patient is ready, takes it far more quietly, not carelessly but with a compassionate matter-of-factness which one sees, of course, with the nuns. The nuns have this quality par excellence: this capacity to be matter-of-fact and to go on doing things while showing deep compassion. We do not move our patients away when they are dying. We have one single room on each floor, but we do not move patients into it unless, perhaps, family tradition dictates that ten members of the family sit around the bed for ten days on end or something like that. But apart from such occasional crises the patients remain in their own beds during their final days. This is vital. I have worked in a setting where patients were always moved out, and the other patients were then far more disturbed. You could see them thinking, "What is it like? We never see it. It must be awful." By contrast, when people die in the ward, it isn't "awful." It is always quiet. "It's as quiet as blowing a candle out" is how patients have described it to me. Often it is because they have seen somebody else die quietly that they are finally able to talk about death themselves. They talk not because they have an extra weight of anxiety but because they feel "Oh! Now it seems that it isn't quite so frightening." What counts the most is that they can see that they are not alone. Since we take care that the nuns say the "last prayers" at the last moment, we have to be good at knowing when this last moment is. We try hard to see to it that patients are not alone at the end. And so they are in the ward, they do have their cubicle curtains drawn at the last moment, and more often than not Sister is actually there, saying her prayers at the very moment that the patient dies. Often the family is there too. While you may think that this sounds disturbing, it is not. It is aloneness that our patients are most afraid of. It is also essential that we should be good at making the end peaceful. The patient should not be confused, fighting for breath, crying out, and that sort of thing. The end is always quiet and peaceful, and nearly always the patient is in a state of sleep or unconsciousness. The patient who dies fully conscious is rare, but a few do.

Another feature is that one must always let the other patients talk about it, if they want to. We do not force talking upon them, but neither do we say, "She went home in the middle of the night," or "We moved her out into a single room," or some other deception like that. I found out that one old lady was mending her nightdress forty-eight hours before she died because the patient in the bed opposite told me. Then we talked about her. Sometimes patients become extremely fond of each other and they have much to give each other, including emotional support and a great deal of individual helping. But—love costs. It always does. It is hard when somebody you are very fond of goes but more than once a patient has said to me, "You know, I gave her her last drink." There is a special communication here.

Sometimes we may have several patients who die, one right after the other. Because we have only about forty-five beds for dying patients out of a wing of seventy-five, the others having long-term illness, we are able to move some around and release the tension. Of course, this is a problem but there are problems in every hospital. My final point on this topic is, we are not afraid of dying ourselves. It is quiet on the ward; there is no sense of panic; it is all right.

Helping The Grieving Family

We always tend to feel guilty in bereavement. Indeed, feelings of guilt are part of bereavement. We go back in memory until we find ways that we let the person down. We remember things that we did and now cannot undo. To know that it is natural and ordinary to feel this way can be very helpful. I think that the nurses can do a great deal for the grieving family. The nurse who said to me, "He didn't open his eyes again after you left, you know. You *were* the last person he saw," helped me more than anybody else. This really did matter to me.

One of the ways we try at St. Joseph's to help the bereaved is just to listen. If a relative wants to say, "Why did God do this to me? Why did He let this happen? Why did the doctor operate?" you must let him do it. You must never stop him. You must never argue. You must let him talk, because expressing these thoughts begins to help toward healing. He may have to express his anguish again and again, but the listener is the person who is needed, and especially the listener who is not a member of the family. The listener from outside can help in a way that another family member cannot. But if we are to learn to help as listeners, we have to learn to accept people as they are. Once when I was complaining about a particularly disturbing and troublesome patient, Sister looked up at me and said simply, "He is himself." People who can allow us to be ourselves are helpful, particularly in bereavement.

One sees that mourning is not just forgetting. It includes a sense of going back to all the ties, and undoing them, and taking out what is really valuable, until in the end what is finally left is no longer grief in the same way, since much has been resolved. This part of the family time together is very important and can make a crucial difference to the whole grieving process.

The Meaning of Dying

A feeling of meaninglessness can be the hardest pain of all for a dying person to bear. Now, you can never impose your own meaning upon another person and his situation, but in a place like St. Joseph's where other people are convinced of the meaning of living and dying, it is easier to find your own way. Sometimes another patient is more help than anybody else. Sometimes the staff have to bear their inability to understand, to feel as if they are not helping at all, yet still go on staying close to the patient. We tend to feel that if we are bringing nothing, then we had better go away. But I think that is just the moment when we have simply got to stay. And if this is the moment when the patient feels that there is no meaning in life and that the weariness of it all is more than he can cope with and we are feeling helpless too, well, we are very much on the same level there. In that place where you share helplessness—there, perhaps, you can help more than you realize.

"Yes, doctor, you can show my photograph to anyone you like," I remember a patient saying, "and you can say to them 'It was all right.'" When she had been admitted to St. Joseph's, it was not "all right" for her, but as she found her way it was she who was telling us the meaning, not the other way around. The answer is found by meeting fate, not by demanding "Why?" but by asking "How?" "How do I live in this situation?" It is like Viktor Frankl finding meaning in the life of the concentration camps; like Dag Hammarskjold deciding to say "Yes" to life; learning from Pierre Teilhard de Chardin to accept our own passivities at the deepest level. But for the woman photographed it was not complicated like that at all. The answer for her was just simple, loving obedience to the daily demands of what was going on in a place where she was continually finding help and meaning, finding that love casts out fear.

The Role of Religion With the Dying

Though there are many similarities among patients who are facing death, each has his unique way of responding. Religion is a real and living thing for a number of our patients, and its meaning grows deeper as death nears. But many of our patients are extremely indifferent to religion, or at least detached from it. I have heard one of the Sisters say kindly of a patient: "His religion's pretty harmless." I doubt that the really aggressive atheist ever reaches us, because the family, knowing that the hospice is run by nuns, would be likely to decide to go somewhere else. In any case, we certainly never do any imposing. I remember one incident when the Sister reported to me, "You know, I went round the ward the other day and I found Mrs So-and-so reading the Bible and I said to her, 'My goodness, Mrs. So-and-so!' and she said, 'It's all right, Sister. It's just for the crossword puzzle!'" The fact that we could all enjoy this as a joke is indicative of the atmosphere at St. Joseph's.

Whatever the religious background of our patients, I often see in them something that could be called "reaching out trustfully." They come to remember things from the past, things that they have been too busy to listen to before, and as death approaches, they find that things begin to make sense. They bring a new attention to the old truths. This is something entirely different from plucking at straws, and is an extremely personal matter for each patient.

What I see over and over again with dying persons, and not only because I hope to see this, are the fruits of the spirit—"love, joy, peace, long-suffering, gentleness, goodness, faith, meekness, self-control." For me this is "truth," and this I continually see. The nuns, I think, represent Christianity in general rather than Catholicism in particular. What we have in common is much more important than what we disagree about. What I see in patients is to be read of in Martin Buber, the Jewish theologian and philosopher, in Teilhard de Chardin, the Catholic, and in many others—they are talking to each other. I am trying to pin down the intangible. If you have seen it—if you have been with these patients—then you will recognize what I am trying to say.

Patients are often shy to ask for spiritual help; at least, they are in Great Britain. So all the more we have to serve as a link. It is often easier for a patient just to mention it to or to have it mentioned by an ordinary person. Perhaps they can accept this kind of help only from an ordinary person. You have to go quietly and very slowly, but you do need to know, I think, about their need for spiritual help, and classify this term as widely as you like. When professionals talk about the care of the dying, they are often careful to omit this topic completely, or they may say, "Well, it's an individual matter." I believe there is a responsibility on us here; otherwise it is just deciding by default. It is part of total care, even if it is not called by that name, or even recognized. At St. Joseph's I have had the good fortune of working with nuns in an atmosphere where religion is totally integrated into all that we do and think, but never forced on anyone who enters. It is there, largely without words. Florence Nightingale, I think, is the one who said, "You should carry the bedpan for the glory of God." Many would prefer to say, "I'll carry it for the dignity of man." But, you know, the two belong together.

I have been trying to talk, in several ways, about "being present" to these people. Underneath there has been a belief in the person in the midst of life and death and in God as the Truth of the moment of truth. Personal, compassionate trust is really what is behind the atmosphere at St. Joseph's.

In my work one is continually seeing people at their most mature. One could look thus far in this work and say that to recognize this moment of greatest maturity, of the greatest depth of individuality, is a totally satisfying and positive aim and ending. But Eissler, in his book *The Psychiatrist and the Dying Patient*, talks about the need for the psychotherapist to have some sort of feeling about the immortality of his patient. I would add: perhaps something more than just "some sort of feeling."

I remember watching one man who could concentrate totally on the white hyacinth plant by his bed. I saw in him the relief of that moment of pure pleasure. Somehow it seemed to be saying to him, "The world to which you also belong is good and can be trusted."

I recall the gaiety of that man and of many others. It was not a euphoria induced by drugs and alcohol. It was the gaiety of having gone through doubts and fears and questions and having come right out on the other side. This, I believe, is why one can go on working with these dying patients, day after day, and month after month.

One patient moved from severe anxiety and denial to an emotional stage where one day, when I was sitting on her bed, she suddenly said to me, "You know, doctor, I couldn't ever really imagine myself dying, but there does come a time when you are ready to lay it down." This reminds me of the always uncanny moment when the body, which even in confusion and pain expresses the person, is suddenly empty. To me, the mind and body are absolutely interwoven, but appear to be no more than the tools of the spirit, which is of much more importance. The spirit seems to lay down the body and the mind when death finally comes.

I recall so many who have been truly ready for meeting this "moment." These patients show man's ability to sum up all that he is in this one moment, this moment of truth. In life, we are always looking ahead and never quite getting there. We are always aiming too far, or we are always tipping over into the depths of self-concern. Even so, we bring all that we are into every moment. The "reason why we're here" is a summing up of everything that has happened before. At this stage, and I have seen it again and again, somehow there is a moment that is fully personal and everything is summed up. When Pope John was dying, he said, "My bags are packed and I can go with a tranquil heart at any moment." This is the "moment" of the bullfight—the whole thing summed up.

I remember talking with a patient the day before her death. Her face showed all the quietness and the weariness of dying. Yet she consented to my taking her picture, knowing that I would use it for lectures. She was a warm person who had been in our wards a long time, and she enjoyed meeting students. That afternoon, she was easily able to talk about death and also to ask me to say one or two things to her family for her. Our students used to come round to visit her. She was the sort of person who was helping our work, and she knew it. She could teach far more during just a short visit by sharing her experience, in whatever way she wanted to at the time, than ever I could do in my talking about it. People who are dying often have a tremendous capacity for meeting, or encountering, because they have put aside the mask that we tend to wear in everyday life. Now they are ready to meet, just as themselves, and I am sure this is why you can get to know these patients in an extraordinarily short time, in fact, even in a brief meeting. As students going round the ward said, "She taught us a great deal of wisdom which we will never forget."

The answer to the question of preparation for this kind of work is that *you learn the care of the dying from the dying themselves*. But only if you look at them with respect and never merely with pity, and allow them to teach you. It is they who show us that the fear of death is overcome. Seeing this, we, too, can come to the place to which I have seen them come so often, and which Ralph Harper describes vividly in his book *Nostalgia:* "We cannot know what is beyond the end of our days, but we can enter into an order of things which can make us say, 'I'm not afraid.'"

CHAPTER VI

THE DEATHS OF OTHER PEOPLE:

BEREAVEMENT AND MOURNING

Introduction

Death comes close to us when a person intimately related to us dies. The first time this happens, for many of us, is when a parent dies. Usually we are protected from the details and protocol of funerals and burials when we are children—whether "overprotected" to our emotional detriment might be debated. Hence the death of grandparents—which for many of us may take place when we are children or young adults and therefore "spared" the burdens of "making arrangements"—may seem unreal or dreamlike. But the death of a parent may bring with it not only the impact of grief and mourning, but also the necessity for making what appear to be essentially business arrangements for the burial. The juxtaposition of two such sharply conflicting demands may be unbearably poignant.

Jessica Mitford was among the first widely read authors to point out the culturally determined nature of funeral practices, and to deplore some of the more pernicious inventions of modern funeral institutions and their personnel. The selection "Fashions in Funerals" is from her well-known book, *The American Way of Death*. In the next selection, Pine (a funeral director) and Phillips (a sociologist) team up to produce a piece of research which underlines the fact that "social demands made of funeral directors... have made certain costly factors part of the American style of death." Despite social change, which has made illness and death increasingly the responsibility of institutions outside the immediate family — e.g., the hospital, the funeral director — bereavement comes to all of us, sooner or later. Is economic expenditure an appropriate expression of grief? Perhaps. Perhaps not.

The final selection in this chapter is an account of the emotional expenditure, albeit mostly supressed emotion, made by a family upon the death of the father. While the economic problems are there, in the background, the dreadful fact is confronted squarely that never will life be the same again, that this death has irrevocably changed everything.

FASHIONS IN FUNERALS   *

by

Jessica Mittford

> ...disposal of the dead falls rather into a class with fashions, than with either customs or folkways on the one hand, or institutions on the other...social practices of disposing of the dead are of a kind with fashions of dress, luxury and etiquette.
>
> *"Disposal of the Dead"* by A. L. Kroeber
> American Anthropologist (New Series)
> Volume 29:3, July-September, 1927

One of the interesting things about burial practices is that they provide many a clue to the customs and society of the living. The very word "antiquarian" conjures up the picture of a mild-eyed historian groping about amidst old tombstones, copying down epitaphs with their folksy inscriptions and irregular spelling, extrapolating from these a picture of the quaint people and homey ways of yore. There is unconscious wit: the widow's epitaph to her husband, "Rest in peace — until we meet again." There is gay inventiveness:

> Here lie I, Master Elginbrod.
> Have mercy on my soul, O God,
> As I would have if I were God
> And thou wert Master Elginbrod.

There is pathos: "I will awake, O Christ, when thou callest me, but let me sleep awhile — for I am very weary." And bathos: " 'Tis but the casket that lies here; the gem that fills it sparkles yet."

For the study of prehistory, archeologists rely heavily on what they can find in and around tombs, graves, monuments; and from the tools, jewels, household articles, symbols found with the dead, they reconstruct whole civilizations, infer entire systems of religious and ethical beliefs.

Inevitably some go-ahead team of thirtieth-century archeologists will labor to reconstruct our present-day level of civilization from a study of our burial practices. It is depressing to think of them digging and poking about in our new crop of Forest Lawns, the shouts of discovery as they come upon the mass-produced granite horrors, the repetitive flat bronze markers (the legends, like greeting cards and singing telegrams, chosen from an approved list maintained at the cemetery office) and, under the ground, the stamped-out metal casket shells resembling nothing so much as those bronzed and silvered souvenirs for sale at airport gift shops. Prying further, they would find reposing in each of these on a comfortable mattress of innerspring or foam rubber construction a standardized, rouged or suntanned specimen of Homo sapiens, U.S.A., attired in business suit or flowing negligee according to sex. Our archeologists would puzzle exceedingly over the inner meaning of the tenement mausoleums with their six or seven tiers of adjoining crypt spaces. Were the tenants of these, they might wonder, engaged in some ritual act of contemplation, surprised by sudden disaster? Busily scribbling notes, they would describe the companion his-and-her vaults for husband and wife, and the approved inscription on these: "TOGETHER FOREVER." For purposes of comparison they might recall the words of Andrew Marvell, a poet from an earlier culture, who thus addressed his coy mistress:

> The grave's a fine and private place,
> But none, I think, do there embrace.

*   Reprinted from *The American Way of Death.* Used by permission of the publisher Simon and Schuster, New York. (1963.) pp 187-201.

They might rashly conclude that twentieth-century America was a nation of abjectly imitative conformists, devoted to machine-made gadgetry and mass-produced art of a debased quality; that its dominant theology was a weird mixture of primitive superstitions, superficial attitudes towards death, overlaid with a distinct tendency towards necrophilism....

Where did our burial practices come from? There is little scholarship on the subject. Thousands of books have been written describing, cataloguing, theorizing about the funeral procedures of ancient and modern peoples from Aztecs to Zulus; but about contemporary American burial practices almost nothing has been written.

The National Funeral Directors Association, aware of this omission and anxious to correct it, recently commissioned two writers, Robert W. Habenstein and William M. Lamers, to explore the subject and to come up with some answers. The resulting studies, *The History of American Funeral Directing* and *Funeral Customs the World Over,* bear the imprint of the National Funeral Directors Association and are the subject of a continuing promotion campaign by that organization: "Buy one for each clergyman in your community!" "Place them in your libraries!" are the slogans. The campaign has had some success. In fact, in most libraries these volumes sponsored by the undertaking trade are the only ones to be found on the subject of the American funeral.

The official historians of American undertaking describe the origin of our burial practices as follows:

"As a result of a long slow development, with its roots deep in the history of Western civilization, it is the common American mind today that the dead merit professional funeral services from a lay occupational group. These services include embalming, the preparation of the body for final viewing, a waiting period between death and disposition, and the use for everyone of a casket that is attractive and protects the remains, a dignified and ceremonious service with consideration for the feelings of the bereaved, and an expression of the individual and group beliefs...." Elsewhere they assert: "The roots of American funeral behavior extend back in a direct line several thousand years to early Judaeo-Christian beliefs as to the nature of God, man and the hereafter.... Despite the antiquity of these roots their importance as regards the treatment of the dead in the world that commonly calls itself Christian today cannot be overemphasized."

In two misinformation-packed paragraphs, we are assured not only that American funerals are based on hallowed custom and tradition, but that they conform to long-held religious doctrine. There is more than a hint of warning in these words for the would-be funeral reformer; he who would be bold enough to make light of or tamper with the fundamental beliefs and ancient traditions of a society in so sensitive an area as behavior towards its dead, had better think twice.

A "long, slow development with its roots deep in the history of Western civilization," or a short, fast sprint with its roots deep in money-making? A brief look backward would seem to establish that there is no resemblance between the funeral practices of today and those of even fifty to one hundred years ago, and that there is nothing in the "history of Western civilization" to support the thesis of continuity and gradual development of funeral customs. On the contrary, the salient features of the contemporary American funeral (beautification of the corpse, metal casket and vault, banks of store-bought flowers, ubiquitous offices of the "funeral director") are all of very recent vintage in this country, and each has been methodically designed and tailored to extract maximum profit for the trade.

Nor can responsibility for the twentieth-century American funeral be laid to the door of "Judaeo-Christian beliefs." The major Western faiths have remarkably little to say about how funerals should be conducted. Such doctrinal statements as have been enunciated concerning disposal of the dead invariably stress simplicity, the equality of all men in death, emphasis on the spiritual aspects rather than on the physical remains.

The Roman Catholic Church requires that the following simple instructions be observed: "1) That the body be decently laid out; 2) that lights be placed beside the body; 3) that a cross be laid upon the breast, or failing that, the hands laid on the breast in the form of a cross; 4) that the body be sprinkled with holy water and incense at stated times; 5) that it be buried in consecrated ground." The Jewish religion specifically prohibits display in connection with funerals: "It is strictly ordained that there must be no adornment of the plain wooden coffin used by the Jew, nor may flowers be placed inside or outside. Plumes, velvet palls and the like are strictly prohibited, and all show and display of wealth discouraged; moreover, the synagogue holds itself responsible for the arrangements for burial, dispensing with the services of the Dismal Trade." In Israel today, uncoffined burial is the rule, and the deceased is returned to the earth in a simple shroud. The Church of England Book of Common Prayer, written several centuries before burial receptacles came into general use, makes no mention of coffins in connection with the funeral service, but rather speaks throughout of the "corpse" or the "body."

What of embalming, the pivotal aspect of the American funeral? The "roots" of this procedure have indeed leaped oceans and traversed centuries in the most unrootlike fashion. It has had a checkered history, the highlights of which deserve some consideration since embalming is (as one mortuary textbook writer puts it) "The very foundation of modern mortuary service — the factor which has made the elaborate funeral home and lucrative funeral service possible."

True, the practice of preserving dead bodies with chemicals, decorating them with paint and powder and arranging them for a public showing has its origin in antiquity — but not in Judaeo-Christian antiquity. This incongruous behavior towards the human dead originated with the pagan Egyptians and reached its high point in the second millennium B.C. Thereafter, embalming suffered a decline from which it did not recover until it was made part of the standard funeral service in twentieth-century America.

While the actual *mode* of preservation and the materials used differed in ancient Egypt from those used in contemporary America, there are many striking similarities in the kind of care lavished upon the dead. There, as here, the goal was to outmaneuver the Grim Reaper as far as possible.

The Egyptian method of embalming as described by Herodotus sounds like a rather crude exercise in human taxidermy. The entrails and brain were removed, the body scoured with palm wine and purified with spices. After being soaked for seventy days in a saline solution the corpse was washed and wrapped in strips of fine linen, then placed in a "wooden case of human shape" which in turn was put in a sepulchral chamber.

Restorative art was by no means unknown in ancient Egypt. The Greek historian Diodorus Siculus wrote: "Having treated (the corpse), they restore it to the relatives with every member of the body preserved so perfectly that even the eyelashes and eyebrows remain, the whole appearance of the body being unchangeable, and the cast of the features recognizable.... They present an example of a kind of inverted necromancy." The Egyptians had no Post Mortem Restoration Bra; instead they stuffed and modeled the breasts, refashioning the nipples from copper buttons. They fixed the body while still plastic in the desired attitude; they painted it with red ochre for men and yellow for women; they emphasized the details of the face with paint; they supplemented the natural hair with a wig; they tinted the nails with henna. A mummy of the XVIIIth Dynasty has even been found wearing some practical burial footwear — sandals made of mud, with metal soles and gilded straps.

Egyptian preoccupation with preservation of the body after death stemmed from the belief that the departed spirit would one day return to inhabit the earthly body; that if the body perished, the soul would eventually perish too. Yet although embalming was available to all who could pay the price, it was by no means so universally employed in ancient Egypt as it is today in the U.S.A. The ordinary peasant was not embalmed at all; yet, curiously enough, his corpse comes down to us through the ages as well preserved as those of his disemboweled and richly aromatic betters, for it has been established that the unusually dry climate and the absence of bacteria in the sand and air, rather than the materials used in embalming, are what account for the Egyptian mummies' marvelous state of preservation.

The Greeks, knowing the uses of both, were no more likely to occupy themselves with the preservation of dead flesh than they were to bury good wine for the comfort of dead bodies. They cremated their dead, for the most part, believing in the power of flame to set free the soul. The glorious period that conventional historians call the Golden Age of Greece is for historians of embalming the beginning of the Dark Ages.

The Jews frowned upon embalming, as did the early Christians, who regarded it as a pagan custom. Saint

Anthony, in the third century, denounced the practice as sinful. His impassioned plea, recorded by Athanasius, might well be echoed by the American of today who would like to avoid being transformed by the embalmer's art and displayed in a funeral home:

"And if your minds are set upon me, and ye remember me as a father, permit no man to take my body and carry it into Egypt, lest, according to the custom which they have, they embalm me and lay me up in their houses, for it was (to avoid) this that I came into this desert. And ye know that I have continually made exhortation concerning this thing and begged that it should not be done, and ye well know how much I have blamed those who observed this custom. Dig a grave then, and bury me therein, and hide my body under the earth, and let these my words be observed carefully by you, and tell ye no man where ye lay me...."

Mummification of the dead in Egypt was gradually abandoned after a large part of the population was converted to Christianity.

The eclipse of embalming was never quite total, however. The death of a monarch, since it is the occasion for a transfer of power, calls for demonstration, and it has throughout history been found politically expedient to provide visible evidence of death by exposing the body to public view. So embalming, of sorts, was used in Rome, and later throughout Europe, but only for the great and near-great, and by the very rich as a form of pretentiousness.

Alexander the Great is said to have been preserved in wax and honey; Charlemagne was embalmed and, dressed in imperial robes, placed in a sitting position in his tomb. Canute, too, was embalmed, and after him many an English monarch. Lord Nelson, as befits a hero, was returned to England from Trafalger in a barrel of brandy. Queen Elizabeth, by her own wish, was not embalmed. Developments beyond her control caused her sealed, lead-lined coffin to lie in Whitehall for an unconscionable thirty-four days before interment. During this time, reports one of the ladies-in-waiting who sat as watchers, the body "burst with such a crack that it splitted the wood, lead, and cerecloth; whereupon the next day she was fain to be new trimmed up."

Although embalming as a trade or cult was not resumed until this century, there prospered in every age charlatans and eccentrics who claimed to have rediscovered the lost art of the Egyptians or who offered new and improved pickling methods of their own invention. These were joined, in the eighteenth century, by French and English experimenters spurred by quite a different motive — the need for more efficient methods of preserving cadavers for anatomical studies.

The physicians, surgeons, chemists and apothecaries who engaged in anatomical research were from time to time sought out by private necrophiles who enlisted their services to preserve dead friends and relations. There are many examples of this curious practice of which perhaps the most interesting is the task performed by Dr. William Hunter, the celebrated eighteenth-century anatomist. Dr. Hunter was anyway something of a card. He once explained his aversion to contradiction by pointing out that, being accustomed to the "passive submission of dead bodies," he could no longer easily tolerate having his will crossed; a sentiment echoed by Evelyn Waugh's mortuary cosmetician: "I was just glad to serve people that couldn't talk back."

In 1775, Dr. Hunter and a colleague embalmed the wife of Martin Van Butchell, quack doctor and "super dentist," the point being that Mrs. Van Butchell's marriage settlement stipulated that her husband should have control of her fortune "as long as she remained above ground." The embalming was a great success. The "preserved lady" (as curious sightseers came to call her) was dressed in a fine linen gown, placed in a glass-topped case and kept in the drawing room, where Van Butchell introduced her to all comers as his "dear departed." So popular was the preserved lady that Van Butchell was obliged to insert a newspaper notice limiting her visiting hours to "any day between Nine and One, Sundays excepted." When Van Butchell remarried several years later, his new wife raised strong objections to the presence of the Dear Departed in her front parlor, and insisted upon her removal. Thereafter the Dear Departed was housed in the museum of the Royal College of Surgeons.*

The two widely divergent interests which spurred the early embalmers — scientific inquiry, and the fascination and financial reward of turning cadavers into a sort of ornamental keepsake — were to achieve a

---

* While on a recent visit to London, I applied to the Royal College of Surgeons of England for permission to see Mrs. Van Butchell. I received this reply from the officer of the curator: "While it is true that the late Mrs. Martin Van Butchell once occupied a place of honour in the historical collection of this college, it is regretted that she was finally cremated along with so much valuable material in the destruction of the College in May, 1941, at the height of the London blitz."

happy union under the guiding hand of a rare nineteenth-century character, "Dr." Thomas Holmes. He was the first to advance from what one funeral trade writer jocularly calls the "Glacier Age" — when preservation on ice was the undertakers' rule — and is often affectionately referred to by present-day funeral men as "the father of American embalming." Holmes was the first to popularize the idea of preserving the dead on a mass scale, and the first American to get rich from this novel occupation.

Holmes developed a passionate interest in cadavers early in life (it was in fact the reason for his expulsion from medical school; he was forever carelessly leaving them around in inappropriate places) and when the Civil War started, he saw his great opportunity. He rushed to the front and started embalming like mad, charging the families of the dead soldiers $100 for his labors. Some four years and 4,028 embalmed soldiers later (his own figure), Holmes returned to Brooklyn a rich man.

The "use for everyone of a casket that is attractive and protects the remains" (*attractive* seems an odd word here) is a new concept in this century, and one that took some ingenuity to put across. Surprisingly enough, even the widespread use of any sort of burial receptacle is a fairly new development in Western culture, dating back less than two hundred years. Until the eighteenth century few people except the very rich were buried in coffins. The "casket," and particularly the metal casket, is a phenomenon of modern America, unknown in past days and in other parts of the world.

As might be expected, with the development of industrial technique in the nineteenth century, coffin designers soared to marvelous heights. They experimented with glass, cement, celluloid, papier-mache, India rubber; they invented Rube Goldberg contraptions called "life signals" — complicated arrangements of wires and bells designed to set off an alarm if the occupant of the coffin should have been inadvertently buried alive.

The newfangled invention of metal coffins in the nineteenth century did not go unchallenged. An admonition on the subject was delivered by Lord Stowell, Judge of the Consistory Court of London, who in 1820 was called upon to decide a case felicitously titled Gilbert vs. Buzzard. At issue was the right to bury a corpse in a newly patented iron coffin. The church wardens protested that if parishioners were to get into the habit of burying their dead in coffins made proof against normal decay, in a few generations there would be no burial space left.

Said Lord Stowell, "The rule of law which says that a man has a right to be buried in his own churchyard is to be found, most certainly, in many of our authoritative text writers; but it is not quite so easy to find the rule which gives him the rights of burying a large chest or trunk in company with himself." He spoke approvingly of attempts to abolish the use of sepulchral chests "on the physical ground that the dissolution of bodies would be accelerated, and the dangerous virulence of the fermentation disarmed by a speedy absorption of the noxious particles into the surrounding soil."

The inexorable upward thrust towards perfection in metal caskets was not, however, destined to be halted by judicial logic. Just one hundred years after the decision in Gilbert vs. Buzzard, a triumph of the first magnitude was recorded by the D. H. Hill Casket Company of Chicago, and described in their 1920 *Catalogue of Funeral Merchandise:* "A STUDY IN BRONZE: When Robert Fulton said he could propel a boat by steam his friends were sure he was mentally deranged — that it could not be done. When Benjamin Franklin said he could draw electricity from the clouds his acquaintances thought he was crazy — that it could not be done. When our designing and manufacturing departments said they could and would produce a CAST BRONZE CASKET that would be the peer of anything yet developed, their friends and associates shook their heads sympathetically, feeling that it would be a hopeless task. All three visions have come to be realities — the steamboat, electricity, and the Hilco Peerless Cast Bronze Burial Receptacle."

The production of ever more solid and durable metal caskets has soared in this century, their long-lasting and even "eternal" qualities have become a matter of pride and self-congratulation throughout the industry — and this in one area of manufacture where built-in obsolescence might seem (as Lord Stowell pointed out) to present certain advantages. As we have seen, the sales of metal caskets now exceed sales of the old-fashioned wooden types. A brand new tradition has been established; how deep are the roots, Messrs. Habenstein and Lamers?

Mourning symbols have run the gamut. In medieval England and in colonial America, the skull and crossbones was the favored symbol, making its appearance on everything connected with death from

128

tombstone to funeral pall to coffinmaker's sign. Funerary extravagance took the form of elaborate mourning clothes, the hiring of mutes (or paid mourners), tremendous feasting sometimes of many days' duration, and gifts to the living, who were showered with rings, scarves, needlework, books and, most customarily, gloves.

Funeral flowers, today the major mourning symbol and a huge item of national expenditure, did not make their appearance in England or America until after the middle of the nineteenth century, and only then over the opposition of church leaders.

From colonial days until the nineteenth century, the American funeral was almost exclusively a family affair, in the sense that the family and close friends performed most of the duties in connection with the dead body itself. It was they who washed and laid out the body, draped it in a winding sheet, and ordered the coffin from the local carpenter. It was they who carried the coffin on foot from the home to the church and thence to the graveyard, and who frequently − unless the church sexton was available − dug the grave. Funeral services were held in the church over the pall-covered bier, and a brief committal prayer was said at the graveside. Between the death and the funeral, the body lay in the family parlor where the mourners took turns watching over it, the practical reason for this being the ever-present possibility that signs of life might be observed.

The first undertakers were drawn mainly from three occupations, all concerned with some aspect of burial: the livery stable keeper, who provided the hearse and funeral carriages, the carpenter or cabinetmaker who made the coffins, and the sexton, who was generally in charge of bell-tolling and grave-digging. In some of the larger cities midwives and nurses advertised their services as occupational layers out of the dead, and were so listed in city directories. The undertaker's job was primarily custodial. It included supplying the coffin from a catalogue or from his own establishment, arranging to bring folding chairs (if the service was to be held in the home, which was often the case), taking charge of the pall-bearers, supervising the removal of the coffin and loading it into the hearse, and in general doing the necessary chores until the body was finally lowered into the grave.

Shortly before the turn of the century, the undertaker conferred upon himself the title of "funeral director." From that time on, possibly inspired by his own semantics, he began to *direct funerals*, and quietly to impose a character of his own on the mode of disposal of the dead.

Some of the changes that were in store are foreshadowed in *The Modern Funeral* by W.P. Hohenschuh, published in 1900. Hohenschuh may have been the first to put into words a major assumption that lies behind modern funeral practices: "There is nothing too good for the dead," he declares. He goes on to advise, "The friends want the best that they can afford.... A number of manufacturers have set an excellent example by fitting up magnificent showrooms, to which funeral directors can take their customers, and show them the finest goods made. It is an education for all parties concerned.... It is to be commended." Hohenschuh's injunctions about funeral salesmanship, although vastly elaborated over the years, remain basic: "Boxes must be shown to sell them. By having an ordinary pine box next to one that is papered, the difference is more readily seen than could be explained, and a better price can be obtained for the latter." And on collections he warns, "Grief soon subsides, and the older the bill gets, the harder it is to collect."

In 1900 embalming was still the exception rather than the rule and was still generally done in the home − although Hohenschuh mentions a new trend making its appearance in California, that of taking the body to the funeral parlor after death for dressing and embalming. He proposes an ingenious approach to selling the public on embalming: "It may be suggested that bodies should be embalmed in winter as well as in summer. It may be a little difficult to have people accept this idea, but after having tried it a few times, and people realize the comfort to themselves in having the body in a warm room, this preventing them against colds, besides the sentimental feeling against having the body in a cold room, it is an easy matter to make the custom general." However, the most profitable aspect of the modern funeral − that of preparing the body for the public gaze − seems to have escaped this astute practitioner, for he opposes the open casket at the funeral service, and remarks, "There is no doubt that most people view the dead out of curiosity."

It was still a far cry from these early, hesitant steps of the emerging funeral industry to the full-fledged burlesque it has become.

THE COST OF DYING: A SOCIOLOGICAL ANALYSIS OF FUNERAL EXPENDITURES *

by

Vanderlyn R. Pine and Derek L. Phillips

Introduction

In the United States, as in all societies, death is met with culturally defined emotional reactions, ranging from resignation to hysteria. The deceased becomes the focal point for the attention of the bereaved, and the occurrence of death provides an occasion for socially conditioned grief reactions and mourning practices. Beginning with the initial psychological impact of loss, there are social and psychological forces that affect the bereaved and condition their responses to death.

Death, however, involves not only the bereaved family, but also has its impact on significant others of the dead and their relatives. As Blauner (1966) observes: "Since mortality tends to disrupt the on-going life of social groups and relationships, all societies must develop some forms of containing the impact." He then goes on to note (Blauner, 1966) that "mortuary institutions are addressed to the specific problems of the disposal of the dead and the rituals of transition from life to death." Funeral rites, which serve as one of the crucial *rites de passage,* attempt to give support not merely to the next-of-kin, but to the community as well (Blauner, 1966; Durkheim, 1961; Firth, 1964; Malinowski, 1948).

Although there have long been scholarly works assessing deaths and reactions to it, these have been primarily historical, religious, anthropological, and psychological in nature (Feifel, 1959; Habenstein and Lamers, 1960; Habenstein and Lamers, 1962; Iron, 1954; Jackson, 1957). Recently, however, several sociological investigations have been published (Fulton, 1965; Glaser and Strauss, 1968; Sudnow, 1967), and a new area of study is developing: namely, the Sociology of Death (Faunce and Fulton, 1958). In these studies, there have been three major approaches. First, several investigators have been concerned with the awareness of dying as a social phenomenon. This approach examines the social and psychological problems of terminally ill patients. Studies by Glaser and Strauss (1965a; 1968) and, more recently, by David Sudnow (1967) assess death from the viewpoint of the dying patient, his family, friends, doctors and nurses, and others with whom he must interact. Second, some sociologists have focused their attention on the functionaries of death, such as clergymen, funeral directors, cemetery administrators, and monument builders. This approach examines such things as the role conflict between clergymen and funeral directors (Fulton, 1961), and the public's orientation toward death and funerals (Fulton, 1963). Third, there have been studies approaching death from the perspective of reactions to the occurrence of death. Important here are the writings of Kephart (1950), the anthropologist Gorer (1965), and Pine (1969).

The results set forth in the present study come from an investigation utilizing the third of the above-mentioned approaches to the Sociology of Death. It follows Kephart's suggestion that the sociologist make use of certain neglected evidence for investigating specific reactions to death. In Kephart's words (1950:637): "... empirical evidence does exist—in the form of church records, burial records, cemetery files, and records kept by the funeral director, although it is difficult to gain access to these sources." Because the senior author of this study did have access to funeral records, we have been in a position to utilize figures on *funeral expenditures* as a possible indicator of reactions to death. As far as we can determine, this represents the first sociological investigation making use of such direct funerary information. However, we do not expect

* The preparation of this paper was partially facilitated by a National Institutes of Health Fellowship No. 1 F01 MH3812401A1 from the National Institute of Mental Health. We wish to express our appreciation to the following persons for their comments and assistance with this paper: James A. Davis, Eliot Freidson, Ronald Maris, Edmund D. Meyers, Michael Polich, Richard Quinney, Bernard E. Segal, and Robert Sokol.

* Reprinted by permission of the authors, Vanderlyn R. Pine and Derek L. Phillips. Published in Social Problems, Vol.17, No.3 (Winter 1970.)

that it will remain alone in the future, for, as Talcott Parsons (1963) has pointed out, a society's mortuary customs and practices are very obvious phenomena which merit attention for the light they may throw on many of the basic problems and values of that society.

We view funeral expenditures in the present investigation as one indicator of the bereaved's sentiments for the deceased. While other indicators connected with funeral rituals also exist—for example, amount of audible crying, number of pieces of flowers, number of friends in attendance at the funeral, the amount of time spent by the bereaved family in the presence of the corpse—there are obvious difficulties in the measurement and utilization of these potential indicators. Funeral expenditures, on the other hand, are not only intrinsically important to funeral directors who depend on the income produced by funerals for their livelihood, but they also present an economic problem to *all* potential purchasers. As a social phenomenon, the large monetary exchange between the bereaved public and funeral directors is an important factor in understanding the American way of death (Mitford, 1963).

In the present study of funeral practices in a contemporary small town, there are a number of other reasons for utilizing funeral expenditures as a measure. First, accurate dollar sales figures *are available* in funeral home records. Second, these expenditures provide a monetary measurement which is common to almost all American funerals, enabling possible future comparisons. Third, in a consumption-conscious society like our own, the way in which people spend their money is associated with such social factors as status, power, and success (Barber, 1957; Kahl, 1966; Lenski, 1966). In light of these social factors, expenditure patterns may offer insights into other social behavior, attitudes, and beliefs. Fourth, there is a common belief in our society that the worth of something is commensurate with its cost. This equates the funeral with other purchases, the implication being that "you get what you pay for."

In our view, the most important single influence upon the magnitude of funeral expenditures is people's location within the status hierarchy of the community in which they live. Especially in small towns, an individual's social status is an important determinant of his beliefs, behavior, and general style of life (Gerth and Mills, 1958; Hollingshead, 1949; Veblen, 1934; Warner, 1960). It also seems likely that his social status strongly affects his reactions to death—including the amount of money he spends on funerals.

One reason for expecting higher status persons to have larger funeral expenditures is rather obvious: They simply have more money available to them. But it also seems true that the manner in which people spend their money is an important criterion for the subjective assessment of status within a community. Veblen (1934:84) emphasized this point more than sixty years ago when he wrote: "The basis on which good repute in any highly organized industrial community ultimately rests is pecuniary strength; and the means of showing pecuniary strength, and so of gaining or retaining a good name, are leisure and a conspicuous consumption of goods." Hence, we expect social status to strongly influence the amount of money which people spend on funerals, in that these expenditures reflect both the availability of money and the common effort of the bereaved to *maintain* status after the death of a family member. Social status is operative throughout life, and its power does not necessarily diminish upon death (Glaser and Strauss, 1965b; Kephart, 1950).

Clearly, however, social status does not exist in isolation from other factors which may also affect funeral expenditure patterns. Even among people of similar social status, the amount of money spent for funerals will be influenced by their sexual status, their ages, their relation to the deceased, and whether or not the death was expected. Thus, systematic data were collected with regard to these factors as well. This means that in our analysis, the effects of each of these additional variables can be examined together with social status for its influence upon funeral expenditures.

Community Description and Data-Collection Techniques

This investigation was conducted in "Collegetown," a small town located in the northeast within a 100 mile radius of a large metropolitan center. Excluding college students, the community's population is approximately 7,000. The work force is employed in a variety of occupations, scattered throughout the town and in surrounding cities. There is no major local industry acting as an important primary source of employment, although the local college—a former teachers' college which is now a liberal arts institution with a student body of 4,000 undergraduates—employs a fairly large number of local residents. Incomes span a wide range, with an annual average of about $7,000. The town contains no enclaves or ghettoes, apparently because there has never been a large local industry to attract recent immigrants.

The analysis presented here is based on data from 351 adult funerals conducted by the Collegetown Funeral Service during the five years 1961-1965, inclusive. The data were collected through a variety of methods by the first-named author, a community resident, who operates the town's only funeral business. These methods include: participant observation; utilization of information from death certificates and burial permits maintained by the state department of health and by local registrars; examination of the local news media, with a special focus on obituaries; interviews with local citizens; and the analysis of funeral home business records.

By employing these multiple methods, we were able to obtain data pertaining to the variables under consideration in this report: social status, sex, age, relation to the deceased of the arranger, whether or not death was expected, and funeral expenditures. Measurement of most of these variables is obvious, but it is necessary to briefly discuss our measure of social status. To place people in the appropriate status positions, we used Warner's (1960) Index of Status Characteristics (I.S.C.), an index based on occupation, source of income, education, and house type. These factors were weighted and combined (Warner, 1960), thus providing an index score for each family within the funeral sample and allowing for the placement of each arranger in the status hierarchy of Collegetown.[1]

As was noted earlier, funeral expenditure is considered here to be an indicator of the culturally defined contemporary reaction to death (Kephart, 1950; Warner, 1965). Further, this monetary measure is useful because money is the common denominator for styles of death in America. Since we contend that the relative status position of a family in Collegetown affects its responses to death as indicated by funeral expenditures, it seems advisable to explain some of the various funeral practices, customs, and patterns in Collegetown.

There are regional disparities between funerals and funeral customs, and, therefore, the following comments are true specifically for Collegetown. They may or may not be true for other small town situations. In Collegetown, the range of available funerals is from $250.00 to $1925.00. The notable exceptions to the $250 minimum involve funeral services of infants, children, and adolescents. These exceptions are not analyzed in the present study because in practice only actual cash expenditures are charged to these families, and the funeral bills are usually very small. For the period 1961-1965 the median funeral expenditure was $753.00. This amount is based on the charges made by the Collegetown Funeral Service, and includes the casket, facilities, equipment, and professional services. The main cost differential between funeral services is determined by the casket selected, of which the least expensive is a rectangular pine box, and the most expensive a solid cast-bronze sarcophagus. However, the most often used type is fashioned of wood or metal, has a rounded lid, full-length handles, and a lined interior.

Upon the death of an individual, the surviving relatives usually contact the funeral home directly and arrange to have the body removed from the place of death to the funeral home. The arranger of the funeral and the funeral director then meet to discuss and decide on the course of the funeral. It is the financial consequences of that encounter which are the major concerns of this report.

Findings

The results in Table 1 show a generally positive relationship between people's position in the status hierarchy and their expenditures for funerals. We see that the smallest percentage of high spenders is in the lower status group where only 18.4 percent spend $800 or more on funeral expenditures.[2] There is a sharp

[1]Our status categories are the same as Warner's except that we combine the Lower- and Upper-Middle into a "Middle Status" group, and what he calls Upper-Lower is herein termed "Working Status" while what he calls Lower-Lower is termed "Lower Status."

[2]Using median expenditures as a measure, results in the same patterns seen in Table 1 and the tables that follow. We chose to utilize the percentage with "high expenditures" because it facilitates the presentation and discussion of our results.

increase to 43.5 percent in the expenditures of the working status, and then a further increase to 56.1 percent among middle status persons. The percentage of people with high expenditures then levels off in the upper status group. It may appear somewhat surprising that those at the upper status level do not spend more than those at the middle level. But, clearly, for most members of the upper status group, expenditures for anything are not usually a matter of the ability to pay. Furthermore, the upper status is traditionally accorded a certain freedom to behave in generally self-fulfilling ways, and they are not expected to conform completely to social conventions. Thus, it appears likely that those at the upper status level select their funeral purchases to please themselves, rather than to try to impress an already impressed Collegetown community.

TABLE 1
Social Status and Funeral Expenditures

Social Status

	Lower (N = 38)	Working (N = 124)	Middle (N = 164)	Upper (N = 25)	Total (N = 351)
Percent Spending Over $800	18.4	43.5	56.1	56.0	48.0

Table 2 allows us to examine the effects of the funeral arranger's sex on expenditures, within different status groups. The first thing to be noted is that women spend more than men at every status level. There seem to be several possible reasons for these disparities between men and women. For one thing, women apparently lack knowledge about realistic funeral costs. Fulton (1961) found that females imagine funerals to cost much less than they actually do, while males estimated funeral costs with great accuracy. Although women may have less idea of what funerals really cost, when they are confronted with making an economic decision about the funeral arrangements, they tend to select more expensive services—a result, perhaps, of their more general lack of familiarity with the values of large commodities (e.g., automobiles, homes, etc.) which they seldom purchase on their own. A second possible reason for larger expenditures among women is that, more often than men, they are the recipients of sizeable insurance benefits. Upon the death of a male family member, there is more often an insurance payment or a pension plan which the survivors may use than when a female

TABLE 2
Funeral Expenditures: By Social Status and Sex
(Percent Spending Over $800)

Social Status

Sex	Lower	Working	Middle	Upper	Total
Men	5.8 (17)	42.5 (54)	47.6 (63)	40.0 (10)	40.3 (144)
Women	28.5 (21)	47.1 (70)	61.3 (101)	66.7 (15)	53.1 (207)

dies. Another possibility is that social norms condition females to be somewhat more emotionally responsive to situations involving the feelings (Krech and Crutchfield, 1964; Parsons and Bales, 1955), and this may contribute to their higher funeral expenditures. Men may feel constrained to display less visible emotional reactions to death. If so, the masculine value of stoic acceptance of death may operate on the economic as well as on the psychological level. Finally, women are perhaps more apt than men to emphasize conspicuous consumption, attempting to impress their friends and relatives with their funeral purchases. Whatever the explanation, it is clear that a larger percentage of women than men have high funeral expenditures in Collegetown.

A second point of interest in Table 2 concerns the relationship between social status and expenditures. Among women there is an increase in expenditures with higher status, while among men, there is an increase from lower to working status and then a general leveling off in the percentage of persons spending over $800 on a funeral. Our final observation about Table 2 concerns the very marked joint effects of social status and sex on the amount spent for funerals. Only 5.8 percent of lower status males spend more than $800, compared to two-thirds of upper status females. While both status and sex exercise strong independent effects on expenditures, the influence of status is considerably greater than that of sex.

Table 3 indicates that the relation between social status and funeral expenses is maintained within the group of persons 50 years of age and under; there is a progressive pattern of increase in expenditures as one moves across the table from left to right. Among older people, however, we find an increase up through the middle status group and then a decline from those of upper status.

TABLE 3
Funeral Expenditures: By Social Status and Age
(Percent Spending Over $800)

Social Status

Age	Lower	Working	Middle	Upper	Total
under 51	7.1	37.2	47.2	55.6	40.5
	(14)	(43)	(72)	(9)	(138)
51 plus	25.0	48.2	64.1	56.3	52.0
	(24)	(81)	(92)	(16)	(213)

We also see that the findings in Table 3 show that, at each status level, expenditures are higher among older than younger persons. This pattern may be partially due to a greater availability of money for funeral expenses among older people, for longer tenure in the work force generally means greater accumulation of economic resources to be utilized for funerals. This does not imply that older persons are better off financially than younger ones, but rather that they have superior access to funds such as saving accounts and, especially, life insurance. Older persons also spend more time under the influence of community norms and have greater exposure to the funeral customs of Collegetown which emphasizes the importance of a "decent" funeral. The lack of disparity in expenditures in age at the upper status level may reflect a lack of desire, and need, to display financial ability among older individuals. Perhaps as tenure and position increase, the general upper status tradition of less required conformity helps older persons of upper status to select less expensive funerals.

Like sex, then, age plays a role in determining how much people spend on funerals in Collegetown. And like sex, age exercises strong joint effects with status on funeral costs. While age shows an independent influence on the amount spent for funerals, it is much less than the independent influence of status level.

The association between expenditures and the arranger's relationship to the deceased can be examined in Table 4. First, we should note that the direct relation between status level and funeral costs exists for persons arranging the funeral of some relative other than their spouse. For those arranging their spouse's funerals, however, there is an increase in the percentage spending over $800 from lower through middle status and then a very sharp decline in the upper status group. We will discuss this finding after we deal with the association between people's relationship to the deceased and their funeral expenses.

It can be seen in Table 4 that the upper status group is the only one in which spouses have a lower percentage of expenditures over $800 than other relatives. In the other three groups, spouses have higher

TABLE 4
Funeral Expenditures: By Social Status and Relationship
To The Deceased
(Percent Spending Over $800)

Social Status

Relationship	Lower	Working	Middle	Upper	Total
Spouse	29.4	50.7	72.5	53.8	56.0
	(17)	(69)	(51)	(13)	(150)
Non-Spouse	9.4	38.1	48.6	58.3	42.0
	(21)	(55)	(113)	(12)	(201)

expenditures than others. It may be, as Firth (1964) and Lindeman (1965) have suggested, that death involving a spouse will be associated with more intense reactions of all kinds than is the case with another family member. Thus funeral expenditures may reflect greater grief reactions associated with the loss of a spouse. The close ties between husband and wife in our society contribute to a tendency for marital partners to spend more on one another for all commodities or services of a sentimental nature. This is evident in anniversary, birthday, and other similar occasions that are usually commemorated by gifts and other financial expenditures. We believe that the effects of this sentimentality play an important part in determining the higher funeral expenditures among most spouses in Collegetown. High affectivity seems to be at work in the lower, working, and middle status groups, although not at upper status level. A possible explanation for this is that the spouses in the upper status group feel less social pressure to prove their affection by material purchases, especially considering that their inherent ability to do so is well-known in the Collegetown community. This same explanation may help to account for the very high percentage of middle status spouses who spend over $800 on funerals. They may feel constrained by the traditions of the community to show that they really care by spending a large amount upon the death of a spouse. Less secure in their status position, their conspicuous consumption more often exceeds that of individuals at the upper status level.

As with the other variables, there are fairly strong joint effects on funeral costs exercised by status and relationship to the deceased. Once again, social status has more independent influence than the other variable on funeral expenditures.

In the final table in this report we can view the association between expectancy of death and expenditures. We can also continue examination of the stability of the relation between status level and funeral spending. Looking at this relationship first, we find that in situations where death was expected, expenditures increase with higher status until the middle status level and then remain virtually the same among upper status

TABLE 5
Funeral Expenditures: By Social Status and Mode of Death
(Percent Spending Over $800)

Social Status

Mode of Death	Lower	Working	Middle	Upper	Total
Expected	12.5	38.8	56.1	55.5	45.5
	(26)	(90)	(114)	(18)	(248)
Unexpected	25.0	61.7	56.0	57.1	54.3
	(12)	(34)	(50)	(7)	(103)

individuals. But in cases of unexpected death, there is no clear pattern. The percentage spending over $800 is smallest in the lower status group and largest at the working status level, with the other two groups having intermediate funeral expenditures. These findings will be discussed shortly.

Considering now the relationship between the mode of death and funeral expenses, it can be seen that expenditures are higher with unexpected than expected deaths. But at the lower and working status levels mode of death has no apparent influence on expenditures among middle and upper status persons.

At least in the two lower status groups, it may be that guilt is an important factor in the larger expenditures for unexpected deaths. In their discussion of people's "awareness of dying," Glaser and Strauss (1965a) imply that the expectation of death is relevant to the next-of-kin not only while the patient is dying, but also the preparations of those *about to be* bereaved play a key role in determining reactions to death. When death is not anticipated, people do not have the opportunity to complete their obligations to the deceased. These deaths "remind the survivors of the social and psychological debts they have incurred toward him—debts that they may have been intending to pay in the coins of attention, affection, care, appreciation, or achievement" (Blauner, 1966). Hence, larger funeral expenditures may often indicate a desire to "make up for" some of these debts. Perhaps in the middle and upper statuses, with their greater educational attainment and more psychological orientation toward life, there is a more "rational" appraisal of their own feelings of guilt toward the unexpectedly departed. Consequently, they do not differ in their funeral spending from those persons of similar status who are prepared for the death of a loved one. This same reasoning may help account for the finding, mentioned earlier, that there is a larger percentage of high expenditures for unexpected deaths within the working status group than in the other status categories. While lower class persons may feel equally guilty, they are less able than working status people to be able to afford expensive funerals. And middle and upper status persons, while better able than the working status group to afford large expenditures, are less likely to allow their feelings of guilt to influence their funeral spending.

Furthermore, extensive illness may deplete available cash reserves in the lower and working status groups, thus suggesting that expected deaths resulting from long illnesses are more likely to be associated with lower expenditures for these persons. In addition, if the sudden and unexpected death is accidental, there may be double indemnity life insurance available, thereby allowing greater freedom of expenditure at all status levels. This may help account for the rather large differences in expenditures among those who did and did not expect death at the working and lower status level as compared to the relative lack of difference at higher status levels.

Since each of the variables examined in this report has had at least some independent influence on funeral expenditures, the obvious next step in the analysis would be to look at the joint effects of three or more variables at a time as they affect funeral costs. But the relatively small size of the funeral population in Collegetown results in many cells with fewer than ten cases. Therefore, these results are not presented here. We should note, however, that our analysis of several four-variable tables revealed patterns generally in line with the findings presented in the previous pages. Each of the variables (social status, sex, age, relation to the deceased, and mode of death) continued to exercise some independent influence on funeral expenditures, while social status consistently had more influence than the other factors examined.

Discussion

Social observers have long recognized the functions of funeral rites and practices (Durkheim, 1961; Firth, 1964; Malinowski, 1948). While funerals are created by death, they are *regulated* by social factors. This is because, as was noted earlier, the problems of death are not solely individual but have broad social consequences as well. Malinowski (1948:53) recognized this when he observed that:

[death]...threatens the very cohesion and solidarity of the group... [and the funeral] counteracts the centrifugal forces of fear, dismay, demoralization, and provides the most powerful means of reintegration of the group's shaken solidarity and of re-establishment.

It is in the funeral that death reactions become visible in most societies. Funeral rites allow the bereaved to pass through the difficult period of adjustment following death with a defined social role, delimit the period of mourning, allow the bereaved to release grief emotions publicly, and aim at helping to commemorate an individual's passing. These rites provide occasion for group assembly, reaffirm social values, and allow for relief from the guilt that is often part of bereavement. As Firth (1964:63) explains, "A funeral rite is a social rite *par excellence.* Its ostensible object is the dead person, but it benefits not the dead, but the living." Firth (1965:63-64) describes some important aspects of the funeral: First, there is "the resolution of uncertainties in the behavior of the immediate kin, by providing social support in the form of 'funeral ritual.'" Second, there is "the fulfillment of social sequence, [by] stressing the dead, they emphasize the value of the services of the living." And, third, there is "the social importance of the economic aspect ... [which] is not incidental ... [for] every funeral means expenditure."

The present study has focused on the third element mentioned by Firth: funeral expenditures. These expenditures represent an effort by the bereaved to express in a concrete, material way their sentiments for the dead (Firth,1964), for funeral expenditures are one tangible evidence of the style of death in America. Social demands made of funeral directors, plus their own efforts to enhance the position of their occupational group, have made certain costly factors part of the American style of death. These costly items include such things as well-appointed funeral homes, modern equipment, and efficient professional services. Such items are generally expensive to provide, but are commonly sought by the bereaved public. The present style of death, as indicated by these services and facilities, emphasizes the continuing trend toward funeral practices of a more secular nature.

In American society, it is clear that the handling of illness and death are increasingly the responsibility of institutions other than the family. At the same time, and partially as a result of the same social forces, death is something that comes primarily to the very old (United Nations, 1961). The general elimination of infant and child mortality and greater control over the diseases of adolescence and middle life work to concentrate death in the ranks of the elderly. There is also a general absence of *direct* contact in American life with deaths resulting from war. Taken together, these facts result in the average person having very little exposure to death and its consequences. Blauner (1966:388) has estimated that "... most people during the first 40 (or even 50) years of life attend only one or two funerals a decade." Clearly, then, most Americans have little experience with death.

Once death does occur, however, Americans turn the death-related activities over to a funeral director. The utilization of a funeral director at the time of death is accounted for by several factors: legal requirements pertaining to the disposal of the dead (Habenstein and Lamers, 1960); the desire of the family and community to have someone else assume the task of getting rid of the corpse which, as Blauner (1966) has observed, tends to produce fear, generalized anxiety, and disgust (Goody, 1966; Malinowski, 1948); bureaucratization which has increasingly removed social functions from the family to specialized institutions; and, as a consequence of bureaucratization, the creation of an occupational group for the sole purpose of handling the final disposition of the deceased (Habenstein, 1962).

Accompanying the diminished presence of death in our society and the increased utilization of funeral experts are diminishing ceremonial observances for the dead. We no longer have the Victorian ceremonial of black-edged invitation cards. Mourning dress is almost a thing of the past. There is less formal cancellation of social engagements for a predetermined period. Visits to the house of mourning and the respectful viewing of the body have declined. Participation in funerals is increasingly restricted to family members and friends rather than involving the larger community. Consequently, family members must shoulder a greater emotional burden than in the past. Funeral ceremonies are of shorter duration and involve considerably less religious ritual than they once did. There is less and less acceptance of the reality of life after death (Glock and Stark, 1960), so that the bereaved can no longer comfort themselves with thoughts about the rewards coming to the deceased in an after-life. In short, religious and ceremonial responses to death have lost significance in American society.

But at the same time that death has become less disruptive and important (Goffman, 1966) to the society, its prospects and consequences have become more serious for the bereaved individual. For with all of these societal changes, one fact remains the same: most people will, sooner or later, experience death's presence as it removes from them a loved one — a spouse, parent, child, other relative, or friend. What this means for the bereaved is that, as Blauner puts it (1966): "He experiences grief less frequently, but more intensely, since his emotional involvements are not diffused over an entire community, but are usually concentrated on one or a few people."

It may be that for those who have, to a great extent, abandoned a religious outlook in favor of a secular one, the act of buying, receiving, and paying for funerals represents a *secular and economic ritual of payment formerly performed by more religious customs and ceremonies.* If expenditures are viewed as a secular ritual, then money spent for funerals is serving a far different need than one of mere exchange of cash between two agents: the funeral purchaser and the funeral producer. While Mitford (1963) sees funeral expenditures as largely an exploitation of the public by funeral directors, it may be that the bereaved funeral purchasers utilize their expenditures for funerals in a manner that is beneficial in their emotional confrontation of death. Should this be the case, funeral expenditures may benefit not only the funeral director but the bereaved as well. Some evidence for this view is found in Pine's (1969) cross-cultural analysis of funeral practices. He found that funeral expenditures by the bereaved seem to be a common element in all societies. For instance, in Russia, where funeral expenses are largely the province of the state, bereaved families still engage in funeral expenditures of their own for memorialization in cemeteries. Even though the funeral arrangements provided by the state are fully adequate for the final disposition of the deceased, there appears to be a desire on the part of many Russian families to assume additional expenses on their own.

Our view is that *because* people increasingly lack both the ceremonial and social mechanisms and arrangements that once existed to help them cope with death, monetary expenditures have taken on added importance as a means for allowing the bereaved to express (both to themselves and others) their sentiments for the deceased. For with so few modes of expression remaining to the bereaved, funeral expenditures serve as evidence of their concern for both the dead and the conventional standards of decency in their community of residence.

REFERENCES

Barber, Bernard
1957 Social Stratification. New York: Harcourt, Brace & World.

Blauner, Robert
1966 "Death and social structure." Psychiatry 29:278-294.

Durkheim, Emile
1961 The Elementary Forms of the Religious Life. New York: Collier Books.

Faunce, William A., and Robert L. Fulton
1958 "The sociology of death: A neglected area of research." Social Forces 36 (March):205-209.

Feifel, Herman (ed.)
1959 The Meaning of Death. New York: McGraw-Hill.

Firth, Raymond
1964 Elements of Social Organization. Boston: Beacon Press.

Fulton, Robert L.
1961 "The clergyman and the funeral director: A study in role conflict." Social Forces 39 (May).
1963 The Sacred and the Secular: Attitudes of the American Public Toward Death. Milwaukee: Bulfin Press.
1965 Death and Identity. New York: John Wiley.

Gerth, Hans H., and C. Wright Mills
1958 From Max Weber: Essays in Sociology. New York: Oxford University Press.

Glaser, Barney G., and Anselm Strauss
1965a Awareness of Dying. Chicago: Aldine Publishing Co.
1965b "Temporal aspects of dying as a non-scheduled status passage." American Journal of Sociology 71 (July):48-59.
1968 Time for Dying. Chicago: Aldine Publishing Co.

Glock, Charles Y., and Rodney Stark
1965 "Is there an American Protestantism?" Transaction 3(November-December):8-13.

Goffman, Irwin W.
1966 "Suicide motives and categorization of the living and dead in the United States." Unpublished manuscript.

Goody, Jack
1962 Death, Property and the Ancestors. Stanford: Stanford University Press.

Gorer, Geoffrey
1965 Death, Grief, and Mourning. New York: Doubleday.

Habenstein, Robert W., and William M. Lamers
1960 Funeral Customs the World Over. Milwaukee: Bulfin Press.
1962 The History of American Funeral Directors. Milwaukee: Bulfin Press.

Hollingshead, August B.
  1949 Elmtown's Youth. New York:
       John Wiley.
Iron, Paul E.
  1954 The Funeral and the Mourners.
       New York: Abingdon Press.
Jackson, Edgar N.
  1957 Understanding Grief. New York:
       Abingdon Press.
Kahl, Joseph A.
  1966 The American Class Structure.
       New York: Holt, Rinehart, and
       Winston.
Kephart, William M.
  1950 "Status after death." American
       Sociological Review 15 (October):
       635-643.
Krech, David and Richard S. Crutchfield
  1962 Individual in Society. New York:
       McGraw-Hill.
Lenski, Gerhard E.
  1966 Power and Privilege. New York:
       McGraw-Hill.
Lindemann, Erich
  1965 "Symptomatology and management
       of acute grief." In Robert
       L. Fulton (ed.), Death and
       Identity. New York: John Wiley.
Malinowski, Bronislaw
  1948 Magic, Science and Religion. New
       York: Doubleday.

Mitford, Jessica
  1963 The American Way of Death.
       New York: Simon and Schuster.
Parsons, Talcott and Robert F. Bales
  1955 Family, Socialization and Interaction
       Process. Glencoe: The Free
       Press.
Parsons, Talcott
  1963 "Death in American society – a
       brief working paper." The American
       Behavior Scientist 6 (May):
       61-65.
Pine, Vanderlyn R.
  1969 "Comparative funeral practices,"
       Practical Anthropology 16 (March-April):
       49-62.
Sudnow, David
  1967 Passing On. Englewood Cliffs:
       Prentice-Hall.
United Nations
  1961 Demographic Workbook. New
       York: Department of Economic
       and Social Affairs.
Veblen, Thorstein
  1934 The Theory of the Leisure Class.
       New York: Random House.
Warner, W. Lloyd
  1960 Social Class in America. New
       York: Harper Torchbacks.
  1965 The Living and the Dead. New
       Haven: Yale University Press.

A DEATH IN THE FAMILY   *

by

James Agee

Chapter 18

When grief and shock surpass endurance there occur phases of exhaustion, of anesthesia in which relatively little is felt and one has the illusion of recognizing, and understanding, a good deal. Throughout these days Mary had, during these breathing spells, drawn a kind of solace from the recurrent thought: at least I am enduring it. I am aware of what has happened, I am meeting it face to face, I am living through it. There had been, even, a kind of pride, a desolate kind of pleasure, in the feeling: I am carrying a heavier weight than I could have dreamed it possible for a human being to carry, yet I am living through it. It had of course occurred to her that this happens to many people, that it is very common, and she humbled and comforted herself in this thought. She thought: this is simply what living is; I never realized before what it is. She thought: now I am more nearly a grown member of the human race; bearing children, which had seemed so much, was just so much apprenticeship. She thought that she had never before had a chance to realize the strength that human beings have, to endure; she loved and revered all those who had ever suffered, even those who had failed to endure. She thought that she had never before had a chance to realize the might, grimness and tenderness of God. She thought that now for the first time she began to know herself, and she gained extraordinary hope in this beginning of knowledge. She thought that she had grown up almost overnight. She thought that she had realized all that was in her soul to realize in the event, and when at length the time came to put on her veil, leave the bedroom she had shared with her husband, leave their home, and go down to see him for the first time since his death and to see the long day through, which would cover him out of sight for the duration of this world, she thought that she was firm and ready. She had refused to "try on" her veil; the mere thought of approving or disapproving it before a mirror was obscene; so now when she came to the mirror and drew it down across her face to go, she saw herself for the first time since her husband's death. Without either desiring to see her face, or caring how it looked, she saw that it had changed; through the deep, clear veil her gray eyes watched her gray eyes watch her through the deep, clear veil. I must have fever, she thought, startled by their brightness; and turned away. It was when she came to the door, to walk through it, to leave this room and to leave this shape of existence forever, that realizations poured upon and overwhelmed her through which, in retrospect, she would one day know that all that had gone before, all that she had thought she experienced and knew—true, more or less, though it all was—was nothing to this. The realization came without shape or definability, save as it was focused in the pure physical act of leaving the room, but came with such force, such monstrous piercing weight, in all her heart and soul and mind and body but above all in the womb, where it arrived and dwelt like a cold and prodigious, spreading stone, that she groaned almost inaudibly, almost a mere silent breath, an *Ohhhhhhh*, and doubled deeply over, hands to her belly, and her knee joints melted.

Hannah, smaller than she, caught her, and rapped out, *"Close that door!"* It would be a long time before either of the women realized their resentment of the priest and their contempt for him, and their compassion, for staying in the room. Now they did not even know that he was there. Hannah helped her to the edge of the bed and sat beside her exclaiming, over and over, in a heartbroken voice, "Mary, Mary, Mary, Mary. Oh Mary, Mary, Mary," resting one already translucent, spinster's hand lightly upon the back of her veiled head, and with the other, so clenching one of Mary's wrists that she left a bracelet of bruise.

Mary meanwhile rocked quietly backward and forward, and from side to side, groaning, quietly, from the depths of her body, not like a human creature but a fatally hurt animal; sounds low, almost crooned, not strident, but shapeless and orderless, the sisters, except in their quietude, to those transcendent, idiot, bellowing screams which deliver children. And as she rocked and groaned, the realization gradually lost its fullest, most impaling concentr...on: there took shape, from its utter darkness, like the slow emergence of the countryside into first daylight, all those separate realizations which could be resolved into images, emotions, thought, words, obligations: so that after not more than a couple of minutes, during which Hannah never ceased to say to her, "Mary, Mary," and Father Jackson, his eyes closed, prayed, she sat still for not more than a moment more, made the sign of the Cross, stood up, and said, "I'm ready now."

But she swayed; Hannah said, "Rest, Mary. There's no hurry," and Father Jackson said, "Perhaps you should lie down a little while;" but she said, "No; thank you: I want to go now," and walked unsteadily to the door, and opened it, and walked through.

Father Jackson took her arm, in the top hallway. Although she tried not to, she leaned on him very heavily.

"Come, now," their mother whispered, and, taking them each by the hand, led them through the Green Room and into the living room.

There it was, against the fireplace, and there seemed to be scarcely anything else in the room except the sunny light on the floor.

It was very long and dark; smooth like a boat; with bright handles. Half the top was open. There was a strange, sweet smell, so faint that it could scarcely be realized.

Rufus had never known such stillness. Their little sounds, as they approached his father, vanished upon it like the infinitesimal whisperings of snow, falling on open water.

There was his head, his arms; suit: there he was.

Rufus had never seen him so indifferent; and the instant he saw him, he knew that he would never see him otherwise. He had his look of faint impatience, the chin strained a little upward, as if he were concealing his objection to a collar which was too tight and too formal. And in this slight urgency of the chin; in the small trendings of a frown which stayed in the skin; in the arch of the nose; and in the still, strong mouth, there was a look of pride. But most of all, there was indifference; and through this indifference which held him in every particle of his being — an indifference which would have rejected them; have sent them away, except that it was too indifferent even to care whether they went or stayed — in this self-completedness which nothing could touch, there was something else, some other feeling which he gave, which there was no identifying even by feeling, for Rufus had never experienced this feeling before; there was perfected beauty. The head, the hand, dwelt in completion, immutable, indestructible: motionless. They moved upon existence quietly as stones which withdraw through water for which there is no floor.

The arm was bent. Out of the dark suit, the starched cuff, sprang the hairy wrist.

The wrist was angled; the hand was arched; none of the fingers touched each other.

The hand was so composed that it seemed at once casual and majestic. It stood exactly above the center of his body.

The fingers looked unusually clean and dry, as if they had been scrubbed with great care.

The hand looked very strong, and the veins were strong in it.

The nostrils were very dark, yet he thought he could see, in one of them, something which looked like cotton.

On the lower lip, a trifle to the left of its middle, there was a small blue line which ran also a little below the lip.

At the exact point of the chin, there was another small blue mark, as straight and neat as might be drawn with a pencil and scarcely wider.

The lines which formed the wings of the nose and the mouth were almost gone.

The hair was most carefully brushed.

The eyes were casually and quietly closed, the eyelids were like silk on the balls, and when Rufus glanced quickly from the eyes to the mouth it seemed as if his father were almost about to smile. Yet the mouth carried no suggestion either of smiling or of gravity; only strength, silence, manhood, and indifferent contentment.

He saw him much more clearly than he had ever seen him before; yet his face looked unreal, as if he had just been shaved by a barber. The whole head was waxen, and the hand, too, was as if perfectly made of wax.

The head was lifted on a small white satin pillow.

There was the subtle, curious odor, like fresh hay, and like a hospital, but not quite like either, and so faint that it was scarcely possible to be sure that it existed.

Rufus saw these things within a few seconds, and became aware that his mother was picking Catherine up in order that she might see more clearly; he drew a little aside. Out of the end of his eye he was faintly aware of his sister's rosy face and he could hear her gentle breathing as he continued to stare at his father, at his stillness, and his power, and his beauty.

He could see the tiny dark point of every shaven hair of the beard.

He watched the way the flesh was chiseled in a widening trough from the root of the nose to the white edge of the lip.

He watched the still more delicate dent beneath the lower lip.

It became strange, and restive, that it was possible for anyone to lie so still for so long; yet he knew that his father would never move again; yet this knowledge made his motionlessness no less strange.

Within him, and outside him, everything except his father was dry, light, unreal, and touched with a kind of warmth and impulse and a kind of sweetness which felt like the beating of a heart. But borne within this strange and unreal sweetness, its center yet alien in nature from all the rest, and as nothing else was actual, his father lay graven, whose noble hand he longed, in shyness, to touch.

"Now, Rufus," his mother whispered; they knelt. He could just see over the edge of the coffin. He gazed at the perfect hand.

His mother's arm came round him; he felt her hand on the crest of his shoulder. He slid his arm around her and felt her hand become alive on his shoulder and felt his sister's arm. He touched her bare arm tenderly, and felt her hand grapple for and take his arm. He put his hand around her arm and felt how little it was. He could feel a vein beating against the bone, just below her armpit.

"Our Father," she said.

They joined her, Catherine waiting for those words of which she was sure, Rufus lowering his voice almost to silence while she hesitated, trying to give her the words distinctly. Their mother spoke very gently.

"Our Father, Who art in Heaven, hallowed be Thy name; Thy kingdom come, Thy—"

"Thy will be d..." Rufus went on, alone; then waited, disconcerted.

"Thy will be done," his mother said. "On earth," she continued, with some strange shading of the word which touched him with awe and sadness; "As it is in heaven."

"Give us this d..."

Rufus was more careful this time.

"Daily bread," Catherine said confidently.

"Give us this day our daily bread," and in those words still more, he felt that his mother meant something quite otherwise, "And forgive us our trespasses as we forgive those who trespass against us.

"And lead us not into temptation; but deliver us from evil," and here their mother left her hands where they dwelt with her children, but bowed her head:

"For Thine is the kingdom, and the power, and the glory," she said with almost vindictive certitude, "forever and ever. Amen."

She was silent for some moments, and still he stared at the hand.

"God, bless us and help us all," she said. "God, help us to understand Thee. God, help us to know Thy will. God, help us to put all our trust in Thee, whether we can understand or not.

"God, help these little children to remember their father in all his goodness and strength and kindness and dearness, and in all of his tremendous love for them. God, help them ever to be all that was good and fine and brave in him, all that he would most have loved to see them grow up to be, if Thou in Thy great wisdom had thought best to spare him. God, let us be able to feel, to know, he can still see us as we grow, as we live, that he is till with us; that he is not deprived of his children and all he had hoped for them and loved them for; nor they of him. Nor they of him.

"God, make us to know he is still with us, still loves us, cares what comes to us, what we do, what we are; so much. O, God..."

She spoke these words sharply, and said no more; and Rufus felt that she was looking at his father, but he did not move his eyes, and felt that he should not know what he was sure of. After a few moments he heard the motions of her lips as softly again as that falling silence in which the whole world snowed, and he turned his eyes from the hand and looked towards his father's face and, seeing the blue-dented chin thrust upward, and the way the flesh was sunken behind the bones of the jaw, first recognized in its specific weight the word, *dead*. He looked quickly away, and solemn wonder tolled in him like the shuddering of a prodigious bell, and he heard his mother's snowy lips with wonder and with a desire that she should never suffer sorrow, and gazed once again at the hand, whose casual majesty was unaltered. He wished more sharply even than before that he might touch it, but whereas before he had wondered whether he might, if he could find a way to be alone, with no one to see or ever know, now he was sure that he must not. He therefore watched it all the more studiously, trying to bring all of his touch into all that he could see; but he could not bring much. He realized that his mother's hand was without feeling or meaning on his shoulder. He felt how sweaty his hand, and his sister's arm, had become, and changed his hand, and clasped her gently but without sympathy, and felt her hand tighten, and felt gentle towards her because she was too little to understand. The hand became, for a few moments, a mere object, and he could just hear his mother's breath repeating, "Good-bye, Jay, good-bye. Good-bye. Good-bye. Good-bye, my Jay, my husband. Oh, Good-bye. Good-bye."

Then he heard nothing and was aware of nothing except the hand, which was an object; and felt a strong downward clasping pressure upon his skull, and heard a quiet but rich voice.

His mother was not—yes, he could see her skirts, out behind to the side; and Catherine, and a great hand on her head too, and her silent and astounded face. And between them, a little behind them, black polished shoes and black, sharply pressed trouser legs, without cuffs.

"Hail Mary, full of grace," the voice said; and his mother joined; "The Lord is with thee; blessed art thou among women, and blessed is the fruit of thy womb, Jesus.

"Holy Mary, Mother of God, pray for us sinners, now, and in the hour of *our* death. Amen."

"Our Father, Who art in heaven," the voice said; and the children joined; "Hallowed be Thy name," but in their mother's uncertainty, they stopped, and the voice went on:

"Thy kingdom come, Thy will be done," said the voice, with particular warmth, "on earth as it is in heaven. Give us this day our daily bread. And forgive us our trespasses, As we forgive those who trespass against us." Everything had been taken off the mantelpiece. "And lead us not into temptation, But deliver us from evil," and with this his hand left Rufus' head and he crossed himself, immediately restoring the hand, "for Thine is the kingdom, and the power, and the glory, for ever and ever. Amen."

He was silent for a moment. Twisting a little under the hard hand, Rufus glanced upward. The priest's jaw was hard, his face was earnest, his eyes were tightly shut.

"O Lord, cherish and protect these innocent, orphaned children," he said, his eyes shut. *Then we are!* Rufus thought, and knew that he was very bad. "Guard them in all temptations which life may bring. That when they come to understand this thing which in Thy inscrutable wisdom Thou hast brought to pass, they may know and reverence Thy will. God, we beseech Thee that they may ever be the children, the boy and girl, the man and woman, which this good man would have desired them to be. Let them never discredit his memory, O Lord. And Lord, by Thy mercy may they come quickly and soon to know the true and all-loving Father Whom they have in Thee. Let them seek Thee out the more, in their troubles and in their joys, as they would have sought their good earthly father, had he been spared them. Let them ever be, by Thy great mercy, true Christian Catholic children. Amen."

Some of the tiles of the hearth which peeped from beneath the coffin stand, those at the border, were a grayish blue. All the others were streaked and angry, reddish yellow.

The voice altered, and said delicately: "The Peace of God, which passeth all understanding, keep your hearts and minds in the knowledge and love of God, and of his Son Jesus Christ our Lord." His hand again lifted from Rufus' head, and he drew a great cross above each of them as he said, "And the blessing of God Almighty, the Father, the Son, and the Holy Ghost, be amongst you, and remain with you always."

"Amen," their mother said.

The priest touched his shoulder, and Rufus stood up. Catherine stood up. Their father had not, of course not, Rufus thought, he had not moved, but he looked to have changed. Although he lay in such calm and beauty, and grandeur, it looked to Rufus as it he had been flung down and left on the street, and as if he were a very successfully disguised stranger. He felt a pang of distress and of disbelief and was about to lean to look more closely, when he felt a light hand on his head, his mother's, he knew, and heard her say, "Now, children;" and they were conveyed to the hall door.

The piano, he saw, was shut.

"Now Mother wants to stay just a minute or two," she told them. "She'll be with you directly. So you go straight into the East Room, with Aunt Hannah, and wait for me."

She touched their faces, and noiselessly closed the door.

Crossing to the East Room they became aware that they were not alone in the dark hall. Andrew stood by the hat rack, holding to the banister, and his rigid, weeping eyes, shining with fury, struck to the roots of their souls like ice, so that they hastened into the room where their great-aunt sat in an unmoving rocking chair with her hands in her lap, the sunless light glazing her lenses, frostlike upon her hair.

They heard feet on the front stairs, and knew it was their grandfather. They heard him turn to go down the hall and then they heard his subdued, surprised voice: "Andrew? Where's Poll?

And their uncle's voice, cold, close to his ear: "In—there—with—Father—Jackson."

"Unh!" they heard their grandfather growl. Their Aunt Hannah hurried towards the door.

"Praying."

"Unh!" he growled again.

Their Aunt Hannah quickly closed the door, and hurried back to her chair.

But much as she had hurried, all that she did after she got back to her chair was sit with her hands in her lap and stare straight ahead of her through her heavy lenses, and all that they could do was to sit quietly too, and look at the clean lace curtains at the window, and at the magnolia tree and the locust tree in the yard, and at the wall of the next house, and at a heavy robin which fed along the lawn, until he flew away, and at the people who now and then moved past along the sunny sidewalk, and at the buggies and automobiles which now and then moved along the sunny street. They felt mysteriously immaculate, strange and careful in their clean clothes, and it seemed as if the house were in shadow and were walking on tiptoe in the middle of an easy, sunny world. When they tired of looking at these things, they looked at their Aunt Hannah, but she did not appear to realize that they were looking at her; and when there was no response from their Aunt Hannah they looked at each other. But it had never given them any pleasure or interest to look at each other and it gave them none today. Each could only see that the other was much too clean, and each realized, though that the more acutely, that he himself was much too clean, and that something was wrong which required of each of them such careful conduct, and particularly good manners, that there was really nothing imaginable that might be proper to do except to sit still. But though sitting so still, with nothing to fix their attention upon except each other, they saw each other perhaps more clearly than at any time before; and each felt uneasiness and shyness over what he saw. Rufus saw a much littler child than he was, with a puzzled, round, red face which looked angry, and he was somewhat sorry for her in the bewilderment and loneliness he felt she was lost in, but more, he was annoyed by this look of shut-in anger and this look of incomprehension and he thought over and over: "Dead. He's dead. That's what he is; he's dead;" and the room where his father lay felt like a boundless hollowness in the house and in his own being, as if he stood in the dark near the edge of an abyss and could feel that droop of space in the darkness; and watching his sister's face he could see his father's almost as clearly, as he had just seen it, and said to himself, over and over: 'Dead. Dead;" and looked with uneasiness and displeasure at his sister's face, which was so different, so flushed and busy, so angry, and so uncomprehending. And Catherine saw him stuck down there in the long box like a huge mute doll, who would not smile or stir, and smelled sweet and frightening, and because of whom she sat alone and stiffly and too clean, and nobody was kind or attentive, and everything went on tiptoe, and with her mother's willingness a man she feared and hated put his great hand on her head and spoke incomprehensibly. Something very wrong was being done, and nobody seemed to care or to tell her what or to help her or love her or protect her from it and there was her too-clean brother, who always thought he was so smart, looking at her with dislike and contempt.

So after gazing coldly at each other for a little while, they once more looked into the side yard and down into the street and tried to interest themselves in what they saw, and to forget the things which so powerfully pervaded their thoughts, and to subdue their physical restiveness in order that they should not be disapproved; and tiring of these, would look over once more at their aunt, who was as aloof almost as their father; and uneased by that, would look once more into each other's eyes; and so again to the yard and the street, upon which the sunlight moved slowly. And there they saw an automobile draw up and Mr. Starr got quickly out of it and walked slowly up towards the house.

CHAPTER VII

SOME CONSIDERATIONS OF

PERSONAL DEATH

Introduction

In the first sentence of his article, "Time, Death and the Ego-Chill," Dr. Leveton suggests: "Among the many experiences possible to man perhaps none is so overwhelming or intolerable as the feeling of panic initiated by thoughts about personal death or non-existence." While we may not all be as neurotic as Dr. Leveton's patient, Alice, so aptly used as an illustration of this profound point, when we confront personal death the dimension of neurotic or non-neurotic becomes irrelevant. The "ego-chill" is universal; we all flee in panic from the void of non-existence of the self. Alice was "hung up" on death, but she differs only in degree from all of us.

What is it like to die? When time runs out for me, how will I react? If I am destined to die, will it be painful? Will I weep? How can I face my own finiteness? Who do I want with me when the unbearable happens to me? When will death come? How will it come? What will I feel? What will I do?

Will I curse? Will I pray? How can I even think about such an unthinkable disaster — can anyone think about it, cope with it? Why can't someone tell me like it is?

But no one has ever been able to tell us about death from personal experience. This is not really a **non sequitur**, if one takes an existential look at the statement. Death is the only life process for which we have no reports of the experiences of those who precede us. Nearest to such accounts are the reports of persons who **almost** died, but in fact did not — or at least, did not die then. Such an account is given in the selection which details the experience of young Don O'Daniel, "Last Thoughts Before Drowning." Who among us who has surveyed the vastly powerful surf of the Pacific Ocean as it meets the Oregon coast has not felt a premonition of the "ego-chill?" Don O'Daniel **almost** died there.

TIME, DEATH AND THE EGO-CHILL *

by

Alan Leveton

I. A Case Study

Among the many experiences possible to man perhaps none is so overwhelming or intolerable as the feeling of panic initiated by thoughts about personal death or non-existence. Those who have experienced these moments remember the dreadful discomfort, the frantic efforts to recover, and the lasting unease that follows. Despite its intensity this panic is sometimes difficult to describe to others. The patient who is fearful of recalling too vividly an unpleasant experience that may repeat itself if described avoids disclosure or indicates vague episodes of "nameless dread." Words, even when gropingly used, seem inadequate to describe this overwhelming, sudden and disturbing event which involves painfully intense emotions, feelings of unreality, fears of insanity, illusions and depersonalizations, and many physiological changes — sweating, vertigo, weakness, or syncope.

The following case study demonstrates the impact of thoughts of time and death in the thoughts and life cycle of Alice X, a 26-year-old woman who stated that she had been thinking about her eventual death in time. This had certain consequences affecting her and the clinician who treated her. This paper describes what can happen when an individual "discovers" the fact of his own finiteness, using Erikson's term, the ego-chill, "... a shudder which comes from the sudden awareness that our non-existence...is entirely possible."[1]

Although many of the observations in this paper were made during work with psychiatric patients, the phenomenon itself is not limited to any particular category of the "sick" or "well" or any diagnostic group. It is a human experience universally possible because of the essential self-awareness of man.

Case Report:

Alice, the mother of two children, had been repeatedly incapacitated by severe migraine headaches which first began in adolescence and later required occasional periods of hospitalization and narcotics for their control. While experiencing the pain of headache, she was in great discomfort, demanded relief, medication and a quiet environment which only the hospital could provide. Her thoughts, although of necessity focused on pain, were orderly and goal-directed. She showed little anxiety.

When free of headaches she was an extremely active person. She was forever plunging into "projects," writing, visiting friends, helping the needy, planning activities around the house and children, all in a very frantic way. Despite this great activity, few of her projects came to fruition. Just when it seemed that something might be finished, she dropped it for something new that was also destined to remain incomplete. Her speech and motions were rapid, intense and intrusive. Although she sought peace and quiet in the hospital, these were now an anathema to her. In contrast, her constant search was for more and more stimulation.

There were times when she could find nothing to do, when her restless activities were insufficient. She was terrified of these moments. "What came to me then," Alice said, "was that time is passing, that the world is moving on, that I am growing older, that some day, in time, I am going to die." With these thoughts came the approach of panic. "I tried to think of something, anything, just to avoid facing the real fact — *time is passing, some day I will be dead and forever gone.*" She began frantic activity, moving from room to room, attempting to reach someone. "But moments came when this didn't work, when I couldn't do this in time. The thought of my real and inevitable death suddenly flooded me. I couldn't stand that. I felt horribly empty, I would be nothing, the bottom dropped out. I felt close to fainting, not as if I was in my own body at all; as if already dead. I tried to scream; I couldn't even do that. I had to stop this. I began banging my head against the wall. The pain was a real relief and I began to feel better." At her worst moments, the "inner void" was filled with chaotic thoughts, illusions, and even what seemed to be hallucinations. "The room dissolved; I saw death within me. Even pain failed to shut it off." In fact, she had had many such episodes, and many terminated

* Reprinted by permission of the Journal of Existentialism, Vol VI (Summer 1966.) Libra Publishers, Inc., Roslyn Heights, N.Y., pp 69-80.

with self-inflicted pain: head-banging, wrist-cutting, knuckle-biting acts with which she always tried to end the dreadful experience of her thoughts of personal death.

Her trait of not being able to finish tasks had been with her for many years. Although intelligent and able to succeed in college studies, she failed to graduate in her major by six months. She continued in school, however, took extra courses, and accumulated extra units, but none that could be applied to her college degree. She vacillated about getting married; her decision was accompanied by severe headaches. Her two pregnancies, unplanned, were difficult. Each delivery was followed by severe depression and the first by hospitalization. Ill at ease with children, she felt she could watch them grow "only out of the corner of my eye." Thoughts of their growing older distressed her, particularly since she thought of their developmental milestones as "meaning that I was growing older."

On occasion she would anticipate periods of isolation and loneliness and attempt to avert panic by getting drunk or using high dosages of stupefying medications "to blunt my sense of passing time, to kill time before it killed me." When her husband was absent, she engaged, as she had before marriage, in promiscuous sexual acting out. Her lovemaking was coarse, painful, sought from strangers, and once orgasm was reached, dissatisfying, "not only because I felt it was wrong, but because once the momentary stimulation was gone, I felt even more strongly the emptiness of time. I would have to get drunk to oblivion; I often thought of suicide."

She was careful with her appearance, quite neat and pleasing to look at, but she disliked spending time before her mirror. She used it for cosmetic functions but actively avoided "really looking at myself." This had its origins in some experiences she had at her mirror.

"I was looking at myself intently; I suddenly saw myself as others must *see* me, as a person among other persons. I wasn't invulnerable; I was mortal. 'That person' over there in the mirror might be killed by a car, might perish. In fact, I suddenly realized that the person in the mirror would surely die, and that the person in the mirror was me. It was a curious and terrifying moment. I was here inside myself feeling comfortably immortal, but seeing myself as destined to die. I was at a distance from myself; all time stretched out before me; I had to bite my knuckles to keep from shaking all over with the knowledge of my death."

It is helpful to know that her family had only helped her achieve a very precarious sense of identity. Her mother was intrusive, depreciating, reproachful, controlling and overly involved with internal problems to which she exposed her daughter. Her mother denied the passage of time by trying to pass as Alice's sister and so dressed herself quite inappropriately for her true age. She had wrongly refused to believe that anything was wrong with her daughter, and dismissed the behavior which led to her psychiatric hospitalization as mere "play acting." Her father, although successful in business, was self-depreciating, distant and aloof. He did not intervene between mother and daughter as Alice tried unsuccessfully to extricate herself from her mother's intrusiveness. Her father was absent or slept. The whole family was suspicious of outsiders, felt that people's motives were essentially selfish, that it was safer to remain distant from the world and distrustful. For the family, time did not hold out a promise of future fulfillment, but merely an opportunity for more disappointment. Despite their spoken praise for achievement, they generally devalued work and its meaningfulness. A younger brother was already repeating the patient's failure to finish school and was at the point of dropping out of school one year before graduation.

Alice had, therefore, underlying convictions that people, she herself, and the future were not to be trusted. She could not finish things, needed intense activity to avoid overwhelming feelings about the passage of time, and fled from the knowledge of her own mortality. At times, this knowledge came suddenly and produced panic; terror was associated with faintness, chaotic thoughts, and fears of insanity. Self-inflicted pain could end experience for the moment should headaches fail to provide a focus of attention. Drugs, alcohol, and sexual adventures might prevent it. Loneliness, isolation, boredom and mirror-gazing were feared as precursors and also avoided. Psychological tests showed her as "well-defended against schizoid emptiness, with both hysterical and obsessive-compulsive mechanisms most prominent." Regardless of her past history or the psychiatric diagnosis, the patient had experienced knowledge of her own death to come and insisted directly on having this issue out within the therapy.

Discussion:

We can examine in detail some elements of Alice's experience as she related it: its relationship to time, to the knowledge of personal death, the sensations involved, methods used by her to terminate or avoid it, the vulnerable periods in her life cycle, the kind of life cycle which these concerns imposed upon her, and finally, the implications for therapy not only for this woman, but also for a wide variety of patients with similar experiences.

Alice's many concerns are unified in the theme of time's passage or, more explicitly, her passage in time. Although time is an essential dimension of all existing things, her relationship with time was one of increasing tension. It moved quickly, bringing adulthood, parenthood and growth towards old age at a faster rate than she could tolerate. She often felt "like a little girl" despite her chronological age. Her self-image was preserved from an earlier time in her life cycle. In her dreadful self-consciousness of time's passage, she attempted vainly to control time by filling it up with activities, avoiding quiet moments, and by being constantly "on the go." Even potentially satisfying experiences eluded her because her concentration on time's passage led to feelings of isolation from herself and others. Her thoughts were fixed on the future or were dragged backwards toward the past and deprived her of a fullness in the present moment. "Killing time" was not only impossible, but led to feelings that "I'm drifting along aimlessly with nothing to do that really counts."

Some of her interest in time found a more adaptive outlet in historical studies, which not only gave her a sense of belonging to the continuity of the past, but also allowed her to step outside momentary dissatisfactions into a consideration of a wider time perspective. When planning a trip she carefully prepared herself by reading in depth about the history or geography of an unfamiliar place. This created a feeling of belonging, however transitory. This woman felt in many ways out of place with herself and, therefore, everywhere. Nonetheless, even historical studies involved some risk to her, for past history disclosed a time in which she had not yet existed; by extension, history would move onto a time just as real as the past in which she could no longer exist. "The people who built this castle," she would think, "are dead. Many people who have seen this castle, as I am doing, have also died. So will I also be dead at some future date."

She had fears that she was wasting time. Her endless almost hypomanic disorganized activity led her to an endless cycle which she experienced as a "too fast conveyer belt," a series of empty present moments which flitted by and evaded her control only to be added to the vast and empty past.

Alice's projects had another quality besides frantic activity — they were usually unfinished. Her school performance might have become a permanent achievement had she been able to complete the work needed for graduation. This pattern was repeated in half-finished poems, stories, paintings and household chores. This was also an attempt to control time: what is not finished is left undone, as if it may be finished "some day," even as she promised herself that "some day I'll get my college degree." There is a covert affirmation that there will be time to complete the task that is left undone. The finished task is one that is over and done with, part of the past. Events like graduation are also milestones in the life cycle and confront the person with a symbolic ritual, with the fact that he is ready for the next step, and the next, and the next. It is precisely in this, that the time-frightened person finds dread. Every milestone is seen as progression toward death.

Further evidence for this interpretation is found in her profound reactions to events which reached conclusion, e.g., orgasm and childbirth. Although orgasm had other meanings to her — in its aspect of being a peak event in time, it distressed her to have it end; she wished that foreplay "would never stop." When climax was reached, she might have an orgasm, but after that "it was all over, I just felt empty with nothing, for the moment, to look forward to." She frequently began drinking at that moment to blunt this feeling. During pregnancy and childbirth, in addition to worries about her parental capacities, she was preoccupied with time and change. She would no longer be a girl herself, she would irrevocably "graduate" to the role of mother. Her thoughts led further: "when they grow up and have children, I'll be a grandmother, and then" — once again the future which contained her death would intrude itself into her thought, and would flaw even a potentially gratifying experience, for the beginning of life implied the end of life. The growth and development of her children had to be ignored as a further reminder of the passage of time. She echoes Rilke's observation: ".. and what a melancholy beauty it gave to women, when they were pregnant and stood there; and in their big bodies, upon which their slender hands instinctively rested, were two shapes: a child and a death. Did not the dense, almost nourishing smile on their quite vacant faces come from their sometimes thinking that they were both growing?"[2]

Alice's experience with mirrors also deserves comment. Mirrors have an uncanny capacity to bring about a vivid stepping back from the self. Many mirror games of children and psychotics use this phenomenon, in which the viewers lose and retrieve themselves by passing back and forth.[3] The crucial question is "what does the person see in the mirror?" Children and animals see other children and animals and may pursue them frantically behind the mirror. It seems uniquely human (and not all have this capacity, i.e., not young children, some psychotics or some primitive peoples) to be able to identify the mirror image as the Self. We see ourselves in the mirror. As we look from the outside, we observe ourselves as we observe others and recognize, perhaps with sudden insight, that we too are part of the ongoing and perishable world.

This, in turn, may give rise to a curious and intense kind of depersonalization which is also an intense experience of self-awareness. The mirror image shows the person that he, too, is plunged into the world and that he is irrevocably embedded in the matrix of time. The image is a threat to our cherished notions of omnipotence over time and death. One would gratefully let the mirror image die or sacrifice it. It is the hateful and fearful reminder of just what one is. As Alice once exclaimed, "Let *it* die, but not *me*. But the image *is* me, it is I who will die, no sacrifice or avoidance is possible. I am here inside, I am there outside." Hence, the turning away from the mirror, even its destruction in anger, as if to destroy the threatening finite self which is implacably reflected there and is forever one's self.

We have all become practiced in using our mirrors for cosmetic functions – to see eyes, hair, lips, cheeks as objects, and not as our finite self. We find time writing on our faces; we smooth out the wrinkles and dye our hair in the hope of revising the aging mirror image into everlasting youthfulness. We put away our mirrors at death, covering them lest the corpse and our own face be caught in the same all-embracing glass.

Exposed to an intolerable and total experience, the person must end it. The void must be filled up, the nothingness replaced by something, and a curtain drawn over memory. It is an easier experience to avoid than to interrupt. Emergency measures must be applied rapidly by using whatever is close at hand. It cannot wait for the leisurely attention of prepared defenses because all that happens mentally and physically is frantic and desperate.

The void may be filled with thoughts and emotions. The person hopes they will be orderly, as a character of Rilke prays, "My God, my God, if any such nights awaken me in the future, leave me at least one of those thoughts that I have sometimes been able to pursue!"[2] Often, however, the thoughts that come, as did Alice's, seem the very essence of madness – a jumble of thoughts and feelings without structure. This, too, is unbearable and frightening. But, even the return of chaotic thoughts, hypnogogic illusions, or hallucinations seem more tolerable than the peak experience of absolute nothingness – reminiscent of those experiences of religious ecstasy that follow "the dark nights of the soul."

A common method of ending these thoughts is through self-inflicted pain – Alice not only struck and bit herself, but hurt her head. Other patients have reported pinching themselves, plunging into cold water or cutting themselves.

Pain can be self-inflicted with little improvisation. It focuses consciousness and thoughts from their wanderings and anchors them to a more well-defined area, such as the skin surface. Pain crowds out other sensations and displaces varied preoccupations with a single, urgent, and simple problem of obtaining relief. Feeling pain binds one to the moment of experience and contracts the limitless horizon of time, i.e., death's field of action. The only point in time that is now important is the moment when pain ceases. The terrible spell of the ego-chill is broken by the time that pain has ebbed away and other or more stable defenses, such as avoidance, denial or "getting busy with other things," can take over. Pain gives our body back to us; it is experienced within. If it is self-inflicted it is under control, it gives some sense of self-mastery. If there is relief in pain, it is the relief expressed by Alice, "I'm really there, really alive."

Chronic illness seems similarly useful. Not only do people like Alice suffer from overwhelming moments of the ego-chill, they are also chronic sufferers of pain – often headaches, beginning at night or at moments in which boredom and isolation threaten to expose them to dreadful self-awareness. When a person becomes preoccupied with illness, his total self seen at a distance in endless time is replaced by a diseased part close at hand. A sick person will say, "it's my head," "my kidney," "my lungs." By replacing the whole with a part, the person protects himself against the threat of dying. ("It is not I that am sick, but a part of me. After all, Doctor, you can give me pills for my headaches, and a person can live, can't he, with one lung and one kidney?")

During sickness one's time sense is contracted as with pain: "When I get better" becomes the unit of measure, not one's entire life span. There is a continual hope for improvement instead of the feeling of the ego-chill, which is essentially one of final and total hopelessness.

Compulsive activity, as in Alice's unfinished and endlessly repeated tasks, isolates and attempts to order and control time through repetition that leads nowhere and, therefore, not to death. The repetition-compulsion has its roots in the past. It is a remnant of the past that may successfully hide the uncertain future and fill up the present. What is repeated endlessly, is endless. Although uncomfortable, it is nonetheless familiar. It is tragic for a person to attempt to control time by filling it with painful, self-defeating experiences and relationships, and to fear change. But change means the abandonment of a familiar past and present for an uncertain and progressing future; the oblation of consciousness and the renunciation of change are heavy prices to pay for fear of one's own death.

The change in Alice which finally came about did not come only with interpretation about family relationships or intrapsychic conflict, although these were important to her. The most important changes resulted from making the subject of her own death a possible topic for real consideration.

II. The Therapeutic Task

The therapist often feels that talk of death will bring him into the realm of philosophy and religion and, therefore, is not a proper area of therapeutic work. At times, in our eagerness to "get to the bottom of things" we move away from the simple and direct expression of the patient's concern with his own death into what may be more comfortable areas of interpretation and miss the vital and valid center of the very source of many symptoms.

Within varied frames of reference, many students have described the effects of a fear of death, horror of the existential vacuum, time-horror, dread of nothingness, the naked anxiety of non-being, and a host of related and perhaps derivatory phenomena — fears of abandonment, castration anxiety and loss of self. Death concern is not always recognized in the patient's symptoms, and when it is, it is often not approached directly. It is often not appreciated that the ego-chill can be a "normative" crisis in the healthy at certain stages of development.

The knowledge that one must die presupposes a sense of self which can be lost as well as a perception that one is joined to a life cycle destined to end in death. This requires a certain conceptual leap, not available to animals in the woods or creatures in the nursery. As children emerge from their omnipotent world of timelessness, they begin to discover that people dear to them can be lost, they learn the word "death" and the verb "to die." They learn that there are children, parents, and grandparents who exist at first in their minds as separate and distinct beings. Later, the child will discover that adults represent a later stage in the life cycle to which he is irrevocably joined. When the child recognizes his own life cycle, and perceives both future and impersonal time, he becomes open to the essential human experience of recognizing personal finiteness, death, and the ego-chill.

Adolescence is a phase in growth and development when people can experience a heightened consciousness of time and personal finiteness and pass through these traumatic experiences as normative crises. During young adulthood, career choices narrow; as one realizes that omnipotent dreams and fantasies are more ruthlessly hindered by reality and a shrinking expanse of available future time, he may experience the dread of death and nothingness. In the thirties and early forties such repeated crises occur, often buried from view by a variety of defenses and diversionary tactics. It is not easy to talk about death or face it. One suspects that the reason that we know relatively little about this kind of crisis during the middle productive years of life is that therapists may be inclined to join their patients in feeling and avoiding the discomfort in the confrontation of the knowledge of death.

As long as one is movng, growing, developing, possessing a strong sense of self, and confidence in place and identity change, the future is tolerable. The ego-chill in thoughts of death is neither pressing nor threatening. Thoughts of death may be a prominent problem, however, during change when identity and self are not in continuity, when there is uncertainty because of great internal pressure, or when ego apparatuses are weakened (as in isolation), or in those with "borderline" adaptedness.

Since catastrophic reaction to thoughts of death seem to come at moments of stepping back from the self, protective measures may include a solipsistic belief that one is unique and unlike others who are destined to die, or omnipotent.

From our vantage point "within" our skin, we look on our world exerting considerable control over its phenomena. We darken it by closing our eyes, silence it by plugging up our ears, and vary its appearance by moving our bodies in space. The apparent division between subject or self, and object or world (one of our most prolonged philosophical and metaphysical debates) may be retained by the person to support his fiction of uniqueness outside the flow of time and decay. Since we generally experience internal continuity and permanence, it is hard for us to see ourselves plunged into that outer world where so many fatal things may or eventually will happen.

The death of others whom we know challenges this solipsism. A death invites fearful identification with the dead and their death; it forces us momentarily away from our secure sense of timeless identity. We are pulled back to the dead and see them through our own transitoriness, "as he died, so shall I. I am no different than he in death. In his death I am looking on what I shall one day be. I am here, but also there." Much of what happens after a death is done to appease guilt over ambivalence, but much is done also to help deny this participation in an eventuality, one's own death. Purification rites or burial and mourning customs serve to place the dead person in some category other than shared humanity with those who survive. Mimicry of the dead through imitation of the dead person's gestures, modes and tones serves to hang onto fragments of the dead and protect them against loss (understood partly by the psychoanalytic concept of introjection) and helps to deny the fact of death itself. "If he is not truly dead, I will not die, death is defeated."

In our own culture particularly, we turn away from death and hide it in the tabooed mortuary and distant hygienic cemeteries. We take an actuarial view of death so that we are not moved by starvation of 25,000 Indians in a famine but a single picture of one dead or dying person sends "a shudder" down our spine. As human beings we are there in that death and momentarily split off from our smug omnipotence; we quickly turn the page. Any defensive strategies which serve to protect against self-awareness may become quite useful in avoiding thoughts of personal finiteness. Many people, therefore, welcome illness as a relief from the more intolerable anxiety of an uncertain fate or their final, inevitable end. In illness, one may recover in time. Some use drugs or alcohol for defense: "The day ends, the long empty night stretches ahead with its waking thoughts of 'what have I accomplished, where am I going, who am I, who loves me, whom do I love, and what will become of me?' " The first drink allows omnipotence to surge up, identity seems certain, and the future seems easily conquered. Later, with more drinks, blunted consciousness induces indifference to the passage of time which moves effortlessly — there is either the pleasant, painlessly empty present or the omnipotent future. With more drinks somnolence intervenes, no questions are asked of the self, no expectations fulfilled, no tasks completed. All that remains is unconsciousness or sleep until sobering-up plunges the person back into the real world where time and life are lived and lived out.

It is not only "dependency, passivity, and oral needs" that make an alcoholic, but boredom, loneliness and the need to crush a sense of passing time and coming death. Not only antisocial tendencies push the adolescent in his search for "kicks," but also a need to re-establish the immediacy of one's physical body in the here and now, where it may be protected against the onrush of the future.

Suicide has been known to occur in persons in whom the uncertainty about the time of their death has been intolerable. A more adaptive and culturally supported defeat of death comes in our beliefs in immortality and a life beyond death. It is an appealing solution and recalls Erikson's remarks that the ego-chill "is at the bottom of our myth making, our metaphysical speculations and our artificial creation of 'ideal' realities."[1] If the soul exists and is the most real part of the self, and is returned or united with the timeless one, then death and the future need hold no fear – terror can turn to ecstasy.[4] Mystics, theologians, and philosophers learn about time and death before they find God or eternal Truth. Many good descriptions of this phenomenon are found in their writings, e.g., Paul Tillich's "threat of non-being."[5] The immediate effect on the mystic who experiences the ego-chill has often been the infliction of pain through scourging and self-mutilation, as well as a "divine madness" as emptiness filled with chaotic thoughts and feelings which are often interpreted as an oceanic reunion with God.

These are problems not only of the extraordinarily sensitive or the very sick, but also seem to be a permanent characteristic of our fragmented times. A general dread of death and dying, feelings of not really living authentic lives, concerns about mass man, mass communications, industrialization, automation, the loss of well-defined religious and social goals, the immensity of government and the destructive forces of war, the palpable presence of evil in such political movements as German National Socialism remind us of our frailty, impotence and aloneness. Our clinical attention is led away from problems of hysteria and psychoneurosis to the difficult problems of "alienation," "the schizoid personality," "naked anxiety," "the existential vacuum," "unauthentic existence," "borderline states," and "apathy and loneliness." [6-11] More people are seen whose defective sense of identity and continuity makes the ego-chill more disruptive and drives them to non-productive and uncomfortable means of dealing with their lives and passage through time. We have also seen what may happen when people surrender to charismatic leaders like Hitler, whose promise of an eternal Reich capitalized partly on fears of nothingness, time, and death by promising an end to uncertainty and union with an indestructible, infinite future – a secular Eternal – if only his followers would become blind "true believers."[12]

Talk about death does not come into therapy with every patient; perhaps it should. Patients and therapists may both be eager to seize upon symptoms, illnesses, drugs, and interpretations to avoid a subject which is unpleasant for both to face. Many aspects of the psychotherapeutic situation support this mutual avoidance. We rest more or less securely in our role as therapists who deal with pathology. The patient, we like to think and hope, brings himself, but often he brings a role or a mask, a portrayal of illness. Talk in therapy, especially ritualistic exchange between role players, can also becomes a meaningless and compulsive activity used to kill time. A prolonged anamnesis can build a real or mythical past as the present slips by, the future remains inaccessible, and the patient waits for something to happen.

"I understand myself," complains the patient after engaging in any therapy that achieves only the level of ritual, "but I still feel empty." Sensitive therapists of whatever theoretical background understand this point, but it is easier to be a technically competent therapist and an understandably ill patient than to be a man or fully human. However, to help a patient deal with thoughts of his own death demands unstructured contact between man and man, something beyond the professional role.

We can be adroit at avoiding the issue in the psychiatric office or in the hospital where patients are actually dying. Doctors frequently cooperate with the dying person's wish to be reduced to a single organ ("It's just my lungs") and, eventually, a thing. In the vocabulary of the hospital ward "The cancer in Room 145 isn't doing well," or "He is dying a renal death."[13]

Identification with the dying confronts the physician with a reality of his own finiteness and death. The impersonal bedside manner, the focus on the patient as a defective physiological machine, the denial of death as a natural phenomenon[14] places the patient in a category other than shared mortal humanity with the physician. Hospital routines which emphasize the dehumanized, mechanized routine production lines of institutional death move towards this goal, often to the great discomfort of the patient.

Even in the calm of our psychiatric offices, we may decide that questions of death, meaningfulness, and values in faith belong to another field, usually philosophy or religion. The uncomfortable and embarrassing presence of death may have to be exorcised by "analysis" into some other category, to the intense relief of the patient and doctor; yet, death is real.

If our formulation and interpretations are confined to such statements as "This is only your fear of retaliation for your aggressive feelings, etc.," we may accomplish only a partial interpretation, however correct, and avoid reality. The patient is going to die; he knows it. Why is it something that cannot be discussed in its unaltered state? It may be that his naked horror has become elaborated into fears of something — abandonment, cannibalism or loss of love. Will it be enough to convince the patient that his fears of abandonment are illusory; of castration, exaggerated; of cannibalism, absurd; of loss of love, improbable, if the final issue rather than its hydra-headed derivative is not engaged. The result may be interminable analysis with series of therapists (the patient never "graduating" from the comforting eternity of an uncompleted analysis), moments of relief as interpretations are given, followed by despair as death remains unconfronted in the proliferation of meaningless activities, and the demand is made for cessation of anxiety through drugs from what is, after all, a real and non-pathological stress.

The ego-chill, the catastrophic confrontation of the individual with his own death, is the business of therapy because it is a psychological experience. It is of great and significant power to those who have encountered it, and is particularly prone to distortion and concealment behind other symptoms. No matter how reductive, scientific and analytic we wish to be, a consideration of this experience draws us inexorably into thinking about our patient's future, his values, existence and need. It is not enough to liberate him from the prison of a repetitious and unsatisfying life pattern which is dominated by the past if he does not know what to do with his present or future. He may need something more than his release, five dollars and a new suit; he needs somewhere to go, something to do.

As "experts" in understanding him and life, it is important for us to know or at least to address the question of what human life should be or might be if we are to do our job fully. All therapists have a goal in mind for their patients, e.g., "authentic existence," "removal of repression," "sublimation," etc., yet the content of these goals is often not examined with the patient. He recovers from his illness, but does not move toward anything and still avoids his future and his death.

When the patient describes the overwhelming experience that relates to knowledge of personal death, the issue must be open rather than hidden and covert. Death and Time concern the patient. This is part of his essential humanness and not necessarily pathological, but the means of dealing with this knowledge may be pathological.

Only man recognizes his future death and can feel it and its coming. It is important and "healthy," not tragic and "sick" to recognize that his future is limited and that time passes whether we are busy or bored, in movement or at rest, engaged or escaping.

Talk must turn to the contents of the future: hopes, aspirations, goals, obligations, ambitions, intentions — in ego-psychologic terms, the ego-ideal. In their attainment, or in striving for their attainment, achievement, pride, and a sense of identity and continuity will be found.

The therapist who limits himself to understanding the patient's past, asks him "why"; the one who attempts to help the patient confront his death, asks him "why not?" Why not dare to use the remaining time in the search for his ideal? Unfortunately, our efforts in this direction are complicated by the fact that the patient's failure to strive after his ego-ideal while killing time results in a profound sense of shame, which, like death and the ego-chill, is difficult to talk about and is often concealed behind a more comfortable diversionary symptom.[14]

Technical skill alone will not always help us to deal with the patient in this moment of realization of finiteness and shame. The confrontation of the normal tension aroused by our own personal death is a task we owe ourselves as human beings and is necessary before we can help that other human being who is our patient. Finiteness binds us to the patient and all others at a level of shared humanity which is more fundamental than our individual roles of doctor and patient. It may call for moments of reaching out beyond the confines of the strategy and tactics of analysis or psychotherapy, a "bearing witness" to the hope that finite life can be meaningful and thoughts of death productive. It is difficult and uncomfortable for the therapist in his humanity and for the patient in his. To grapple with these problems in therapy is, in Buber's words,[15] "a way of frightened pause, of unfrightened reflection, of personal involvement, of rejection of security, of unreserved stepping into relationship, of the bursting of psychologism, this way of vision and of risk."

Summary

Man is finite and dies in time. He is also aware of his own finiteness. The sudden awareness of personal finiteness and eventual personal death comes as a shock to the person who was once secure in his sense of omnipotence. The catastrophic reaction named the ego-chill by Erikson was described in greater detail through the case history of a woman very concerned with thoughts of her own death and who used frantic action, sex, drugs, alcohol, uncompleted activities and self-inflicted pain to avoid a sense of passing time and finiteness. The therapist who tries to "look beneath" the patient's straight talk about time and death for castration or abandonment anxiety may be missing an extremely important and vital experience with which the patient needs help. Inevitably the therapist must consider issues that relate to the possible meaningfulness of life if he is to help himself and the patient face a shared finiteness and mortality.

References

1. Erikson, E. H. *Young Man Luther.* London, Faber & Faber, Ltd., 1958.

2. Rilke, R. M. *The Notebooks of Malte Laurids Brigge.* New York, Capricorn Books, 1958.

3. Elkisch, Paula. The psychological significance of the mirror. J. Am. Psychoanalyt. Assoc. 5:235, 1957.

4. Lewin, B. Some psychoanalytic ideas applied to elation and depression. Am. J. Psychiat. 116:38, 1959.

5. Tillich, P. *The Courage to Be.* New Haven, Yale University Press, 1952.

6. Guntrip, H. The manic-depressive problem in the light of the schizoid personality. Intl. J. Psychiat. 43:98, 1962.

7. ——Ego-weakness and the hard core problem of psychotherapy. Brit. J. Med. Psychol. 33:163, 1960.

8. Weiss, F. Self-alienation: Dynamics and therapy. Am. J. Psychoanalysis 21:207, 1961.

9. Fromm-Reichmann, Frieda. On loneliness. *Psychoanalysis and Psychotherapy,* Chicago, University of Chicago Press, 1959.

10. Heilbrunn, Gert. The basic fear. J. Am. Psychoanalyt. Assoc. 3:447, 1955.

11. Frankl, V. E. Logotherapy. J. Exist. Psychiat. 8:1, 1962.

12. Hoffer, E. *The True Believer.* New York, Mentor Books, 1951.

13. Guttentag, O. The meaning of death in medical theory. Stanford Med. Bull. 17:165, 1959.

14. Leveton, A. F. Reproach: The art of shamesmanship. Brit. J. Med. Psychol. 35:101, 1962

15. Buber, M. Healing through meeting. *Pointing the Way.* London, Routledge and Kegan Paul, 1957.

LAST THOUGHTS BEFORE DROWNING *

by

Charles J. Thurmond

Several hours' delirium followed an unusual accident and the amazing survival of a good swimmer. During the delirium the boy recited many of the thoughts that had gone through his mind while he was out in the ocean struggling for his life and fearing he would certainly drown. A college teacher was present and recorded every word he said. The transcript is presented in this article.

Don O'Daniel, a 19-year-old engineering student at Oregon State College, was swept out in the Pacific Ocean about 4:30 Saturday afternoon, November 29, 1941. He had been "jumping the breakers" at Wakonda Beach, south of Waldport, Oregon, when he lost his footing and was carried out by undertow in an outgoing tide.

A husky football player, Don made good use of his powerful physical strength and his long-accumulated knowledge of the ocean, kept himself alive until his limp body was picked up at 8:30 Saturday night.

Either he had swallowed no water or he had vomited it all before he was picked up; he had no water in his lungs at all when he was carried in the house and given first aid; he was suffering only from the shock of his experience and the complete exhaustion of several hours' battling the ocean.

Small drinks of warm coffee excessively sweetened to replace what his body had spent in exertion were given him every half-hour. Until 11:20 he lay completely motionless except that he suffered violent cramps, groaned, and arched his body up off the bed convulsively after each drink. A spoon of coffee against his lips caused him to swallow involuntarily; but he did not move, he lay lifeless. His hair was matted heavily with wet sand; his face was red and bruised; his arms and legs were badly scratched; the skin was torn off several toes.

At 11:20 pm. Don started writhing and moaning as if he were in great mental agony. He started talking but his eyes were closed and he appeared to be talking in his sleep. Everything he said was repeated several times precisely the same way. He spoke in a low voice but very distinctly and clearly so that everybody in the room could understand everything he said.

Chuck taught English, always carried a pocket notebook. He started taking down exact notes of every word Don said. Mr. and Mrs. Pennington were both present and commented at times. Don spoke slowly and distinctly as well as repeating every phrase so that there never was any doubt what he was saying. Both the Penningtons and Chuck were interested to hear what he was saying because this was their first glimpse (after hours of anxiety for Don's safety) into what had actually happened to him. These notes are presented in the next section exactly as they were made.

Parentheses are used around any material which has been added later. *Italics* indicate Don's *exact words.* Other notes without editing of any kind are given here exactly as they were recorded originally on the scene.

I

11:20 pm, Saturday night, November 29, 1941.
moaning
stay out past breakers until tide changes
wept pitifully
the wind is pushing you past
you won't make it 3 times
you can't make it over and over; pitifully anguished
float for a while
float for a while
maybe I can make it
cramps
take it easy or you are going to cramp

* Used by permission of the publishers of the Journal of Abnormal and Social Psychology. Ed. Gordon W. Allport, Evanston, Ill. The American Psychological Association, Inc. (1943.)

156

do you think you can make it?
it's getting dark
water logged
keep moving to keep warm
what will my folks think
mother will go crazy
I have been out here two hours already
I'm crazy
Rose Bowl
you won't get to see it
I won't be able to collect it
you are all through in school
you have wasted your folks' money
what will Rose think of this
you won't pass your exam
you are going to make it

frantic moaning (body tense and rigid as if preparing for great exertion)
dive under it
dive under the breaker to get back
(tension subsided; he relaxed)
don't drink any salt water
don't swallow any salt water
take off your pants and shirts
they will help you float
don't take them off it will help you float
keep them on
take it easy
you will be all right
try to hold your own until the tide turns
you will be O.K. but you're getting tired repeated several times
you were crazy to come out in the first place
you have gone out too far
you know better than that
don't swallow any water
it'll choke you
(rather calm, reviewing the above thoughts slowly and philosophically)
(then) sudden mental anguish
body writhing in agony:
dive under that breaker!
(3 times very rapidly; strained painful tone)

(Mrs. Pennington insisted that Chuck try to wake Don or stir him to prevent his suffering in these episodes of mortal agony, tortured twisting, as if summoning his strength to *dive under the breakers.* Chuck did not touch Don and persuaded Mrs. Pennington not to. Chuck thought it was good for Don to reconstruct the situation, at least up to where his life was safe. If Don had stopped his reconstruction before he reached safety on the beach he might have suffered later from unverbalized recurrences of these disturbing thoughts. He was doing for himself in this delirium what an expert psychiatrist has to do for patients.)

Mother...she'll go crazy
What will she do when she finds out?
She is not well enough to stand it
You got out of your wreck all right
they said you wouldn't
you'll be all right (very calmly as if to soothe himself)
it's getting dark
the tide's turning
see that light
it's getting plainer
take it easier
you'll be all right
the water stings my face just like needles
(whimpering, complaining tone: like a child's)
(then deadly serious again):
you are going to make it to the breakers
swim with the breakers
you are going to make it
　　* 　* 　* 　* 　* 　* 　*

that sand stings my face
it's cold
drag yourself
why doesn't somebody come?
take it easy
you're out of the water
I can't yell
why doesn't my flashlight work?
moaning
I can't yell
my voice doesn't work
my throat is all stopped up
crawl out of the water before it takes you back out
(several times; some tension)
　　* 　* 　* 　* 　* 　* 　*

(Long silence during which he lay completely quiet and motionless.)

(Reconstructing the whole experience in his mind, he had at this point reached relative safety. He could afford to rest. He knew he would not drown, that his life was safe now that he was *out of the water.*)

During a pause in his talking, the Penningtons said how remarkable it was that he beat his way back against an outgoing tide.

Where are you?
I don't remember this
this is all new to me
where is this?
where were you before you came here?
where was I before I came here?
where are your folks?
where do they live?

wait 'til you come to
you don't know anyone
strangers
you don't know anyone
they are all strangers
can't I remember where I am?
better go back and see where you lost your senses

(Mrs. Pennington repeated this to Mr. Pennington who was standing over by the door. They both laughed heartily.)

    * * * * * * *

you are starting all over again
what are you gonna do here?
get to the light
this doesn't seem familiar
crawl through the bank
crawl through the canyon

(Mr. Pennington went outside to investigate to see where he actually did crawl up.)

where are you? repeatedly
moaning
this is the end of the line
you can't make it any farther
you can't go on
you're just a weakling repeated many times!
you can't make it
this is as far as you can go
you're just a weakling
you still got your rabbit foot?
your mother bought that for you
it's a good thing you took that along
your 165 pounds is too heavy
you can't pull it repeated many times.
it's too heavy
there's a log
lean over it and throw up
stick your finger down your throat
throw up and then you can breathe
you can't get up the bank
you'll have to go up the canyon

Mr. Pennington came back in the house and reported that there were marks in the sand where his wrist and rabbit's foot had imprinted. He tried to crawl up the bank at the back of the house, but a boarded-up wood-shed prevented his getting up. He then had to crawl farther south and come up through a little gorge which he called *canyon*. The marks of his hands, rabbit's foot, and dragging body were abundantly evident in the sand.

*　*　*　*　*　*　**

(several minutes' silence indicated in original notes)
(Then):
pitiful anguished moanings
spasmodic pained weeping reactions (sometimes with tears)

gee, that makes lots of noise
beautiful ocean
still a lot for you
dive under the big ones
you can't ride 'em all
it's getting so dark
if it wasn't for that light you might be going the wrong way
I hope they don't turn it out
you've learned lots of things
that phoney girl
talking about Hollywood
crazy people
Seaside
she's stringing you along
she thinks she's big time
Chuck's on to her
think about something
keep your mind busy
don't worry
you're an Irishman
as good as any of them
they don't let down
you're Irish and you don't quit 8 times
that girl is just trying to pull the wool over somebody's eyes
peculiar people
sort of cute
but she thinks she's good
don't be a dink
it's a good thing you didn't ask her for a date 3 times
you're better than she is 3 times
she talks too much 4 times
you won't get to go to Puget Sound next year 4 times weeping
you're a fool
they always told you you were dumb
you're trying to bluff your way through
you can't bluff now
you gotta produce the goods

dreadful writhing and anguish

you'll make it 4 times
just take it easy 5 times
God, you have been out here a long time
you must have stepped in a hole

the tide took you out
it's a good thing you know how to swim
but don't swim too hard
get out past the breakers before you get caught
you thought you had it figured out
how you'd make it
now's your chance
you can't play shuffleboard out here
you can't dance
you haven't got a boat
you're making it the hard way
your 19 years are going to be over quick
you are not even going to know what life's about
break it to them gently
my heart belongs to you
kiss them good bye
only thing smacks you is a wave
God, I never knew there could be so much water 4 times
on the bumpy, bumpy road to hell 2 times
you're doing fine 3 times
you'll be a success 5 times
why couldn't a boat come?
break it to them gently
that my heart belongs to you
kiss them good bye
I got one over on them 4 times
eleven men go to the Rose Bowl 3 times
one kid gets the whole Pacific Ocean
what are you going to do with it?
it is not half as crowded as it will be in the Rose Bowl
Father Dailey 4 times
Sister Mary 5 times
laughed when you got me out of the other wreck 3 times
I'll never laugh again if you'll get me out of this one 5 times
any time that you would spend two hours on knees for me why
should I laugh?
I'll never laugh again
I can't remember back any more
what's happening to your mind?
what's your name?
how'll they know your folks?
why worry about that when you are out in the ocean?
I always said I would be buried at sea 4 times
you always wanted to be buried at sea 3 times
here's your chance 3 times

moaned and wept
I hope you never wash up on the beach 8 times
if mother should find you
the birds'll pick your eyes out
that's fine...you'll go a long ways.

I hope I don't wash up on the beach 6 times
I saw a guy that did once 5 times
you know what he looked like
one leg was gone
crabs ate the eyes out of his head
he fell off the jetty
you might as well shake hands with yourself
this is the last time you'll have both of them
why don't people sit by the fire like this and talk more often?
I hope a fish doesn't grab you
I wonder if there are fish on the bottom
that old saying "paddle your own canoe" 6 times
you can't hand the paddle to the guy in the back
you've got to paddle your own canoe
get a grand-daughter and lose a son 4 times
what will my folks think? 3 times
she looks like you...mother says 2 times
you've been awfully damned ornery 5 times
this'll finish it sure 3 times
you'll have a nice Christmas 6 times

wept bitterly
tears poured down his cheeks

you can come home 5 times
you can come home and be with us 3 times
you are going to have your Christmas all by yourself
it's a good thing Chuck didn't come along
with those big boots
it's a good thing he didn't come along
he couldn't have made it
he has gone a long way
he has a long way to go
but you, you are losing nothing
come home for Christmas with us 5 times
you'll be like this for all time 8 times

wept particularly bitterly

I remember when you lost your little boat 3 times
I never knew then you were going to be next 4 times
we'll have Christmas together
isn't that ocean pretty? 3 times
it looks like hell! 4 times
you can have Christmas just the three of us
we'll all be together
it's a good thing you wrote just before you left
I hope they call and tell them
break it to them gently
you played football to get out of high school

162

you are going to have to swim to get out of the ocean
I'm getting so tired
being out here for hours 4 times
give up
just give up
give one more try
what difference does it make if you do drown?
sailors are drowning in Europe every day
you're no better than they are
the mighty Pacific 4 times
it's gonna defeat you
aye, an' sure enough you're from Ireland 5 times
you can make it 4 times
everything is beginning to spin 3 times
if I can just make it 3 times
either make it all the way or not make it at all 3 times
if your mother found you on the beach she'd go crazy
you know how that other fellow was
his hand gone
his eyes gone
his bones showing through his skin
that girl
that's a laugh
think of something else
Seaside 3 times
Hell! that's a laugh 3 times
she probably stopped there to get a drink of water
keep your fingers crossed 4 times

Don opened his eyes and looked at Chuck.
2:25 a.m. Sunday morning, November 30, 1941.

II

When Don woke up at 2:25 a.m., Chuck gave him coffee and medicine according to the doctor's instructions. He was lying there, complaining of how his arms and legs hurt, but otherwise lying there peacefully, looking straight at Chuck.

He had sudden attacks of violent cramps and held his breath and grew as rigid as a board, his arms clenching the side of the davenport as if he were in mortal pain. These came every fifteen or twenty minutes after he drank the hot coffee.

He was looking at Chuck and yet seemed not to see him. His eyes were glassy, unnatural, un-alive looking. His eyes had no expression, none of the twinkle and mischievous look which normally characterized Don's smiling Irish eyes.

He was lying very still (very sick) looking up at the ceiling and at Chuck who had note paper down beside the bed. Don did not know that Chuck was jotting down his responses. The following responses are Don's words and represent only half the conversation:

"I can't remember where I've been or where I'm going"
"where is this?"
"Wakonda Beach?"
"where is that?"

"where am I going?"

"home?"

"where is home?"

"I go to school?"

"No, I finished school!"

"Who are you?"

"Chuck?"

"Chuck at Camas?"

"How did I get here?"

"Is this the Navy?"

"What is this on me?"

"Sugar?"

"Chuck?"

"Go to school?"

"Chuck?"

"School?"

"This is like the time in football when I was knocked out for 5 hours"

"Corvallis?"

"school?"

"I remember when I used to go to Corvallis when my brother was down there"

"out have I ever gone to school there?"

"ocean?"

"swimming?"

"have I been to the ocean?"

"how could I get here and not know a thing?"

(Looking at ceiling. Disgusted with himself, trying to get things clear. Straining to think through things and get it all connected up.)

3:15 A.M., Sunday morning, November 30, 1941.

"God, my head starts whirling again"

"All I can remember is my folks' trying to talk me out of going to the Navy"

"it's just like jumping off of something"

"it's not clear"

"we're going to Corvallis tomorrow?"

"I am going to school there?"

"You're an English teacher?"

"No, my English teacher was a woman"

Chuck decided Don was not going to die and lay down himself at 4:30 a.m.

Chuck got up at 6:00 and again about 8:00 and kept the fire going. It was bitter cold outside. He kept Don thoroughly wrapped and covered up.

Shortly after 10:00 a.m. Don sat up, ate breakfast, and seemed to recognize Chuck. He was still too weak to do anything but lie in bed. But he said, "It's all right. It's beginning to get clear. I remember you now, Chuck. I am beginning to remember Oregon State. Gosh, my shoulders hurt me, and my arms and legs."

Sunday afternoon (24 hours after the accident) when Don was able to talk the Penningtons and other neighbors came in to sit with him and talk over everything. Don explained:

"I had always planned what I'd do. I knew if I thrashed around trying to swim against the outgoing tide I'd wear myself out. So I swam out and stayed out past the breakers until the tide started back."

Mr. Pennington explained: "The tide was going out when you went out. The tide was still going out when you swam in. It did not change until after you were in."

MacGregor (a neighbor): "One of the worst storms of the year."

Pennington: "Nobody ever came in against an out-going tide that I ever heard of before."

Don: "Undertow kept knocking me off my feet — like when you roll down a hill — you regain your feet, but you keep on rolling."

III

The total transcript notes contain 190 lines. Thoughts out in the ocean occupy 134 lines; thoughts on the beach occupy 41 lines; thoughts on the bed in the house after his rescue occupy 15 lines.

The transcript falls into five distinct groups of thoughts: (*a*) out in the ocean, 64 lines; (*b*) on the beach, just out of the water, 13 lines; (*c*) on the bed in the house, 15 lines; (*d*) on the beach, trying to crawl to the house, 28 lines; (*e*) out in the ocean (different tone), 70 lines.

If, under hypnosis now, Don recited from beginning to end every thought that went through his mind from the time he lost his footing until he started talking; or if, by an imaginary process, an electrical recording had been made of his entire stream of thought during his experience; we should have an absolutely complete transcript. What we do have is a collection of fragments verbalized as he wandered over the complete record of thoughts. The analogy of a giant disc may serve here. If the complete record of his thoughts is represented by a large phonograph disc and Don's verbalized sampling is represented by placing the needle about at various places on the disc, Don's talking during delirium falls into these groups:

1. Very little is apparently given of what he was thinking the first two hours from about 4:30 P.M. to 6:30 P.M. Undoubtedly the eight lines figuring out what had happened to him and determining his course of action were thoughts that went through his mind shortly after he lost his footing:

you must have stepped in a hole; the tide took you out; it's a good thing you know how to swim; but don't swim too hard; get out past the breakers before you get caught; you thought you had it figured out; how you'd make it; now's your chance.

2. It is logical that in his delirium he should verbalize the most intense moments of anxiety. Apparently the great bulk of his thoughts recorded in the transcript falls in the period from about 6:30 P.M. to 7:30 P.M. when he was deciding that the tide had turned and he was swimming back toward the light on the coast.

stay out past breakers until tide changes; the wind is pushing you past; you won't make it; you can't make it; float for a while; maybe I can make it; cramps; take it easy or you are going to cramp; do you think you can make it; it's getting dark; water logged; keep moving to keep warm; I have been out here two hours already; you are going to make it; dive under it; dive under the breaker to get back; don't drink any salt water; don't swallow any salt water; try to hold your own until the tide turns; you will be O.K. but you're getting tired; you were crazy to come out in the first place; you have gone out too far; dive under that breaker; you'll be all right; it's getting dark; the tide's turning; see that light; it's getting plainer; take it easier; you are going to make it to the breakers; swim with the breakers; you are going to make it; dive under the big ones; you can't ride 'em all; it's getting so dark; if it wasn't for that light you might be going the wrong way; I hope they don't turn it out; you'll make it; just take it easy; God, you have been out here a long time; I'm getting so tired; being out here for hours; give up; just give up; give one more try; the mighty Pacific; it's gonna defeat you.

3. It is possible that Don was not out of the water even by 7:30 pm; but it seems apparent that he was on the beach for quite a time. His struggle to crawl out of the water and drag himself across the beach is well recorded in 41 lines. He unfortunately went through discomfort which could have been spared him if his friends had not already given him up as drowned. Nobody dreamed of his fantastic plan to swim out past the breakers, stay out for hours, and then swim back.

that sand stings my face; it's cold; drag yourself; why doesn't somebody come; take it easy; you're out of the water; I can't yell; why doesn't my flashlight work; I can't yell; my voice doesn't work; my throat is all stopped up; crawl out of the water before it takes you back out; you are starting all over again; what are you gonna do here?; get to the light; this doesn't seem familiar; crawl through the bank; crawl through the canyon; where are you?; this is the end of the line; you can't make it any farther; you can't go on; you're just a weakling; you can't make it; this is as far as you can go; you're just a weakling; you still got your rabbit's foot?; your mother bought that for you; it's a good thing you took that along; your 165 pounds is too heavy;

you can't pull it; it's too heavy; there's a log; lean over it and throw up; stick your finger down your throat; throw up and then you can breathe; you can't get up the bank; you'll have to go up the canyon.

4. Sometime between 9:00 pm and 10:00 pm Don thought the questions which puzzled him as he tried to figure out where he was. He was lying on a davenport in the Pennington's living room at Wakonda Beach, the cottage nearest where he had gone swimming.

where are you?; I don't remember this; this is all new to me; where is this?; where were you before you came here?; where was I before I came here?; where are your folks?; where do they live?; wait 'til you come to; you don't know anyone; strangers; you don't know anyone; they are all strangers; can't I remember where I am; better go back and see where you lost your senses.

IV

On Monday December 1, 1941, Chuck took Don back to Corvallis and put him in the infirmary at Oregon State College. As he regained his strength and felt like talking, the transcript was discussed with him.

"You see, Chuck, I had lived on the ocean all my life. I had seen lots of people get drowned. I had made up my mind what I'd do if I ever got caught myself." His plan was to stay out past the breakers until the tide changed, keep himself up by swimming and floating, and then return easily with an incoming tide. He followed his plan exactly; the plan explains why he stayed in the ocean several hours.

1. HIS EXPLANATION OF WHAT WAS HAPPENING TO HIM was revealed in his delirium: *you must have stepped in a hole; the tide took you out; get out past the breakers before you get caught; you thought you had it figured out; how you'd make it; now's your chance.*

2. HIS RESIGNATION TO A FATE OF DROWNING was revealed in his delirium: *you won't get to go to Puget Sound next year; your 19 years are going to be over quick; you are not even going to know what life's about; what difference does it make if you do drown?; sailors are drowning in Europe every day; you're no better than they are; break it to them gently; kiss them good bye; only thing smacks you is a wave; get a grand-daughter and lose a son; it's a good thing you wrote just before you left; I hope they call and tell them; I always said I would be buried at sea; here's your chance; I hope you never wash up on the beach; the birds'll pick your eyes out; this is the last time you'll have both of them; you'll be like this for all time; I remember when you lost your little boat; I never knew then you were going to be next.*

Don explained that he had planned to attend the College of Puget Sound on a football scholarship, had come to Oregon State for his first year, wanted to go to Puget Sound the second year.

He was convinced at times out in the ocean that he was going to drown and he wanted the news broken to his parents gently. He was thinking of his mother out in the ocean: *get a grand-daughter and lose a son.* His married brother had a new little baby girl: the news of the arrival reached Don shortly before he started to the coast for this trip.

As he was growing up his mind had been deeply shocked by sights and stories of men who drowned in the Pacific Ocean. Sights of dismembered bodies had left a horror in his memory of people who *wash up on the beach.*

HIS REMINISCENCES OF A PLEASANT EVENING were revealed in his delirium: *why don't people sit by the fire like this and talk more often?* Friday night had been a wild and stormy night, windy and rainy outside. Don had listened contentedly to Chuck's poetry as they sat comfortably gazing into a big log fire.

Don explained that his mother enjoyed sitting before a log fire but that he was not satisfied unless his evening could be filled with dancing, dating, and active social pursuits. It was gratifying to Chuck that the delirium revealed that Don had enjoyed the evening of quiet philosophical musings which he had expected to find tedious.

4. HIS RELIGIOUS FEELINGS AND MINOR SUPERSTITIONS were revealed in his delirium: *You got out of your wreck all right; they said you wouldn't; Father Dailey; Sister Mary; laughed when you got me out of the other wreck; I'll never laugh again if you'll get me out of this one; any time that you would spend two hours on knees for me why should I laugh?; you still got your rabbit foot?; your mother bought that for you; it's a good thing you took that along; keep your fingers crossed.*

Don explained that he was a Catholic, that he had been taken to a Catholic hospital when he had a bad auto wreck. The naive credulity of *if you'll get me out of this one* is happily offset by the healthy skepticism of *laughed when you got me out of the other wreck.* The *rabbit's foot* and *fingers crossed* are more of a jest than anything serious; he laughed about them later.

5. HIS APPRAISAL OF A GIRL was revealed in his delirium: *that phoney girl; talking about Hollywood; crazy people; Seaside; she's stringing you along; she thinks she's big time; Chuck's on to her; that girl is just trying to pull the wool over somebody's eyes; peculiar people; sort of cute; but she thinks she's good; don't be a dink; it's a good thing you didn't ask her for a date; you're better than she is; she talks too much; that girl; that's a laugh; think of something else; Seaside; Hell! that's a laugh; she probably stopped there to get a drink of water.*

Don explained that this girl was Sheila Patrick and that Chuck knew her. She was one of the most beautiful co-eds on the Oregon State campus, very proud and very sophisticated. She had spent considerable time in both Hollywood, California, and swank Seaside, Oregon, but Don thought she was only trying to impress him, "*to pull the wool over*" his eyes. He had never dated a girl with such urbane bearing and manner; he was embarrassed and lacked self-confidence. Actually, as a matter of fact, they might have been ideally matched; they had identical Catholic and Irish backgrounds; he was a football hero, she was enormously popular socially. But his inferiority complex was too strong; he walked home with her from class but he never got the nerve to *ask her for a date.*

6. HIS REFLECTIONS ON SCHOOL AND MAKING GOOD IN LIFE were revealed in his delirium: *you are all through in school; you have wasted your folks' money; what will Rose think of this; you won't pass your exam; you're a fool; they always told you you were dumb; you're trying to bluff your way through; you can't bluff now; you gotta produce the goods; you can't play shuffleboard out here; you can't dance; you haven't got a boat; you're making it the hard way; you're doing fine, you'll be a success; that old saying "paddle your own canoe;" you can't hand the paddle to the guy in the back; you've got to paddle your own canoe; you played football to get out of high school, you are going to have to swim to get out of the ocean.*

7. HIS REGARD FOR HIS PARENTS was revealed in his delirium: *what will my folks think; Mother will go crazy; what will she do when she finds out?; she is not well enough to stand it, break it to them gently; my heart belongs to you; kiss them good bye; either make it all the way or not make it at all; if your mother found you on the beach she'd go crazy.*

8. HIS ADVICE TO HIMSELF was revealed in his delirium: *float for a while; take it easy or you are going to cramp; water logged; keep moving to keep warm; you are going to make it; dive under it; dive under the breaker to get back; don't drink any salt water; don't swallow any salt water; take off your pants and shirts; they will help you float; don't take them off it will help you float; keep them on; take it easy; you will be all right; try to hold your own until the tide turns; you will be O.K. but you're getting tired; you were crazy to come out in the first place; you have gone out too far; you know better than that; don't swallow any water; it'll choke you; you'll be all right; it's getting dark; the tide's turning; see that light; it's getting plainer; take it easier; you'll be all right; the water stings my face just like needles; you are going to make it to the breakers; swim with the breakers; you are going to make it; that sand stings my face; it's cold; drag yourself; take it easy; you're out of the water; I can't yell; my voice doesn't work; my throat is all stopped up; crawl out of the water before it takes you back out; your 165 pounds is too heavy; you can't pull it; it's too heavy; there's a log; lean over it and throw up; stick your finger down your throat; throw up and then you can breathe; dive under the big ones; you can't ride 'em all; think about something; keep your mind busy; don't worry; you're an Irishman; as good as any of them; they don't let down; you're Irish and you don't quit; it's a good thing you know how to swim; but don't swim too hard.*

9. HIS RECOLLECTIONS CONCERNING THE ROSE BOWL GAME were revealed in his delirium: *Rose Bowl; you won't get to see it; I won't be able to collect it; I got one over on them; eleven men go to the Rose Bowl; one kid gets the whole Pacific Ocean; what are you going to do with it; it is not half as crowded as it will be in the Rose Bowl.*

Don explained that he had listened intently to the radio version of the game which determined that Oregon State would go to the Rose Bowl on New Year's Day. This news was so exhilarating to him that he decided to go swimming in the ocean, or literally "jumping the breakers" which is a pleasure known to all ocean lovers.

V

What we have here is nothing more than the report of a normal person's delirium due to extreme exhaustion. Similar deliria recurring after the accident would have been abnormal. It is true that Don's sleep for some months afterward was interrupted by terrifying dreams during which he would call out: "I can't make it" or "I won't make it." But these symptoms would seem to fall well within the range of normal under the circumstances and would seem to indicate only the intensity of the original shock. Characteristic amnesia followed the delirium. Instead of persisting, nowever, it fortunately cleared up automatically as Don regained his strength.

A great deal of the time during the delirium he talked to himself in such phrases as *you won't make it* and *I hope you never wash up on the beach.* A curious cleavage exists here. It seems as though the *you* (the person asleep) is being lectured by the "unconscious mind" which is suppressed by the "conscious mind" during the day.

An interesting illustration of this phenomenon is shown also in the case of a psychologist at Oregon State who in a dentist's office had himself put under gas to see what happened. He kept thinking, "Why doesn't that guy do something about his shins' being kicked?" The dentist was kicking his shins. But the shins belonged to the "guy" who was in charge during waking hours (the "conscious mind") and the "unconscious mind" was observing as an outsider looking on.

Don, of course, had no flashlight with him when he was crawling across the beach and was thinking to himself: *Why doesn't my flashlight work?* Don had carried a flashlight the night before (1) when he went out back of the cabin to get firewood, (2) when he went "jumping the breakers" in infinite blackness on the beach with Chuck. The night of his accident was equally dark.

The temperature of the ocean was 46. Swimming three hours in water 46 degrees is a feat in itself. Small wonder that he was so exhausted when it is remembered that Don fought an outgoing tide and a dreadful storm that added bitterly cold rain and high wind.

168

CHAPTER VIII

THE SIMULATION OF PERSONAL DEATH:

A T-GROUP EXPERIENCE

Introduction

Our final chapter, an original paper by Saul Toobert, reports the origin, rationale, and development of the week-end experience which culminates the seminar "Confrontations of Death." We can add only that the teacher planning to try to duplicate these experiences should obtain the very best, most thoroughly experienced, emotionally mature trainers he can find; additionally, it seems best to have the same trainers, rather than different ones, time after time. Trainers themselves have profoundly insightful experiences as they help with "Confrontations of Death," and it is only after assimilation of these experiences that the trainer can most effectively assist you in planning a meaningful and exciting series of exercises, or a "laboratory," for your students. The teacher has no better ally than an experienced mature trainer who has confronted and come to terms with his own feelings about his own personal death.

In Appendix B we list all National Training Laboratories branch offices and officials in the United States. The inexperienced teacher will be most likely to find an effective trainer from NTL; we hasten to say, however, that not all NTL trainers are experts on laboratories dealing with feelings about personal death. The teacher is also advised to consider the resources of his own university or organization.

For the student, Dr. Toobert's article is a preview of things to come — although the details will be different for each class, our objective is always the same. We want to "turn you on" to life. We feel the most effective way to do this is to "turn you on" to a confrontation of your own death.

THE SIMULATION OF PERSONAL DEATH: A T-GROUP EXPERIENCE

by

Saul Toobert

In this paper, an attempt is made to describe in detail the set of experiences which, taken together, comprise the "laboratory" or week-end T-group experience which climaxes the "Confrontations of Death" seminar offered at the University of Oregon. Experienced trainers will recognize some of the exercises, or will realize that a more or less basic exercise can be changed in a detail or two to accomplish another task than that for which it was originally designed. One of the strong points of the T-group method in an educational setting, it seems to us, is the ability of the instructor or of the trainer to innovate and to design — almost on the spot, once he has mastered some basic group processes and the exercises that give practice in coping with these — a laboratory experience that will unerringly meet the needs of the particular group with which he is working. Therefore, we emphasize that the trainer contemplating design of a laboratory experience in "Confrontations of Death" regard what follows in this paper as suggestive and illustrative only; literally thousands of variations and innovations can be thought of — and should be implemented, at least on a trial basis — by the creative trainer.

Before we discuss the labs themselves, perhaps a description of the human relations warm-up which began the seminar is in order.

The Human Relations Warm-Up

The aim of the seminar is to offer an opportunity for students to deal with their own feelings about death. An attempt must therefore be made to create an atmosphere in which social fears are reduced and trust is established. The warm-up is conceptualized as an attempt to get the class acquainted with one another in a short period of time, to "unfreeze" them, since they are usually strangers to one another, to teach them certain communication skills, and to form three permanent small groups for the remainder of the seminar. The theme of the seminar, death, is also introduced into the warm-up. The instructors always participate along with the students in the warm-up. The writer, who has been a trainer in the week-end laboratory experience for each seminar, conducted the warm-up the first two times the seminar was offered. Another trainer conducted the warm-up in Winter, 1970. The warm-up has been composed of essentially the same set of exercises each time.

With the above goals in mind, the warm-up proceeded as follows:

1. **Pairing**. The instruction given is, "Approach someone you do not know and talk to him about anything you want to." (2 minutes). Pairing is repeated about a half dozen times. Its purpose is to offer social approval for talking to a stranger, and to begin getting the group acquainted with each other.

2. **Blind Exercise**. The trainer says, "Now leave the person you are talking to and approach a new person. One of you close your eyes and pretend to be blind. The other person in the pair is sighted. Now continue to talk under these conditions." (2 minutes). After switching roles for another two minutes, the instruction is, "Pair up with an adjacent couple and make a foursome. Talk about your feelings about being blind." (4 minutes) The purpose of this exercise is to offer an experience in role playing and an experience in debriefing or talking about feelings. The use of the foursome expands the number of people with whom one feels comfortable talking about his own feelings.

3. **Non-verbal Encounter**. The instruction is, "Now leave your foursome. Approach someone you don't know and have an encounter with him without words." (2 minutes). "Now pair up with an adjacent couple, make foursomes again, and talk about your feelings about this experience." (4 minutes). The purpose of this exercise is again role playing, but with the addition of an "unnatural" or unusual communication restriction, i.e., being unable to talk. The debriefing gives further experience in putting feelings into words. It should be pointed out that by

this time the class is usually stimulated and noisy. The atmosphere is freed up, the students are trying to examine their feelings about these experiences and to share them with one another.

4. **Role Playing**. The trainer says, "Leave your foursome, find someone you don't know or don't know well, and sit down with him somewhere in the room. One of you is to role play being a patient with a terminal illness. The other role plays being a physician who is telling the patient that he is going to die." (4 to 5 minutes). "Now the physician stands, while the patient remains seated." (2 minutes). "Now the patient and the physician continue discussing the problem but the physician stands on a chair while the patient remains seated." (2 minutes). "The physician comes down from the chair and stands behind the patient while they continue talking about the problem." (2 minutes). "The physician remains behind the patient, but puts his hands on the patient's shoulders." (2 minutes). "Form foursomes again with a pair nearby and talk about your feelings as a patient and your feelings as a physician." (4 minutes). The purposes of this exercise are manifold. Experience in role playing is heightened, additional trials at talking about feelings are provided, a first exposure to the subject of death and to talking about one's own death is brought about, changes in the way the problem is verbalized depending upon changes in the positions or statuses of the "doctor" and "patient" are brought home — these and a myriad of other new perceptions and new ideas usually are brought out in the debriefing.

After this exercise the instructors are asked to stand aside. The class is requested to organize themselves into three groups of equal size, with equal resources. "Resources" are defined as such characteristics as age, sex, major, and anything else one can think of that is considered a resource to the group. When they are so organized, the trainer asks the groups to look at themselves and decide if their resources are distributed equally and, if not, to do some shifting about until they are equal. He also tells them that if any married couples are in the class they should arrange to place themselves in different groups. We have found this less likely to inhibit married couples. Instructors are then assigned to each group by the trainer. The remainder of the evening is spent getting acquainted within the group by debriefing the whole evening, talking about feelings generated by the

warm-up, and working on a task decided upon by the instructor and the group together.

We have found this type of warm-up to be a successful design in getting the seminar off to a good start. The seminar then proceeds like most other classes which meet for three hours each week. The nature of the presentations or "in-puts" have been described in a previous chapter and are detailed for one semester's work in Appendix A. The unique experience for each evening is the debriefing in small groups, wherein feelings and attitudes toward the content are examined and shared with the group.

The Week-End Laboratories

For the first week-end laboratory, two trainers were assigned to each small group, along with an instructor, for a total of 3 staff for each 10-12 students. Trainers were either associates of the National Training Laboratories or people experienced in conducting groups. Three of the trainers were also certified psychologists in the State of Oregon. The staff were prepared for all eventualities by anticipating trouble in this new venture and having enough personnel to deal with it; the legal responsibility of the university as well as our moral obligation to our students, was protected by the presence of the certified psychologists.[1]

The laboratory took place in a large private home. The house easily accommodated the three groups in separated rooms, and provided a large living room where the entire seminar could meet together. The laboratory began Saturday morning, ended before dinner, reconvened Sunday morning, and ended late Sunday afternoon. Participants went home to sleep Saturday night.

On the first morning, the group opened with a warm-up consisting of brief non-verbal sensory awareness and space exploration exercises. As the groups had shared experiences throughout the term not shared by the trainers, the decision was made to break up the groups and reconstitute new ones. Participants were instructed to move around the

[1] The trainers were: Richard Schmuck, Patricia Schmuck, Carolin Keutzer, Dan Langmeyer, Charles Pyron and Saul Toobert. Norman Sundberg, Marvin Janzen and Frances Scott were the instructors.

room and mingle with one another, then to select a partner. The pair in turn selected another pair and continued this procedure until three groups of equal size were formed. The groups were examined for equal distribution of resources, adjustments were made and trainers and instructors assigned to groups.

The remainder of the morning was devoted to a birth-death continuum exercise; each individual was asked to place himself at the present time where he thought he was on a graphic continuum beginning with birth and ending with death. The debriefing was the most important aspect of the exercise. In the writer's group, participants who expected to live a short time, a medium length of time and a long time subdivided into three mini-groups to seek out other common characteristics.

After lunch, in total session, each individual wrote his own **eulogy** and **epitaph**. Included in the exercise was a notation as to age of death and how death took place. The epitaph is a short statement the person wishes to have appear on his tombstone. The eulogy is an account which might appear in a newspaper or might be given at one's funeral.

Triads were formed within the small groups for debriefing. Each person read his eulogy and epitaph while the other two asked questions and shared feelings about his account. The small group then debriefed as a whole dealing with questions like: What did you feel as you read? What did you die of? What did you leave when you died? How old were you?

Sunday morning within each small group eight participants role-played an extended family in a conflict situation. The other members stood back to serve as resource persons. The trainers, at the height of the conflict, selected to "die" the member of the family most crucial to the family's communication network. The group then spent the remainder of the day role-playing all of the problems and emotions that face a family when a member dies.

In the writer's group the family was assembled at dinner when the role playing began. The father and oldest son were in a heated argument; it was obvious that the father in this family was the communication "hub" or the most central figure. At the height of the conflict, the father suffered a heart attack; the trainer indicated this by covering him over with a coat. The family then role played the entire scope of proceedings following such an event, including calling the doctor, the undertaker's interview, the obituary for the local newspaper, dealing with helpful neighbors and father's lodge members, the minister, the church service, the problems attendant on the smaller children, the widowed mother's reactions, and so on. The intensity of the role playing was limited only by the imagination of the group members. The resource people (the small group members who were not role-playing the family) were called upon to serve as doctor, newspaperman, minister, etc., as needed. The final scene was after the funeral at the cemetery. The entire episode extended from about 9:00 am until about 2:30 pm, with the group simply ignoring the lunch hour. It was not until after the role-play funeral that the group finally went to lunch. Debriefing after lunch lasted until 5:00 pm. The general consensus was that this role playing was the highlight of the laboratory. Participants became emotionally involved in the episode and felt very close to one another in this shared experience. Many reported that the "Confrontations" seminar and the laboratory week-end were the high points of their university careers.

We learned several useful things from our students as a result of this first laboratory. First, there is no need in reconstituting the groups for the week-end experience; this makes enough people uncomfortable that it is not justified. We discovered later, however, that a special effort to incorporate the trainer into the group must then be made, or groups are likely to spend valuable time "testing out" the trainer and may even end by not accepting him at all. Second, a retreat situation is far preferable to one where participants are allowed to return to their usual routines at night. The laboratory needs the increased informal contact of the residential retreat. We have been able to provide this kind of setting at a nominal charge to the students since this first laboratory. Third, we learned it is impossible to grade "Confrontations of Death," so it is now offered only on a "pass — no-pass" or ungraded basis. Fourth, we discovered that while tears are common, explosive emotional "blow-ups" are not likely; one trainer per group is quite sufficient, with only one of them a certified psychologist.

The next time the seminar was taught the week-end laboratory was held at a YMCA camp in the country. Participants brought sleeping bags, spent the night and had meals together.

The design very much resembled the first laboratory with minor exceptions. The warm-up included a *trust-walk* in the wooded area surrounding the camp. Participants first mingled, selected a partner, were issued blindfolds and told to walk outdoors, with the sighted member of the pair offering to the blindfolded person rich tactual experiences. After 10 minutes, the pair switched roles and blindfolds and the exercise continued for 10 minutes more. Students then debriefed this experience in the same small groups in which they had participated all term. Each small group this time was joined by one trainer who worked with the group and the instructor. [2]

The highlight of this laboratory was again the family role-playing exercise. Feedback from the students was the same as the previous term for the most part, but there were some interesting exceptions. Apparently the student sub-culture had picked up certain information about "Confrontations . . ." Briefly, it was considered to be a course which would give everyone a peak experience like nothing ever had done before; it was highly recommended to friends and acquaintances. We were inundated with students who were essentially "thrill-seekers." With this kind of orientation, a number of students not surprisingly failed to achieve the anticipated peak experience. They were let down and disappointed. We resolved 1) to intensify our screening efforts, 2) to be more creative in changing the laboratory exercises each time the seminar is offered, and 3) to give students more factual information about what they could expect from the seminar, so unrealistic expectations would be less likely to develop.

In addition, the closest thing to an unpleasant episode in our entire experience with "Confrontations . . ." occurred during this laboratory. In one group, a graduate student who had done laboratory training himself unwittingly utilized the group to try to work through some emotional difficulties he was encountering, to the detriment of the group itself; the trainer was unable to cope with this more

experienced group member. We began to see that we must 4) utilize trainers of considerable experience and expertness, and preferably those who have worked with "Confrontations . . ." previously.

For the next term the design of the laboratory was changed significantly. The retreat setting was in a former Benedictine monastery, a beautiful and picturesque site on the forested banks of the McKenzie River.[3]

The lab started with a non-verbal warm-up wherein participants paired off and engaged in a series of non-verbal tasks; they said "hello" with their hands, had a conversation, played, had a fight, and made up — all with their hands without the use of speech. They then sat back-to-back on the floor, experienced each other's life and warmth. Then they pulled apart slowly and went to their original small groups without talking. After assembling in their small groups they debriefed the experience.

The next exercise involved writing ten sentences beginning with "Dying is like . . ." and another ten beginning with "When I die . . ." The sentences were first shared in triads for debriefing, then debriefed in the entire small group.

Before the large group assembled for each meal, the trainers taped two "X's" either to the bottoms of coffee cups, plates, or chairs. It was announced that the individuals thus randomly selected as "zapped" were to "die" immediately after the meal, and to remain "dead" for an hour. During this time the "zapped" persons could communicate with no one. After an hour, the "zapped" person returned to his group and debriefed the experience. This innovation proved to be a very worthwhile addition to the laboratory both for those who experienced "death" directly in the "zapping" as well as the others who heard reports of their feelings and experiences. One such experience is recounted in Chapter I.

During the afternoon of the first day, the **birth-death continuum** was repeated, with debriefing in the small group. The next exercise was an innovation in which the group constituted themselves as a working "machine," with members as "parts." The trainer

2 The trainers were Carolin Keutzer, Vincent Manion and Saul Toobert who worked with instructors Steven Saturen, Phoebe Baker and Donna McKenzie.

3 The trainers were John Wallen, Donald Murray and Saul Toobert, who worked with instructors Marvin Janzen, Frances Scott, and Phoebe Baker.

then pulled names from a hat. As each name was pulled, that individual "died" by sitting motionless and not taking further part in the "work" of the "machine." It was apparent that as individuals left the "machine," those remaining had to work harder to perform the same tasks. The experience was debriefed in each small group.

After dinner, the **eulogy-epitaph** exercise described above was repeated with some excellent innovations. Participants were instructed to include in the eulogy the circumstances of death, the nature of the last hour and how they would like their remains disposed of. Each person in turn gave his written eulogy and epitaph to a member of the group to read for him, while he lay supine in the center of the group with a jacket over his face to represent a shroud. After the eulogy was read, he was interviewed about his life while he remained in his "coffin," then brought back to life to be interviewed again about how it felt to be "dead."

The eulogy, of course, is really a description of one's life, rather than one's death. The participant may choose to write what he thinks people **will** say about him after he dies or what he **hopes** they will say. The laboratory thus presents the participant with a confrontation of his own life.

The individual eulogies and their debriefing consumed the evening and next morning. Needless to say, the eulogy exercise was fraught with emotion. At one point in the writer's group, the entire group was in tears over the "death" of a key group member.

This laboratory omitted the family role-play which had been so successful before, and emphasized the eulogy-epitaph innovations.

The laboratory conducted in Spring, 1970, manifested a wider degree of difference between the experiences of the three small groups than ever before, but it also provided more participants with the opportunity to experience simulated death than we had been able to do before. In staff debriefing about the reasons for this, we came to these conclusions: 1) experienced trainers arrive at the same place by different methods, or, the more experienced the trainer, the more difficult it is for him to stay within the bounds of a pre-determined

laboratory protocol, even one he helps to design, but the less important it is that he do so because he can be trusted somehow to help his group experience the generalized objectives of the laboratory, and 2) it is important to provide in the design of the laboratory an over-abundance of opportunities and methods for participants to experience the simulation of death; the randomness of the "zap" and "machine" exercises, the intensity of the epitaph-eulogy role-playing and of the birth-death continuum, provided each individual with at least one meaningful confrontation of his own personal death.

SUMMARY

As a trainer working with "Confrontations of Death" seminar, I suggest serious consideration of the following points by those interested in conducting similar courses:

1. Students should be screened prior to admission to the course. Emotionally unstable people, those with a history of hospitalization or treatment for mental illness, and those who have undergone recent bereavement should not be admitted.

2. A simple human relations warm-up at the first meeting of the seminar seems crucial in helping the instructors and their small groups get started well; if possible, a trainer who intends to be present at the week-end laboratory should conduct this warm-up, although any trainer (who is not one of the instructors) may do it. Instructors should participate along with students in the warm-up.

3. The small groups which have been together throughout the seminar should probably remain intact for the week-end laboratory. Special consideration must then be given to introducing the "stranger" (in the person of the trainer) into the small group quickly and expeditiously.

4. The week-end laboratory experience should be conducted in a residential retreat situation, away from any pressures competing for the attention of participants.

5. It is advisable to have a certified clinician on hand in the event of difficulty with a participant. While we have experienced no such problems as yet, it is possible a future laboratory might produce them.

6. Creativity and innovation in constantly changing the content and the emphasis of laboratory exercises is essential if students are not to feel cheated. "Confrontations of Death" is one course that *must not* be taught the same way year after year or it will most certainly lose its impact and importance to the student.

7. Students should be advised from the first what to expect in this seminar; unrealistic expectations should be dealt with by the instructors before the laboratory, if possible.

8. There is no substitute for experienced trainers; the trainer will find that as he conducts more laboratories he has greater insight and more ideas for further innovation. It is probably a good idea for the same instructors and the same trainers to work together over time, but not necessarily in the same pairs. For the instructors and trainers, as for the students, change is not only fascinating but necessary, and change can be brought about by pairing different instructor/trainer teams, as well as by different laboratory designs.

APPENDIX A

Course Outline and Syllabus

The course outline presented here should be regarded as an example only; it happens to follow the order of the book of readings, but we do not use this order each term. Each instructor should decide for himself how much of the reading material to use and which topics seem to make the best psychological progression from week to week. Used as an example is a recent University of Oregon course.

CSPA 407:   Confrontations of Death

Instructors: Marvin Janzen, Donna McKenzie, Isabelle Moser and Consultants

Human-Relations Group Leaders: Saul Toobert, Frances Page and Peter Maher

Rooms: Quonset 7, Quonset 5 and 8

Text: *Confrontations of Death: A Book of Readings and a Suggested Method of Instruction*

Course Outline and Readings

Week I   Preliminary Considerations of Life and Death

POSITION PAPER 1: Your philosophy of life and death

HUMAN-RELATIONS WARM-UP: Saul Toobert

READINGS (Text):

(1) (Optional) Chapter I: Orientation to a Concept and a Method.

(2)   Chapter II: Some Taxonomies of the Phenomena of Death (especially Nettler's article)

Week II	Philosophical Considerations of the Meaning of Life and Death

Week II   Philosophical Considerations of the Meaning of Life and Death

Class will meet in **Studio B** of the Library

FILM: "Ikiru"

READINGS (Text):

(1)   Chapter III: Some Philosophies of Life and Death (all selections)

Week III   The Theme of Death in Poetry

GUEST READERS: (To be announced)

READINGS (Text):

(1)   Chapter IV: The Theme of Death in Poetry and Literature (all selections)

Week IV   The Theme of Death as Presented in Classical and Contemporary Music

Class will meet at 1410 Parnell (Marv Janzen's house)

AUDIO TAPE: Classical and Contemporary music
T-GROUP DISCUSSIONS: Class and Instructors

READINGS (In Reserve Book Room of Library)

(1)   Laura A. Huxley, *This Timeless Moment: A Personal View of Aldous Huxley.* Farrar, Strauss and Giroux, 1968.

(2)   Lael T. Wertenbaker, *Death of a Man.* Random House, 1957.

Week V   Doctors and Hospitals

GUEST LECTURER: (Physician, name to be announced)

T-GROUP DISCUSSIONS: Class and Instructors

READINGS (Text):

(1)   Chapter V: Doctors and Dying Patients (especially Saunders article)

Week VI   The Process of Dying

Class will meet in **Studio A** of the Library

VIDEO TAPE: Documentary on Death

T-GROUP DISCUSSIONS: Class and Instructors

READINGS (Text):

(1)   Chapter VI: The Deaths of Other People: Bereavement and Mourning (especially excerpt from James Agee)

Week-end   Personal Death: A Sensitivity Group Week-End T-Group Experience

Benedictine Retreat, McKenzie Bridge, Oregon

TRAINERS: Saul Toobert, Frances Page, and Peter Maher

READINGS: (Text)

(1)   Chapter VII: Some Considerations of Personal Death (all selections)

(2)   Chapter VIII: Confrontations of Death: To Each His Own Understanding

Week VII   Final Session

POSITION PAPER II: Your philosophy of life and death (to be written in class)

DEBRIEFING OF WEEK-END: Class and Instructors

APPENDIX B

Directory of National Training Laboratories Personnel

Listed here are the current offices of the National Training Laboratories Institute in the United States. If you contact the office nearest you, you will be given assistance in locating an experienced trainer who will help you apply the T-group method in the educational setting.

Members of the Board of Directors will also be helpful to you, and in some instances you may wish to contact one of them through the regional offices of the Institute.

HEADQUARTERS

Leland P. Bradford, Executive Director
Jerry B. Harvey, Deputy Director
1201 Sixteenth Street, N.W.
Washington, D.C. 20036
(202) 223-9400

CHICAGO METROPOLITAN OFFICE

Thomas R. Bennett II, Acting Director
20 North Wacker Drive
Chicago, Illinois 60606
(312) 641-2633

INTERMOUNTAIN DIVISION

William G. Dyer, Director
P.O. Box 200
Salt Lake City, Utah 84110
(801) 322-6491

MIDWEST DIVISION

Oron P. South, Director
2 West Fortieth Street
Kansas City, Missouri 64111
(816) 531-3136

NORTHWEST DIVISION

Charles Hosford, Director
One Plaza S.W.
6900 S.W. Haines Road
Tigard, Oregon 9723
(503) 639-7651

NTL BOARD OF DIRECTORS

BIBLIOGRAPHY

The theme of death has been explored by philosophers, theologians, sociologists, psychologists, psychiatrists, poets, and writers of fiction throughout man's history. A truly exhaustive bibliography would be a fascinating and monumental undertaking. Regretfully, it is not within the scope of this book.

The following bibliography is a selection of contemporary contributions to the literature on death which will enlarge upon and enhance the readings. It is not intended to be comprehensive. Some facets of the subject such as suicide or death in war are deliberately omitted as they are a distraction from the main theme. Undoubtedly some significant works may be overlooked. Most students, though will find these references adequate for the course.

BOOKS:

Barker, J.C. *Scared to Death: An Examination of Fear, Its Cause and Effects.* Letchworth, Hertfordshire, The Garden City Press, Ltd., 1968.

Bendann, Effie. *Death Customs. An Analytical Study of Burial Rites.* New York. Alfred A. Knopf, 1930.

Berezin, Martin A., and Stanley H. Cath. *Geriatric Psychiatry: Grief, Loss and Emotional Disorders in the Aging Process.* New York. International Universities Press. 1967.

Eissler, Kurt Robert. *The Psychiatrist and the Dying Patient.* New York. International Universities Press. 1955.

Farberow, Norman L., ed. *Taboo Topics.* New York. Atherton. 1963.

Feifel, Herman, ed. *The Meaning of Death.* New York McGraw Hill. 1960

Fiedler, Leslie. *Love and Death in the American Novel.* New York. Meridian Books. 1960.

Fulton, Robert. *Death and Identity.* New York. John Wiley. 1965. (Extensive bibliography included)

Glaser, Barney and A.L. Strauss. *Time for Dying.* Chicago. Aldine. 1968.

———— *Awareness of Dying.* Chicago. Aldine. 1965.

Gorer, Geoffrey. *Death, Grief and Mourning.* Garden City. Doubleday. 1965.

Group for the Advancement of Psychiatry. *Death and Dying: Attitudes of Patient and Doctor.* New York. GAP. 1966.

Harrington, Alan. *The Immortalist.* New York. Random House. 1969.

Herzog, Edgar. *Psyche and Death.* New York. G.P. Putnam's Sons. 1966.

Hinton, J. *Dying.* Baltimore. Penguin Books. 1967.

Huxley, Laura Anchera. *This Timeless Moment: A Personal View of Aldous Huxley.* Farrar, Strauss and Giroux. 1968.

Kübler-Ross, Elisabeth. *On Death and Dying.* London, Macmillan, 1969. (Includes extensive bibliography)

Lepp, Ignace. *Death and Its Mysteries.* New York. Macmillan. 1968.

Levin, Sydney and Ralph J. Kahana, eds. *Psychodynamic Studies on Aging: Creativity, Reminiscing and Dying.* New York. International Universities Press. 1967.

Mitford, Jessica. *The American Way of Death.* New York. Simon and Schuster. 1962.

Munnichs, J.M.A. *Old Age and Finitude: A Contribution to Psychogerontology.* Basel. S. Karger. 1966.

Pearson, Leonard, ed. *Death and Dying.* Cleveland. Case Western. 1969.

Quint, Jeanne C. *The Nurse and the Dying Patient.* New York. Macmillan. 1967.

Sudnow, David. *Passing On.* Englewood Cliffs, N.J. Prentice-Hall. 1967. (With bibliographic notes)

Switzer, David K. *The Dynamics of Grief, Its Source, Pain and Healing.* Nashville. Abingdon. 1970.

Vernick, Joel J. *Selected Bibliography on Death and Dying.* Washington. U.S. Government Printing Office. 1970.

Verwoerdt, A. *Communication with the Fatally Ill.* Springfield, Ill. Charles C. Thomas. 1966.

Weisman, Avery D. and Robert Kastenbaum. *The Psychological Autopsy: A Study of the Terminal Phase of Life.* Community Mental Health Journal Monograph No. 4. New York. The Journal. 1968.

Wertenbaker, Lael Tucker. *Death of a Man.* New York. Random House. 1957.

SINGLE CHAPTERS IN BOOKS:

Back, Kurt W. and Hans W. Baade. "The Social Meaning of Death and the Law," in John C. McKinney and Frank T. DeVyver. *Aging and Social Policy.* New York. Appleton-Century-Crofts. 1966.

Payne, Edmund C., Jr. "The Physician and His Patient Who is Dying," in Sidney Levin and Ralph J. Kahana, eds. *Psychodynamic Studies on Aging: Creativity, Reminiscing, and Dying.* New York. International Universities Press, Inc. 1967.

Shneidman, Edwin S. "Orientations Toward Death: A Vital Aspect of the Study of Lives," in White, Robert W. ed., *The Study of Lives.* New York. Atherton. 1963. Chapter 9.

Strauss, Anselm L. "Problems of Death and the Dying Patient," in Simon, Alexander and Leon J. Epstein, eds. *Aging in Modern Society.* Washington, D.C. American Psychiatric Association. 1968.

Turney-High, Harry Hilbert. *Man and System.* New York. Appleton, 1968. (See Chapter 28, "Human Involution.")

PERIODICALS:

Journals:
"The Process of Dying." Entire issue of *Voices: The Art and Science of Psychotherapy*. Spring-Summer, 1969.

"Sociology of Death." Entire issue of *Sociological Symposium*. Fall, 1968.

Mental Hygiene. Vol. 53 July, 1969. Entire issue devoted to articles on death and bereavement, suicide and its prevention.

Omega. An international journal for the psychological study of dying, death, bereavement, suicide and other lethal behaviors. Vol. 1, No. 1, February, 1970.

Averill, James R. "Grief: Its Nature and Significance," *Psychological Bulletin*. 70:6, pp.721-48. 1968.

Calloway, N.O. "Kinetics of Senile Death,"*The Gerontologist*. 7:4 (December, 1967)

Faunce, William A. and Robert Fulton. "The Sociology of Death. A Neglected Area of Research." *Social Forces*. 36: pp. 205-09.

Gorer, Geoffrey, "The Pornography of Death," *Encounter*, October, 1955. p. 46-52.

Greenberger, Ellen. "Flirting with Death: Fantasies of a Critically Ill Woman," in *Journal of Projective Techniques and Personality Assessment*. Vol. 30, No. 2 (April, 1966) pp. 197-205.

Havighurst, Robert J. and Bernice L. Neugarten. "Attitudes Toward Death   Older Persons: A Symposium," *Journal of Gerontology*. 16:   pp.44-66.

Kastenbaum, Robert. "As the Clock Runs Out," *Mental Hygiene*, 50::   pp. 332-36. 1966.

_____,"Death as a Research Problem in Social Gerontology: An Overview," *Gerontologist*. 6:1, p. 67 ff.

Kidorf, Irwin, W., "Jewish Tradition and the Freudian Theory of Mourning." *Journal of Religion and Health*, 2: pp. 248-52

Kneisl, Carol. "Thoughtful Care for the Dying," *American Journal of Nursing*. 60:(March) pp. 550-53.

Koenig, Ronald R. "Fatal Illness: A Survey of Social Service Needs," *Social Work*, Vol. 13, No. 4 (October 1968) pp. 85-90.

Krupp, George R. and Bernard Kligfeld, "The Bereavement Reaction: A Cross-Cultural Evaluation," *Journal of Religion and Health*. Vol. 1 No.3 (April 1962) pp. 222-246.

Lieberman, M.A. "Psychological Correlates of Impending Death: Some Preliminary Observations," *Journal of Gerontology*. 20: 1965. pp.181-90.

"The Right to Die," *Nursing Outlook.* Vol. 16 (Oct. 1968) pp. 19-28.

Rogers, Jean L. *et al.,* "How Aged in Nursing Homes View Dying and Death," *Geriatrics* 25:4 (April, 1970) pp; 115-119.

Root, Maurice T. "Making Aging and Death Count," *Medical Opinion Review.* Vol. 5 No. 4 (April, 1969) p.96.

"Serious Gap Between Theory and Practice Seen in Physicians' Management of Terminal Patients," *Geriatric Focus.* Vol. 9 No. 8 (September 1970)

Wolff, Kurt."Helping Elderly Patients Face the Fear of Death," *Hospital and Community Psychiatry.* 18: May. 1967.

Popular Articles:

"Death: the Way of Life," *Harvest Years.* Vol. 9 (April 1969) pp. 19-34.

Gossage, Howard Luck. "Tell Me, Doctor, Will I be Active Right Up to the Last?" *Atlantic,* September, 1969. pp. 55-57.

Harrington, Alan. "The Immortalist," *Playboy,* May, 1969. p. 116.

Psychology Today. Vol. 4 No. 3. (August 1970). Entire issue devoted to aspects of death including attitudinal questionnaire.

Wainwright, Loudon. "A Lesson for the Living," *Life,* Vol. 67 No. 21 (Nov. 21, 1969) pp. 36-43.

Woodward, Kenneth L. "How America Lives with Death," *Newsweek,* April 6, 1970. pp. 81-88.

Note: *Psychological Abstracts* carries an extensive list of citations on the subject *Death.* Anyone interested in additional readings should consult this valuable source.

A